TOUGH STUFF

Raymond Cross

Published by Raymond Cross, 2024.

TOUGH STUFF

First edition. June 30, 2024.

ISBN: 979-8224448319

Written by Raymond Cross.

Table of Contents

NOTHIN' LIKE IT

TOUGH STUFF is like nothin' you've ever encountered, providing answers, answers, answers to problems, problems, problems, perplexing problems, deer in headlight problems, startling, disorienting, disabling problems. Solutions boiling up from a steaming hot teapot of trouble, sensing all the stresses while looking up to God for solutions.

INTRODUCTION

The Christian Church began with vigor, boldness and spiritual power. From the beginning faithful proclamation of new life in Christ produced dramatically changed lives. (Acts 5:12-16). As now, however, what followed the movement of God was resistance, even persecution (Acts 5:17-40). In response, with exemplary determination, the Apostles stood firm in obeying God rather than bending to the threats of the ungodly, even going so far as to rejoice in "being counted worthy of suffering for Him" (vs. 41-42). Should it be any different today, especially with our churches surrounded by society that is straying far from the will of God? Sad to say, what is around us has a way of seeping into our churches and the hearts and minds of our congregants. New converts bring it in as well - the renewing of their minds takes time. Pastoring that is faithful to the Lord is not an easy ride. It raises a question we must face and answer. Do we approach Christian pastoral ministry as a calling, or as a career? If as a calling, you will persevere despite the inevitable persecution that Jesus promises to come with ministry. (John 15:19–20) If merely a career, inevitable disappointments will likely derail us. To pastor, according to Jesus' calling, we must be prepared to count the cost and persevere in making all we are and have available to and for Jesus - Matt. 16:24-25. Anything less than this is insufficient.

Acts 16:25-31 demonstrates this even more dynamically. Paul and Silas were snatched from the streets of Philippi and thrown into prison for preaching Jesus. In the midst of the gruesome physical anguish and perplexity of wondering what comes next, in the blackness of the night they did not despair but broke through in praise, singing prayers to their Lord. Their captive audience listened, reports the Scriptures. Then at midnight the locks in stocks and confining doors flung open. The influence of Paul and Silas was so impactful that no prisoners sought to escape. They stay with Paul and Silas awaiting the arrival of their shocked jailer, who fell on his knees before God's servants in desperation for the salvation they preached and lived. Out of the darkness, revival for the jailer and his family, and who knows how many prisoners as well. Stay true, who knows what God will do. The darkest time may be just before the dawn. Keeping our poise is an essential skill and will enable us to navigate adeptly through moments of uncertainly. You may actually be closer to victory than we think.

While all of this is true, I do not believe that much of what clergy go through in ministry today is necessary. It is my conviction that much of what drags us down is due to our lack of skill in removing obstructions. With proper training we could become more adept at navigating clergy challenges more positively and effectively, like Paul and Silas, and the Apostles. The Bible provides what we lack. So I propose to share what will enable us to pastor more effectively to the glory of God and for the health and evangelistic strength of His Church. I visualize God blessing us who walk in purity and godly boldness to pursue His will in the building of His Church to the glory of the God we serve.

"For my part, whatever anguish of spirit it may cost, I am willing to know the whole truth, to know the worst and provide for it." – Matthew Henry

"If you fail to plan, you are planning to fail." — Benjamin Franklin

Anticipation

Pastoral ministry, as I anticipated it, and often experienced it, offers many pleasing benefits. In churches, I have relished getting to know some of the sweetest people this side of heaven. Most were kind, understanding, supportive and encouraging. It's natural to love such people. But, if we are truly a pastor, called by God, our love will flow out to all, whether supportive or not. When they hurt, we hurt. When they hurt us, we will still hurt for consequences their actions bring upon themselves, us and others. Pastoral ministry is truly a roller coaster of highs and lows, helps and hurts. We need to develop the dichotomy to experience appropriate outrage with wrong without losing our love and joy. So, in the midst of everything, we are to keep our eye on opportunities to honor our Savior Who loves us and wants the best for us and our ministry. But recognize also that there are those hidden within churches that may set all our expectations in disarray, enough to drive godly pastors to distraction and even destruction.

Years past, I enjoyed regional meetings with fellow clergy. In the confidential atmosphere of a church we enjoyed a bag lunch and bared our souls about what was happening in our lives and ministries, then encouraged and prayed for each other. Non-competitive understanding and support was uplifting. What most sticks in mind is a time that one pastor shared hellish struggles he was experiencing with a power group in his church. As I remember it, we all listened attentively, with sympathy and understanding, since we also had fumbled with similar challenges through the years, but we offered nothing specific to help manage his situation. A room full of seasoned clergy and none of us seemed able to offer specific helpful advice. At the conclusion of our time and prayer together, he left in tears. A short time later he committed suicide

Horrible anguish seeped into my soul from this heart-wrenching news – such disappointment, discouragement, disillusionment, desperation and futility, driven by church people into the soul of their gentle, caring, godly pastor. I've never recuperated from the sense that we should have done something more – but what?

That heartache sticks with me. He came to us for help. He poured out his soul. We gave him nothing. What if we could have provided that sensitive spiritual pastor with tools for action, would he be ministering even now? What if I had a book like this to share with him? Oh the need – THE NEED!!

That's my driver. I have groveled in the heartaches and hardships of pastors, bleeding with them. I have mixed their blood with my own. This tragedy, and more, again and again along the way, has pulled on my spirit to do something. Nothing has been tougher, but there was no other way to unearth effective, biblical and honorable solutions to the greatest perplexities of ministry. My goal is to enable exceptional clergy competence through proper preparedness for all the tussles of the task.

An " IF ONLY!!!" Book

"Life has to be lived forward but can only be understood backward." Kierkegaard

This is very much an "if only" book. Over and over again, while writing, I have literally wailed, "Oh, if only I had known this before I launched into pastoring! If only I had been taught this so I didn't have to figure it out through hardship and laborious investigation along the way! If only I had known this when I needed it!"

This is my backward look at Christian ministry through the lens of my experiences and of Scripture, with earnest dependence on God's help, help that often brought me to my knees in amazement and adoration. In perplexity, I often felt God pick me up and carry me. I am not an expert, but God sure is. There have been a lot of tears shed over these words, tears of anguish and of appreciation as the Lord stepped in to help and guide me.

Meip Gies was protector of the Frank family from WWII Nazis and of Anne Frank and her Diary. To end her inspirational speeches later in life she shared, "Even an ordinary secretary or housewife or a teenager can, in their own way, turn on a small light in a dark room." That is what I want, to bring light into dark places in pastoral experience so we stand more assuredly and stumble less.

Targeting Pastoral Responsibilities

"When I die, I want to go peacefully in my sleep like my grandfather. Not screaming in terror, like the passengers in his car." Jack Handey

In this humorous quip I see two types of values appropriate to different levels of relations and responsibilities.

The passengers bore no concern for the progress of the vehicle. Their issues were only getting along with each other and not interfering with the driver.

The driver, however, while remaining civil with his passengers, his social graces are not substantially connected to his responsibilities concerning all aspects of vehicle safety – speed, direction, maneuvering and braking.

Likewise, Jesus' universal values for personal relations, (turn other cheek, go second mile etc.) are not adequate to back Christian leadership of churches, official representation for God and the care and protection of individuals, which are the focus of this book.

As leaders we must not lose our skilled grip on the steering wheel or allow another to interfere. We must not be distracted toward soft-peddling dangerous threats to safety, health, peace, love and care.

Pastors stand between the devil and the Church he hates so we must be prepared to thwart his efforts to destroy the effectiveness of Christian ministry and ministers by whatever medium or person he enlists.

Bullies beware – there is a leader in residence, a shepherd ready and able to neutralize all threats to our flock.

Leadership Development Slant

I'm sure it will be noticed and criticized by some that my book is oriented toward male leadership. This is intentional, based on my study of Scripture and on my experience of seeking to build strong Christian churches. I noticed that male leadership was primary throughout the Bible. When it came to structuring the New Testament church the delineation of pastoral and deacons qualifications are inclined toward the masculine. While this may raise the hackles of some, I merely sought to understand how things work best. This became starkly evident when pioneering a church for twelve years. I sought to build a new church from new believers, not merely shuffling people from other churches to mine. For me, this latter course was not real church growth, since I viewed the Christian Church as one, expressed in various congregations and denominations. Building my church should not be at the cost of other godly churches.

So, as the church I was founding began its life, flooded intentionally with those I led to the Savior, I noticed a clear characteristic that women began with more enthusiasm for spiritual things than did men. This was a concern that needed to be addressed. I wanted to build a healthy Christian church, with healthy, strong families – dad, mom and kids, not a harem or the appearance of a harem. So I drew together the dynamic spiritual women of the church for a consult. I asked them what they hoped for their men concerning the church they were attending. Did they want their men to be attending church in five years? Did they want their men to be spiritual leaders in their homes in five years? Did they want their men to be leaders in their church in five years? Without exception they desired this for their men. I continued to explain that if that is the goal they would need to slow down. I encountered a tendency in men to view church as unmasculine. At that time, I shared my awareness that men tend to live in a dirty, vulgar, unchristian work world all week. When it comes to church attendance on Sunday men often feel contaminated and uncomfortable even if they have accepted Christ. They tend to move forward spiritually more slowly than their mates that may be provided more time to read Scripture, pray and gather for Bible studies. I encouraged them to invest in their men, ask them questions about their faith rather than running to their pastor, so that their men are motivated to get into the Scriptures and into greater involvement.

The ladies caught the wisdom of my guidance. They eased back to gently, almost imperceptibly, nudge their men forward. Over the years we all noticed the benefit of this subtle, behind the scenes purposeful program to address a clear problem. Men became more regular in church and they began to stand forth to serve, to grow and to lead. They exhibited more respect and honor for their wives' as a side effect of their wives wonderful ministry of subtly extending to them room to grow into the leaders they sensed they should be. Their families as well developed a stability under kind and care-filled spiritual male leadership. From my perspective, it's hard to knock what works so well for all, for the long term.

It is not gender- preferential but biblically purposeful. This approach may be criticized but I am convinced that it is biblical and functional. Men should not be allowed to languish in spiritual lethargy and irresponsibility. They should be nudged forward to lead honorably and with godly grace. They should shoulder the load of leadership responsibility, with no intent to diminish their mates or their offspring. The Bible establishes differing roles for different genders because it is a basis for healthy homes, churches and societies. This should not be imposed but creatively structured into the church environment for the sake of healthy development, as it was in the church I pioneered. It was genuinely delightful to watch the women working their encouragement mission and enjoying their sense of satisfaction as they helped to develop the type of husbands they could better honor and follow, while encouraging their offspring to do likewise. It's a respectful change of church atmosphere that transforms a church into a wholesome, spiritual male leadership generator.

No apology. I'm for what follows God's wisdom in His Bible. I'm for what works in building properly balanced responsible leadership in homes and churches.

"Please Lord, use what you have been teaching me to ease stress on pastors and unify churches toward what will most glorify You. Amen"

"It is possible to last, to be faithful, to be resilient—not by might, not by power, but by the same Holy Spirit who sustained the church throughout the centuries." Glenn Packiam

CHAPTER 1
Graduated to What?

―――

"Pastors Share Top Reasons They've Considered Quitting Ministry in the Last Year".

This is the title of an online survey conducted by The Barna Group among 413 Protestant Senior Pastors from January 22–27, 2021 and again, among 510 Protestant Senior Pastors from March 10–16, 2022. It netted the following:

The report began, "The number of pastors who have given serious consideration to quitting full-time ministry has risen dramatically over the past year....two in five pastors [42%] have thought about leaving ministry...it confirms the growing number of pastors who are considering resignation—up...from 29 percent in January 2021."

Major reasons pastors reported are: "immense stress, loneliness, isolation, divided church politics, effect on their family, sense of futility, frustrated vision, lack of respect, lack of support by key leaders, ill-equipped for ministry demands....These factors negatively impact their ability to lead their church." http://barna.com/research/pastors-quitting-ministry April 27, 2022

Evidently, the disconnect between pastors and churches is growing systemically wider and worse.

Dr. Dallas Speight has even gone so far as to declare forced resignation / termination of pastors from churches "a pandemic", with devastating consequences on pastors, their families and their churches. It is my hope that the spiritual vaccination therapies of this book will prove crucial in battling this contagion.

Preparing

Hypothetically, picture yourself perusing college catalogues to assess where we might want to train for Christian ministry. The two colleges we are considering are equally committed to Christian standards of conduct and faithfulness to the Bible. As we read on, we take note of their Biblical description of their goal for their graduates. One college declares, "We send graduates out like sheep among wolves." The second one declares, "We send graduates out as shrewd as snakes and as innocent as doves." While both are biblical, neither of them seems to have the right tone. What's your choice? What type of graduate, what type of competence would you like to bring to ministry?

The tone of college number one says to me, "We send out graduates as lambs to the slaughter." While none would actually advertise themselves in this fashion, it is my assessment that much clergy education boils down to just this.

College number two is more attractive to me because it offers hope, but it seems that shrewdness is not required with everyone. It has value when dealing with wolf-like people, people on the hunt, perhaps in packs.

The wisdom of our Lord is to put both awareness and honorable strategic effectiveness together, "I am sending you out like sheep among wolves. Therefore be as shrewd as snakes and as innocent as doves." (Matthew 10:16)

Sadly, my Bible College education and ministry research reveals lack of the balance Jesus advises. There actually seems Bible College naivety that ministerial training should condition graduates for ministry among wonderful people, leaving graduates blinded to the realities Jesus proclaims. We graduate and enter ministry with no preparation for ministry among the wolves of which Jesus speaks.

After graduating from Bible College, while earning a bachelor's degree in a liberal arts university, I became aware of the difference between university courses of study and what I received in Bible College. My university training was theoretical, with little possibility of application to everyday life. In contrast, Bible College instruction was personally enriching and life changing. It instilled values. It taught the riches of God's Word and skills for interpreting it. Courses in theology exposed the essence of God, His good will toward us and challenged us to share this good news with others. I really appreciated learning how to knowledgeably live and share the best kind of Christian lifestyle. Problem was, I was unaware that Bible College wasn't following through to provide skills training I would desperately need.

I enrolled in a four-year degree program entitled, "Pastoral Bachelor of Theology", which means I went to Bible College to learn to pastor, but that is the one thing I did not learn. The one course that might have provided practical instruction was entitled, "Pastoral Theology". Such a vague title. Maybe, if it were titled "Pastoral Practicum" it might have at least been pointed in the right direction. The "Pastoral Theology " course included no theology and almost nothing about the biblical and functional role, responsibility or authority of pastors. Virtually no practical guidance. I didn't object because I was unaware of what I was missing. As far as I was able to discern, the course of study and Christian service opportunities were as they should be. But I graduated more as an enhanced layperson than as trained clergy. The Pastoral Bachelor of Theology I earned was a college bluff – theology without pastoral preparation. It was only through challenges in ministry that I became aware of the devastating voids in my education.

After four years of Pastoral Bachelor of Theology studies I knew little more about pastoring than when I began. I was left to launch into ministry with no clear concept of a pastoral role. I was writing it as I went along from a template spawned mostly from my observation of pastors I had known and demands from my parishioners. So, with little understanding of what a pastor is and does, with no parameters for its functioning, I lived in constant struggle of trying to fill a role that seemed limitless. My desperate, unmet need was education for competence.

A favorite Bible College professor warned us, "You think it's tough here. Wait till you get out there. They're going to crucify you out there!" Sad to say, he did not follow through with answers for us to manage the challenge ahead. Nobody did. I learned later, when he was my faculty adviser, that he was speaking from experience. Pastoral ministry had broken him, leaving him dependent on tranquilizers. I wonder how many Bible College teachers come to the role out of similar failure, unable to discern and pass on practical answers for debilitative pastoral problems that had broken them, that they had not solved.

Blind Side

I came to recognize that a major weakness in training clergy is failure to give adequate attention to the greatest challenge in pastorates. We may be well trained in theology, in preaching, in Christian education, in Bible interpretation and the like, but what will likely decide our success or failure is left out. So, to great discouragement, we are blindsided by the realities of our role. Our training focuses on the most fulfilling dimensions of our service but fails to recognize that what will prove most debilitating along the way will be church politics—managing individual congregational relations and church mechanics for peace in the fellowship and for the sake of leadership toward God honoring endeavors. Church politics, sometimes even disreputable politics, is what will wear us down more than anything else, especially if we lack the skills needed to manage them most effectively. We are not so nice and winsome that we will be insulated from this experience. There is much more at work than personalities. Along with everything else, ministry is complicated by a decline of respect for leadership in North America, and probably elsewhere, as well as spiritual forces at cross-purposes with God's desires. It is so important that we begin ministry aware of what we are walking into and the wisest processes for managing challenges we will face.

Most pastors I have encountered are sincere. They have invested thousands of dollars and years of earnest effort in education in preparation for their role. They want to do a good job for their Lord. So I tend to side with pastors when they receive negative assessments by people in their congregations. God's critique is harder to side step, but if the pastors are sincere it is my sense that a lot of our failings are because we do not know any better. We are ill-prepared for the complex, even crushing, concerns and challenges we will almost certainly encounter in modern pastoral ministry.

A TURN THE TIDE BOOK

As I probed current church problems in the light of Scripture, it became evident that the crux of the challenges relate to pastors and how they fulfill their duties. God declares that there is no church role more important than pastoring. Prophets and evangelists do their thing but it is pastors that are left on the front line holding the fort – God expects them to feed, lead and protect the flock.

"For the shepherds [of the people] have become [like brutes,] irrational and stupid, And have not searched for the LORD or asked about Him or realized their need for Him; Therefore they have not been wise and have not prospered, And all their flocks are scattered." Jeremiah 10:21 Amplified Bible

"Woe to the shepherds who are destroying and scattering the sheep of My pasture!" declares the Lord." Jer. 23:1

"Therefore thus says the Lord God of Israel concerning the shepherds who are tending My people: "You have scattered My flock and driven them away, and have not attended to them; behold, I am about to attend to you for the evil of your deeds," declares the Lord." Jer. 23:2

Yet again...

"He who is a hired hand, and not a shepherd, who is not the owner of the sheep, sees the wolf coming, and leaves the sheep and flees, and the wolf snatches them and scatters them." John 10:12

Furthermore...

"Seeing the people, He felt compassion for them, because they were distressed and dispirited like sheep without a shepherd." Matt. 9:36

God is desperately concerned for the quality of pastoral leadership of His flock.

In the midst of this there is the reality that Satan recognizes the importance of pastors, so targets them with all he can muster, especially, it would seem, from within the church itself, among those who ought to serve alongside their pastors. Satan knows that betrayal by lay leadership cuts deeply. We bleed. "If an enemy were insulting me, I could endure it; If a foe were raising himself against me, I could hide from him But it is you...my companion, my close friend, with whom I once enjoyed sweet fellowship as we walked with the throng at the house of God." Ps. 55:12-14

It is biblically clear; God views pastors as the most essential human agency for the health, biblical fidelity, spiritual vitality and protection of churches. Faithful pastors instill intimacy with and faithful obedience to their Lord, accurately present biblical truth through word and life and lovingly and vigilantly care for and protect God's sheep in the congregations they serve. This is foundational. If there is weakness here, cracks permeate all. As the Scriptures proclaim again and again, concerning the Savior and His shepherds:

"Strike the shepherd that the sheep will be scattered," Zech. 13:7

From God's own lips, pastors are the primary target to weaken and destroy His Body, the Church. There can be nothing more important; therefore, than to upgrade the capability of clergy skills to succeed in ministry despite current head winds. To the glory of God, pastors must be enabled and congregations must be groomed to allow their pastors to lead to the glory of God. No bullying of pastors by parishioners. No bullying of parishioners by pastors.

So my goal has been unearthing flaws in pastoral ministry and determining God's guidance for resolving what is amiss. With much prayer and research God led me step by step through the maze of matters for pastoral ministry in church life. Among other things, I was drawn to understanding and management of meekness weakness and stress, call substantiating and sustaining, time management, marriage and family life, the biblical role of deacons and demon interference. These are easy to describe, but difficult to resolve.

Over and over again I sighed, "I wish I had known this while I pastored! I wish I had received this training in preparation for pastoral ministry!" While under the stress of pastoring, it was so difficult to pull back to develop perspective. Now, retired, I was able to pour six years of intensive research into these essential issues –

how pastors and Christian churches can be strong and resilient to the glory of God and His purpose for mankind.

Let's turn the tide of ministry weakness and Church decline that God may be glorified by our churches and denominations.

It is my goal to make clergy aware of the currents against which they will swim in pastoring, and how to navigate them successfully to God's glory.

The Pressure of Church Politics

This heavy stress of managing church politics became so clear as I left pastoring to providing ministry outside of churches. I came to wonder how I survived for more than thirty years under such pressure. While guest preaching and providing ministry to weddings and funerals in the community I experienced the joy of sculpting challenging sermons and beautiful ceremonies to remember the deceased and to join couples in marriage. There was preparation. There was consultation. There was preaching. There was officiating. Then ministry ended to those individuals. No on-going politics. If there were complaints, they were left behind. I merely moved on to the next challenge. Likewise, when serving as chaplain on cruise ships, each cruise was short duration. I led Bible studies and worship services. I met with cruisers along the way, then, contact ended with the end of the cruise. No long term consequences to badger and burden me. I was free to do ministry as I had been trained to expect it – preparing and delivering inspiring messages to win and feed the Word of God to hungry souls. There was none of the decline of respect for leadership so characteristic of church congregations these days. No pouring out my heart and soul only to be picked apart by some supercilious soul for one word or illustration deemed to be inappropriate. No battles with the defiant. It was ministry as I had always hoped it would be – hungry souls happy to be fed, inspired and encouraged in their faith. Though inadequate to make a living, it is wonderful Christian ministry as Bible College led me to expect.

These latter years of Christian ministry have been encouraging to those I serve, no less so to me. It has been a renewing retirement, and respite sufficient to provide room for me to ruminate over the struggles of pastorates, as I have experienced them and observed them, in hopes of releasing pastors by what I have come to know though never taught and many times was unable to develop when I needed it under ongoing pastoral pressures.

Personal observation and objective investigation supports that I have not been alone in this quagmire. The Rev. Dr. Lester Dennis shared his research into the curriculum of more than a hundred North American Bible Colleges and Seminaries. His assessment was that these training centers are thorough in academic theological training but abysmally lacking in practical instruction. Another student's observation was that it seemed his pastoral bachelor training focused on preparation for masters or doctoral studies. Since not all will choose that track, why not provide a functional alternative majoring on practical know-how for pastoring? Why not focus on teaching pastors-in-training survival skills for challenges they will most definitely encounter in their ministry for the Lord? Kind of a community college approach so graduates don't just come out knowing but knowing how. In my opinion this would go a long way to encouraging new candidates to ministry and for ministry. It would be a kindness much valued by clergy throughout their lives of service. A track to which degree components can be added as a student might desire. Let's learn priority skills first then expand upon them.

Elder Track

Elder Track is an approach that churches themselves might develop to prepare candidates for practical aspects of pastoral service. I first encountered this during a lengthy senior pastorate of Dr. K. Rick Baker at Calvary Baptist Church, Oshawa, Ontario, Canada. The carefully designed stages for this merits close examination for their rich benefits. It represents a careful application of the Scriptural injunction..."Lay hands on no one suddenly." (1 Tim. 5:22) What it amounts to is pastoral ministry apprenticeship that provides opportunity to learn skills for the trade of pastoring possibly along with the convenience of living at home, with their family, earning additional funds to provide adequately for dependents, and worshipping with their church family. The thought is that perhaps other churches might implement something similar to considerable benefit.

1. The Calvary model begins with church elders/ pastors taking note of possible men eligible for elder track—they are members serving diligently already who they sense could be vocational servants. These men, young or not young, are approached to consider interning at Calvary.

2. Those who take the invitation are employed at first as "Ministry Associates". These begin as interns at Calvary. They have to be a Calvary Church member or, in the event there is no one within Calvary's membership to develop, a member of another church with appropriate beliefs. Interns are paid lightly for one or two months to assess their purpose for inclusion, then payment is increased.

A strength of this approach is in bypassing a necessary weakness in the bible college and seminary system. For survival, schools of higher education depend on the tuition of students, especially schools unsupported by government funds. Schools therefore advertise for any and all to attend their institutions. To my knowledge students are minimally vetted. Student bodies can be a hodgepodge of any who avail themselves of the opportunity and have the money to pay, whereas the Elder Track selects and vets those who exhibit promise for the role they seek. This process is focused completely on what is good for the intern and benefits in ministry for the cause of Christ, without being co-mixed with a survival need for money.

3. Ministry associates are observed in their internship for evidence of elder qualities. At some point, these men either continue as excellent ministry associates fulfilling a needed role at Calvary or in some cases express a sense of call from the Lord toward eldership.

4. Those who are excellent at their service, sense a call to vocational eldership, are desiring to give their lives full time, are recommended by the elders to the deacons to be invited into the elder training track.

5. From this point, these men are observed, trained and instructed toward eldership, usually for four or five years. With deacon and elder approval these are channeled through pastoral supervised ministry experiences and leadership. By this means those who sense a call into vocational ministry are given opportunity to venture into ministries in their own home church for church Elders (Pastors) to assess if they have the gifting and qualifications for pastoral ministry. By these means pastoral interns learn the basics of what they will need to succeed in a pastorate. Practical know-how and personal skills precede higher learning that, while valuable, can lack crucial practicality. Along the way they are also trained in biblical spiritual principles and character qualities essential to Christian clergy as taught in I Timothy 3 and Titus 1. Most crucial is a servant's heart, humility and submission to pastoral leadership. Training that inflates egos requires removal from the Elder Track.

6. Their mates are very much involved, in the case of elder candidates. Their wives must also qualify to be the wife of an elder in accordance with 1 Tim 3:11. Their wives are also first in line to give a formal assessment of their husband's qualifications by answering a series of character and behavioral questions.

7. If approved by both Deacons and Elders as they proceed through the Elder Track, these interns may then be presented to the church for consideration for a pastoral position in that congregation or a recommendation for ministry elsewhere. As part of the assessment process congregants are invited to affirm or present concerns from their involvement with and impressions of the applicant. If this stage of vetting draws approval, the membership is invited to an official affirmation service into "eldership" at Calvary or to be commended as affirmed elders to another ministry setting. If there is a role for which they qualify at the local church, they are installed as pastor of that area of local ministry.

8. These men are appointed elders/pastors by Calvary.

9. At a later date, after more elder, deacon, congregational observation and practical and spiritual readiness and theological education, the elder may be considered for ordination.

In this way, over a number of years, hosting churches may groom and increase its staffing with capable clergy, faithful to church leadership and knowledgeable about their church and its ministries. These paid staff are able to provide expertise and work hours inappropriate to expect of volunteers. As well, these churches create a pool of capable clergy to serve elsewhere in their denominational churches. It's a win, win, win - more skilled clergy for better local ministries and

As able, while serving as an associate pastor, these are encouraged to pursue bible college or seminary educational credentials toward ordination, but it is not demanded as a prerequisite for full pastoral ministry. Unordained, the only ministry they cannot provide is the government controlled solemnization of marriages. Churches with multiple pastors do not need all to provide this service.

The evident benefit to Calvary Baptist Church in Oshawa has been an expansion of their pastoral team with trained, capable staff who are already faithful to the leadership and fine tuned and turned on to the vision and mission of the church they serve. The growth has been peaceful and powerful for the Lord. There is a reassuring team spirit.

ELDER TRACK RESOURCES:

1. Elder Development Program (EDP) – for select resources

(https://www.BiblicalLeadersip.com/wp-content/uploads/2018/ 04/Elder-Dem-Prog.pdf}

2. ***Discover the Spiritual Gift in You*** book by Raymond Cross – Another turn the tide book for synergistic biblical team building skills.

(https://www.smashwords.com/books/view/620527)

Unprepared and Fumbling on the Field of Ministry Can Bring a Shake Down

Entering pastorates with blurred skills, knowing no better than to know any better, leaves so many lacking sharp enough focus to adequately take the reins of churches, leaving them vulnerable to debilitating manipulation. Trouble is that, when needed, pastoral skills are required. Having to research the basics before implementation, and then implementing with the hesitancy of a clinical trial, is wasteful and not conducive to confidence and respect for leadership. Lay people expect more than trial and error leadership from trained clergy. Lacking it, they tend toward looking elsewhere, and the roots of mutiny begin. Lack of practical training is definitely a travesty for which clergy, churches and the cause of Christ pay dearly.

This inadequacy grates on me, for the price I paid and for the anguish I watched it inflict on others. It hurt me deeply to observe other pastors likewise set up for failure by inadequate preparatory education for the position we assumed. Conflict. Marital and family overload. Burn out. Bitterness. Escape. Rejection. Suicide.

Having now pastored for thirty-five years, I have considerable experience in managing congregationally governed churches. Like most with lengthy pastoral histories, I have experienced the good, the bad and the impossible. Though I retired from the rigors of pastoring more than fifteen years ago, I never relinquished my call. All I have experienced and observed demands my ongoing attention and contributes to this book. I am seeking to address deeply ingrained flaws in the structure of churches and pastorates. Out from under the push of pastoring was like taking my transmission out of gear so I could take pause, look at things with a more critical eye, measure them more carefully against biblical standards and frame them into tools and templates functionally designed to resolve the ills. This toolkit is meant for wise action no matter what may come our way—composed of mental and spiritual implements for pastors to survive and thrive to the glory of God,

So, to address this need, especially with regard to threatening situations least likely to be dealt with in other education programs, I set out to plug holes in the dyke of pastoral preparedness. It is my hope that this toolkit will serve as an arsenal for survival in ministry for the Savior. It is my one shot to slay the dragon of unpreparedness, but I also hope that what I share might become part of future Bible College and Seminary curriculums.

"We cannot solve our problems with the same thinking we used when we created them." Albert Einstein

CHAPTER 2
The Perfect Church

Jesus declared, "I will build my church, and the gates of Hades will not overcome it."(Matt 16:19) What a triumphal description! What a church! The perfect church! I'd want to be part of such a church, a church with such spiritual power and resilience that the devil buckles before its church building ministry of saving and nurturing souls. Who would not want to pastor such a congregation—a church that fulfills the ideals of the Savior?

To this description, Jesus added, "Remember what I told you: "A servant is not greater than his master. If they persecuted me, they will persecute you also. If they obeyed my teaching, they will obey yours also." (John 15:20) Later on, Paul challenges us to, "be strong in the Lord and in his mighty power....against the devil's schemes". (Eph.6:10-11)

Warfare with the forces of darkness casts a shadow on Christian ministry. The vision of Jesus remains. It will be fulfilled, but not without struggle. Early in my pastoring I expected this to be based on the contrast between Christianity and the culture around, pressure from without to slow down our church's growth.

While there are countries and cultures that actively resist and persecute Christianity, history reveals that the cause of Christ is not crushed in such circumstances. These churches adapt, perhaps move underground in small group gatherings, often grow stronger through enhanced cohesion and prosper with vigor that draws many to their orb and efforts.

In cultures and countries where Christianity is tolerated, however, the Church too easily grows fat and lethargic. In this circumstance, eager clergy are shocked to realize that the enemies with which they struggle are not generally outside the church, but within the church itself. In this situation clergy can blend with what exists for a pleasant career of ineffectiveness, like a happy party host. But is that the type of pastor that follows the lead of Jesus toward the perfect church Jesus visualizes?

Leaving college uninformed, so inadequately prepared, it can be a shock that most of the resistance to church spiritual health and ministry effectiveness may not come from outside churches we pastor but is spawned within churches, among church attendees and even leaders responsible to assist the pastor's ministry. In every church we will encounter Christians of all shades, from salt of the earth supporters through to censoriously determined destroyers. Being unprepared for this, naivety may prove a disabler, taking the shine off enthusiasm as they obstruct our leadership, even if it is in accord with God's Word and guidance.

A

Apparently pastoral leadership, with all of its biblical promise, is not an easy ride. Launching in hopes of finding and pastoring the perfect church is an illusion we will never find this side of heaven. The first century church in Jerusalem was not perfect (Acts 6:1). The early churches addressed in Revelation were not perfect (Rev. 2-3). Churches we pastor will not be perfect as we begin or as we serve them. All churches are works in process, hopefully moving toward the Lord's described ideal. It is the vision of our Head to which we commit, pursue and to which we contribute. Even if we pioneer a congregation, spoilers will join and need to be redirected. So don't be surprised by resistance. Walk forward through it in the power of God. Time to brush aside naivety to prepare for reality.

> All authority in heaven and on earth has been given to me. Therefore go and make disciples of all nations, baptizing them in the name of the Father and of the Son and of the Holy Spirit, and teaching them to obey everything I have commanded you. And surely I am with you always, to the very end of the age. (Matt. 28:18-20)

"Troublesome church members just proves they need a pastor." Rev. Dr. K. Rick Baker

CHAPTER 3
Sitting Ducks - the Meek Weak

J. Upton Dickson, in his book entitled Cower Power, wrote of a submissive group called DOORMATS, "Dependent Organization of Really Meek and Timid Souls—if there are no objections." Their symbol, he claimed, was the yellow traffic light, and their motto, "The meek shall inherit the earth—if that's okay with everybody." (christianlibrary.org, by Grady Scott re. Matt 5:5)

Dickson pokes his comedic finger at a ridiculous misunderstanding of Matthew 5:5 that persists among many church-going Christians—"Blessed are the meek, for they shall inherit the earth." More specific and insightful research has demonstrated a serious flaw concerning this declared profoundly powerful success principle taught by Jesus. Due to the intensity of their drive to please their Lord, pastors are sitting ducks for this incapacitating weakness.

A Tremendous Success Promise

At face value, this verse says that God wants people who exhibit meekness to succeed, even in a big way, but the declared means, as it is understood in English, falls flat in getting there. This depletion of meaning comes from the early 1500s, when William Tyndale translated the New Testament from Greek to English. In Matthew 5:5 he encountered a challenging Greek word that, to this day, defies any one English word equivalent. At the time, and to the present, Tyndale's translation of "meek" picks up on only the softer side of the Greek word "praeis". From the start, Tyndale's translation was too weak to approximate the full meaning in "praeis", but because it was universalized by the King James Translation, it has been enshrined and bound to this Beatitude ever since. We love the poetry of it, but meekness makes inheriting the earth as a reward so far-fetched as to be ludicrous. This problem of bad translation has never been repaired because it is still impossible to do so by an English one word equivalent.

Powder Puff

English dictionary definitions for the English word, "meek", include – 'compliant, passionless, passive, unassertive, yielding, easily imposed upon, willing to go along with whatever other people want'. These definitions of "meek" as a translation for "praeis" miss its muscular side needed to achieve the promised benefit. There is too much wimpiness drooping from the word "meek" for it to lift anything. Misunderstanding Jesus' intention through this mistranslation of Matthew 5:5 confuses and ruins people, situations, relationships, careers, lives, ministries, pastors – everything. Limiting "praeis" to insipid, spineless, divinely instituted and enshrined mediocrity dooms us to a flattening of personal dynamism, short circuited initiative and extinguished passion. It is the disease of the dull.

Spiritual Only? - Rights is Wrong!

Clearly, meekness as we know it does not work to achieve the promised goal. It's a tremendous promise with great attraction, but the means is obscured. Perhaps there is a secret behind it that makes it feasible. This leads us to another perspective designed to stare down the inadequacy created by the "meekness" mistranslation, an attempt to evade the weakness of the word by spiritualizing meekness as a virtue only fully applicable to those in relationship with the Lord.

So, in accord with this, much commentary about meekness restricts Matthew 5:5 to spiritual significance only. After all, spiritualization can be justified, so they think, since this Beatitude came from the lips of Jesus and is recorded in the Bible. But, I ask, is limiting Matthew 5:5 only to the spiritual supported by accurate exegesis?

For clarification, as we view the format of the Beatitudes, except for the last two, each Beatitude is a capsule, disconnected from the meaning of the one on either side, and three of these encapsulated truths are of general application, while six are of spiritual merit.

Matthew 5...

3. Blessed are the poor in spirit,

for theirs is the kingdom of heaven.—SPIRITUAL

4. Blessed are those who mourn,

for they will be comforted.—GENERAL

5. Blessed are the meek,

for they will inherit the earth.—GENERAL

6. Blessed are those who hunger and thirst for righteousness,

for they will be filled.—SPIRITUAL

7. Blessed are the merciful,

for they will be shown mercy.—GENERAL

8. Blessed are the pure in heart,

for they will see God.—SPIRITUAL

9. Blessed are the peacemakers,

for they will be called children of God.—SPIRITUAL

10. Blessed are those who are persecuted because of righteousness,

for theirs is the kingdom of heaven.—SPIRITUAL

11. Blessed are you when people insult you, persecute you and falsely say all kinds of evil against you because of me.

12. Rejoice and be glad, because great is your reward in heaven, for in the same way they persecuted the prophets who were before you.—SPIRITUAL

Notice that the three "m"s, mourn, meek and mercy, offer reciprocated blessings available to all, without restriction related to heaven or seeing God. Matthew 5:5 contains nothing to restrict it to the spiritual. Restricting "praeis" to Christians and their relationship with God is unwarranted. So, unjustly spiritualizing the meaning of Matthew 5:5 in terms of submitting personal rights to God, so God's rights and plans take precedence, distorts the true intent of the word "praeis" and of Matthew 5:5 in the context of the Beatitudes. It's wonderful idealism with no biblical basis and no basis in the meaning of the Greek word "praeis". In my experience of real life situations, rights-meekness doesn't work.

Rights in Conflict

As I sought to apply this in my ministry, meekness proved downright destructive of decisiveness and effectiveness. I hope, by baring my soul concerning this distortion I might deliver many from the twist that disabled me when I most needed to be determined and persistent.

When godless forces muster, surely it is a distortion of God's truth to view our role meekly, doomed to curl up and let them win, without rights unless God or others step up in our defense. We are incorrect to acquiesce to letting others walk on us when we are responsible to act. Not only that, but, since we don't appear to want to win, we isolate ourselves from assistance. There is nothing to take the wind out of attackers' sails and nothing to invite others to stand with us in our defense. What we hope for by laying aside our rights is curtailed, leaving us alone, hoping God will protect us. I've watched this work its way out. Antagonists accost the pastor. Congregants, though sympathetic to their pastor, observe their pastor offering no objection. Thus they are incapacitated in bewilderment about what they should do since their pastor's apparent submission provides no direction. Then they bewail the loss of their beloved "leader".

God always considers it is our responsibility to exercise our responsibilities. Rights need to be exercised according to the responsibility of one's role and the authority required to fulfill that responsibility. As shepherds of a flock, our responsibility is to act when our role demands action – to defend truth, righteousness, God's reputation and that of His Church, for protection of sheep in our flock and of the viability and continuance of our role. Bewilderment while we debate within ourselves the appropriateness of exercising our rights is off base. It is part of our role to earnestly and zealously advocate for God's calling on our lives as shepherds.

Little recognized within congregations, but well understood by antagonists, rights confusion that restricts advocacy by clergy can contribute to the appearance of disinterest in protecting our ministry. In interaction with strong contrarian groups or individuals, troublemakers take advantage of any weakness available, often raising issues meant to paint pastors poorly. Artisans of this will often be people a pastor could destroy with what we know. (In the process of pastoring we become privy to embarrassing details many would not want exposed.) As a professional caregiver, however, we are bound by integrity to keep secret things private. It will soon become apparent that those who attack feel no compunction to be bound by similar restriction. They can dance around issues that are actually to their detriment but present them in a manner to hurt their pastor, knowing that pastors are limited in what truth they can speak. This is personally aggravating, even emasculating, especially as we sense their delight that they know our arms are tied behind our back as they punch. We are limited to publicly acceptable information to represent our position, to do the best we can to ethically share our truth wisely and assuredly in hopes of accurate understanding prevailing.

God has not called us to be punching bags. He has called us to hold His standard high and build His Church, not by being walked on, but by standing on biblical and functional principles and practices in our leadership.

By exercising "praeis" wisely, like an ethical hidden weapon, we can send a shiver down attackers' spines by inviting witnesses of our verbal mugging to get involved in our defense by speaking the truth as they know it. "Since, on the basis of professional confidentiality, we may not be free to comment, others might choose to do so, on the basis of what they know." Hopefully God will move others, not bound as we are, to divulge significant details in our defense. If prayer prevails, if the integrity of our manner and professionalism stands firm, if godly people stand up for their pastor and if God desires our ministry to continue in that place, hopefully God's will in His church will prevail through the efforts of godly advocates. The issue is to be prepared, prayer conditioned and at peace with God for His ongoing presence and power to prevail through the exercise of His power and will through our efforts and through the efforts of the congregation. If this fails, bow out boldly to continue ministry elsewhere. Be unflappable. Don't dilly dally ruminating over rights. Fulfill your responsibility to lead responsibly. When overwhelmed, In "praeis" continue to keep your attitudes right, and your adherence to truth faithful.

Blessed are those who are persecuted because of righteousness, for theirs is the kingdom of heaven. "Blessed are you when people insult you, persecute you and falsely say all kinds of evil against you because of me. Rejoice and be glad, because great is your reward in heaven, for in the same way they persecuted the prophets who were before you. Matthew 5:10-12

Unwrapping "Praeis"

So let's take a look at what the Greek word "praeis", translated "meek", actually means. We could delve so deeply into its multi-facetted meaning as to be engulfed by its complexity, which is not my intent here. A book about meekness I intend to release will do that. For now, just a quick functional summary:

As I said, "meek" as a translation of "praeis" leans to one side. it picks up the soft side of "praeis" only. Catching both sides I'd like to propose "sweet-spirited, purpose-driven living" as a brief, balanced expression of "praeis".

Pulling all strands of "praeis" together reveals it as a balanced atmosphere of activism characteristic of good leaders.

STRENGTH – "Praeis" inspires cooperative, constructive creativity focused unrelentingly toward worthwhile goals.

GENTLENESS - Recognizing the importance of people, "praeis" also exudes purposeful winsomeness for the good of others and for the sake of shared endeavors that benefit the best for the most. Such winsomeness encourages and uplifts rather than denigrating, belittling, exerting superiority or stooping to the tactics of troublemakers. This inspires team-spirit that lubricates purpose-driven leadership. The "praeis" do not back off or back down, but stay focused on tasks without distraction or retaliation.

Simplistically, it reminds me of times I became so focused on work projects that I was not aware of injury or pain. Like the time I sensed a squishing sensation in my shoe. When I took off my shoe it was full of blood from an injury I was unaware of because I was so focused on my task.

Likewise, take special note of the purpose focused nature of "praeis", as it puts some otherwise confusing guidance into perspective. The "praeis" do not operate by "eye for an eye" standards. They choose issues that merit their attention and purposely limit themselves to those priorities. So Jesus' guidance in Matthew 5:38-42 concerning personal offenses applies outside the focus of "praeis", outside the higher priorities of purpose that is the essence of "praeis".

> You have heard that it was said, 'Eye for eye, and tooth for tooth.' But I tell you, do not resist an evil person. If anyone slaps you on the right cheek, turn to them the other cheek also. And if anyone wants to sue you and take your shirt, hand over your coat as well. If anyone forces you to go one mile, go with them two miles. Give to the one who asks you, and do not turn away from the one who wants to borrow from you. (Matt. 5:38-42)

"Praeis" is so purposefully focused that personal affronts roll by like scenery at the side of the road while driving. Personal abuse is naturally handled with grace, without intention of pay back. There is no time or energy to fight for personal matters. Like firefighters putting out fires, we do not stop to look at ourselves in a mirror, even painful irritations do not distract us from our role. The "praeis" set aside ego and selfishness for the sake of higher purpose beyond themselves. We will not be dissuaded.

> Do nothing out of selfish ambition or vain conceit. Rather, in humility value others above yourselves, not looking to your own interests but each of you to the interests of the others. (Phil. 2:3-4)

So, if others try to take advantage, as long as it does not impede chosen outcomes, the "praeis" are magnanimous, open-handed and generous. Only when an affront interferes with our ability or responsibility to provide as we are required by our role, is it confronted, and that decisively. Selfish interference must not be allowed at the expense of higher good. When a cause is greater than ourselves it is the merit of that cause that dictates our responses to ensure that that important cause that we pursue is not compromised. Irritations are deemed inconsequential, whereas attempts at sabotage are too serious to ignore.

Those who live according to this Beatitude, lead with biblical "praeis", not the distortion of unbiblical meekness-weakness. These are not victims, but victors, overcomers. As Jesus declared, this quality of service and leadership is a clear universal basis of even earth encompassing impact. May we who serve Jesus in leadership take up this mantle to be imbued with these rich Matthew 5:5 qualities of enduring, gracious and determined strength for the measure of success Jesus promises. Surely Jesus' Great Commission challenges us to this vision for ministry effectiveness with promised possible global impact.

Lead with praeis. Be on track for the consequence Jesus promises.

"I'm fighting a battle that You've already won.

No matter what comes my way I will overcome." Bryan Fowler, Shane Barnard

Instilling "Praeis"

It is important to realize that people may bring ungodly attitudes with them, even from other churches. These flow out from them as a contagion as they join our churches and enter leadership positions. Unfortunately, there are always those in every congregation who are likewise inclined so tune in with subversives.

The rarest fully mature quality is finely tuned Matthew 5:5 "praeis"—purposefulness with gentleness, even under pressure or confrontation by problematic people. Not surprising that it is rare in churches because it is even more rare in society. Where are they going to learn this life-changing, world-changing attitude but by our teaching and by the contagion generated in our fellowships. If we can get this ball rolling in our alley, it will go far to producing the peace, collegiality and teamwork we crave, and that will make our pastor's role pleasurable rather than painful. We must take up the challenge to herd our flock toward honorable focus on values and causes beyond self. Being channeled together according to honorable, higher purpose grooms each to stand together for, not merely what is right for ourselves, but for what is right and good for everyone.

"Praeis" in Administration

As an example, in the absence of definite divine directives, in democratically governed congregational churches, "praeis" allows for choice within the framework of appropriate honorable means to reaching God's goals. For this, it is not me and my rights, but us and our rights under God and for His glory. Our churches would be much different if selfishness were set aside. If all congregants, at all levels of church government, set aside their personal power mongering to focus together on achieving God's goals, whatever the challenges to be faced, loving respect within the fellowship would be enhanced. Such an approach to church interactions would contribute richly to effectiveness and enjoyment of pastoral ministry and leadership.

Who Is in Charge?

This is the core of systemic Christian church functionality or dysfunction. If the Lord is not leading His Church, someone else is. This disconnection keeps churches ineffective and on life-support. It is Christ's Church. He is the Head. We are His Body. Godly pastors, submissive to the Lord as His undershepherds, are commissioned with instilling loyalty to the Lord. Which makes sense since, by biblical definition, as born again believers, all are to live and serve under Jesus, unified by the indwelling Holy Spirit. As representatives of the Lord, leading the church according to the Lord's requirements, pastors should exude and be respected for divinely directed authority, rather than being expected to submissively solicit parishioners for support of their leadership.

Hindrances

While we might expect that this endeavor would be welcomed, it might actually be resisted, even by deeply entrenched members. It flies in the face of western mores. All week long most people live amidst unrest due to perceived and often proven ruthless inequalities and injustices. How do they, for the sake of church cohesion, adjust their goals away from objectives to get the biggest piece? How do they extinguish dissatisfaction related to those selfish pursuits and change gears for harmonious "praeis" selflessness? Such preaching and teaching can come across as impractical pie-in-the-sky.

Yet, it is here that the "praeis" must draw the line and stand for goals and standards that are right and good for God, for His world and for His enterprises being pursued. Substandard plans, and purposes, must not be allowed to hinder or destroy what is and promises the most good. For this, the "praeis" stand their ground and, with kindness and consideration, move themselves and others relentlessly forward and upward under God's leading, even against minority resistance by stragglers, objectors and obstructers.

So "praeis" as Jesus intended it to be understood and applied is not passive acquiescing or submissively putting up with things, but rather determined participation and teamwork—active attitude and deliberate involvement for improvement, with acceptance of the costs and consequences involved.

Bring It On

Years ago, a visit to a parishioner recovering from hernia surgery, without anaesthetic, prompted discussion about high pain tolerance. He had been a Green Beret, tortured when captured, but never broken. Slight and wiry, yet formidable, he shared, "I never started a fight, but I always finished it." I like that, "Never start a fight, but always finish it."

Skills to Milk Positives from Negatives

"If you are going to take me on, I will give you my best to win with God."

That seems to me a good motto for pastoral ministry. Like the muscle bound bullies that pick a fight with a sleek martial arts expert who allows them to make the first move, then defeats them by control, redirection and pressure points. So the essence of what I hope to impart is not capability for the sake of cocky belligerence or intimidation, but rather a personal sense of preparedness that imparts assured confidence for our manner of ministry. Standing with God and His intention to bring good even out of evil. Using skill to gain the upper hand without unnecessary bravado or brutality. Settling for success by smooth action sufficient to disable attacks, while protecting from injury to self and others under our care. Be about what we're about. Resist being distracted or disabled. Stand our ground for the cause of Christ. Let the effect be what it should be.

Let's pastor, from beginning to end, as though we never get hurt.

Miscalculation

As a refrigeration repair man, my Dad carried to his calls a fully stocked tool box. By this means, he assured himself that he had every tool he needed to handle any required repair. Observing church situations suggests a different scenario. Church problems related to pastors support the view that trouble-makers usually assume that clergy do not have the tools or know how to handle their assaults. This is logical to them. Not surprising at all. It has been their experience over and over again, as pastor after pastor has folded under their characteristic onslaught.

A Tuning Fork for Leadership in Ministry

"For God did not give us a spirit of timidity or cowardice or fear, but [He has given us a spirit] of power and of love and of sound judgment and personal discipline [abilities that result in a calm, well-balanced mind and self-control]." (II Timothy 1:7 Amplified Bible)

Now, imagine how unnerving it would be for those seeking to throw us off balance to sense our fearlessly unperturbed anticipation for the encounter. We exhibit confidence based on God's support of spirituality and integrity, coupled with determination and capability in wielding pastoral tools specially designed to disable their attack. This unflappable assurance and anticipation for opportunity in everything, no matter how threatening, is so disarming to opposition that it needs to remain as a standard for ministry. We need to determine, no matter what, to look for opportunity in every circumstance, to conscientiously and constructively pursue positive possibilities in everything and everyone. This assurance of capability and preparedness may actually smooth our ministry road by signaling a yellow light of caution to antagonists, preempting their attacks as they re-evaluate prospects from proceeding with their evil endeavors.

So, my goal is to stock our pastor's toolkit with templates and tools we know how to use to minimize stress in handling whatever ministry sends our way. As challenges arise, we can rest assured that our toolkit contains the means to wise leadership toward creative resolution. With this orientation we may approach everything with positive anticipation for opportunity for progress in every challenge. Managed wisely, everything has within it the possibility for greater good and glory for our Lord. Our toolkit releases creative skill despite stress. Most importantly we don't have to invent tools on the run. We have a kit of tools chosen for their proven ability to address specific challenges to maintain wellbeing, health and divine intention of ministries and churches. Rather than stiffening with dread of consequences, we'll stay limber to possibilities. No more intimidation. No more off balance. No more unnerved. No more freezing in fear. No more run and hide. In a tussle, we will turn the table on attackers to win the prize of our high calling in Christ Jesus.

So this is a book about preparing for things that go wrong and tools for solving problems.

"Never give in, never give in, never, never, never, never - in nothing, great or small, large or petty - never give in except to convictions of honor and good sense. Never yield to force; never yield to the apparently overwhelming might of the enemy!" Winston Churchill

CHAPTER 4
Our Ministry Stance

Christian pastoral ministry is not meant to be fulfilled like a job, eight to four. Christian ministry has a Follow Me Function that is meant to flow from our inner being, twenty-four seven - a calling. Like the Apostle Paul, we are to lead by example for others are to follow. "Whatever you have learned or received or heard from me, or seen in me—put it into practice. And the God of peace will be with you." (Phil. 4:9) By sharing biblical truth through what we have become in Christ we seek to move others to be what they can be in Christ. We share what the Holy Spirit is able to do through saving faith in Jesus Christ. It is this that makes Christian ministry so eternally transformative, the most astounding calling to officially represent God as agents of His grace and goodness. We are to Live What We Lead

Stage One of Our Pastoral Ministry Stance – Wrap Them in God's Love

I am writing this during the run up to Christmas this year. Fresh baked pies are cooling on the countertop. A robust turkey is being basted in the oven. Sweet aromas fill the air. We so look forward to the celebrative arrival of friends and family knowing that, as they enter, they will be wrapped in delectable fragrances we have prepared for their visit.

It all reminds me of Jesus' description of His Church - "A new command I give you: Love one another. As I have loved you, so you must love one another. By this everyone will know that you are my disciples, if you love one another." (John 13:34-5)

7 Dear friends, let us love one another, for love comes from God. Everyone who loves has been born of God and knows God.

8 Whoever does not love does not know God, because God is love.

9 This is how God showed his love among us: He sent his one and only Son into the world that we might live through him.

10 This is love: not that we loved God, but that he loved us and sent his Son as an atoning sacrifice for our sins.

11 Dear friends, since God so loved us, we also ought to love one another.

12 No one has ever seen God; but if we love one another, God lives in us and his love is made complete in us.

18 There is no fear in love. But perfect love drives out fear, because fear has to do with punishment. The one who fears is not made perfect in love.

19 We love because he first loved us.

20 If anyone says, "I love God," yet hates his brother, he is a liar. For anyone who does not love his brother, whom he has seen, cannot love God, whom he has not seen.

21 And he has given us this command: Whoever loves God must also love his brother. (I John 4:7-12, 18-21)

This is the aroma Jesus wants surrounding Christianity and Christian worship. No matter the messes we encounter, it's the atmosphere

Jesus wants released by those who serve Him. Like a hosting parent managing the hubbub but somehow never missing a step in communicating love for all around. This is the kind of love Jesus wants His faithful pastors and their churches radiating. It's the first stage in our pastoral ministry stance.

As every parent knows, there will be times when children declare their hatred of parents who are responsibly and lovingly firm. So our idealism needs to be buffered by reality. Our role as pastors is to create, by means of the consistent, caring protectiveness of agape love, a secure, wholesome and safe environment for incubating new life and nurturing all to full maturity in Christ. Those that challenge this, we as pastor-protectors, must quench their unsettling influence. Pure, unselfish love is always Jesus' objective for His Church. Those who dance to a different tune must not win

Stage Two of Our Pastoral Ministry Stance – Buoyancy

We are not to be naive but nor are we to mirror or mimic the attitudes of attackers. We are not to become like that which we fight for God.

1... stand firm in the Lord in this way, dear friends!..,

4 Rejoice in the Lord always. I will say it again: Rejoice!

5 Let your gentleness be evident to all. The Lord is near.

6 Do not be anxious about anything, but in every situation, by prayer and petition, with thanksgiving, present your requests to God.

7 And the peace of God, which transcends all understanding, will guard your hearts and your minds in Christ Jesus.

> 8 Finally, brothers and sisters, whatever is true, whatever is noble, whatever is right, whatever is pure, whatever is lovely, whatever is admirable—if anything is excellent or praiseworthy—think about such things.
>
> 9 ...And the God of peace will be with you." (Phil. 4:1, 4-9)

All of this stands together well, until we run it through the complexity of our nature. When we give our best and the benefits are disappointing, or even destructive, our natural tendency is to recoil. So how do we keep our attitudes pure when we feel broken or betrayed - battered in mind and spirit? It's a problem of the just - we know we deserve better. If we succumb to this downward draw the devil wins.

The devil and his demons are drawn to bad attitudes. To them bad attitudes are like handles they grasp and twist for control and manipulation downward into a morass of self pity and recrimination. To whatever measure that the devil is in control, the Lord is not.

It reminds me of the time I spied an antique boat anchor while snorkeling. Wow! I had to have it! So I dived down, grasped it and pumped for the surface. Was that ever educational! It's tough to keep your snorkel above water when you're holding on to an anchor. Likewise, bad attitudes weigh us down. They can drown us. So scripture advises holding on to the buoyancy of positivity. It is as though, nurturing positive attitudes even in the midst of abuse is like keeping our snorkel above water.

Salt and Light for Tough Stuff

The title of this book makes it plain that this is not a book about pie in the sky idealism. It hearkens back to the words of Jesus in description of what lies ahead for those who faithfully live for Jesus, serving and proclaiming His truth as they should:

> If the world hates you, keep in mind that it hated me first. If you belonged to the world, it would love you as its own. As it is, you do not belong to the world, but I have chosen you out of the world. That is why the world hates you. Remember what I told you: 'A servant is not greater than his master. If they persecuted me, they will persecute you also. If they obeyed my teaching, they will obey yours also. They will treat you this way because of my name, for they do not know the one who sent me. If I had not come and spoken to them, they would not be guilty of sin; but now they have no excuse for their sin. Whoever hates me hates my Father as well. If I had not done among them the works no one else did, they would not be guilty of sin. As it is, they have seen, and yet they have hated both me and my Father. But this is to fulfill what is written in their Law: 'They hated me without reason.' When the Advocate comes, whom I will send to you from the Father—the Spirit of truth who goes out from the Father—he will testify about me. And you also must testify, for you have been with me from the beginning. John 15:18-27

It seems to me that New Testament church leaders were better Christ-conditioned for this resilience. Jesus was the Perfect One, perfect in heart, and life and love. It was that very perfection that brought upon Him the wrath of naysayers. So, being faithful for Jesus projects an ominous "tough stuff" shadow over what ministry will mean for us. Our principles will breed problems that will need to be dealt with. Will these overcome us, or will we be prepared to work them for the best possible benefits to God's glory?

The New Testament church leaders considered it a privilege to walk in the Saviour's footsteps. They were irrepressible –

> They called the apostles in and had them flogged.
>
> Then they ordered them not to speak in the name of Jesus.
>
> The apostles left the Sanhedrin, rejoicing because they had been counted worthy of suffering disgrace for the name." (Act 5:40-41)

In post WWII Germany, its capital, Berlin, was divided to the point that east Berlin erected a wall to separate east and west. Apparently, one day East Berlin dumped a truckload of garbage on the west Berlin side of the wall. West Berliners could have reciprocated with the same, but they didn't. Instead they neatly stacked a truck load of canned goods, bread, milk and other provisions, on the east Berlin side. They reached out to the need they saw rather than retaliating. On top of their stack of food they placed a sign, "EACH GIVES WHAT HE HAS."

Who are we? What do we have that others need? What will we give? Skilled and orderly delivery of God's love in place of hate? Divine peace for violence? Eternal life for death? Love that has no boundaries, kindness no borders? How else will they know if we do not live it? How will our world ever understand, appreciate and experience the incredible wonder of Jesus' message of love, if they do not see it demonstrated by His shepherds, fostered among His sheep and shared with those in such desperate need of the redeeming message and life transforming gift of God's Son?

What we pastors need so desperately is a godly atmosphere of love and the buoyancy of positive attitudes that lifts us out of potholes of self-centered discouragement that rob us of uplifting ministry so necessary to transformative influence in the lives of persons in need of our Savior, Jesus Christ. Where we live we lead.

For the Spirit God gave us does not make us timid, but gives us power, love and self-discipline. (II Tim.1:7)

"The LORD is my strength and my shield; my heart trusts in him, and he helps me. My heart leaps for joy, and with my song I praise him." (Psalm 28:7)

"Do not grieve, for the joy of the Lord is your strength." (Nehemiah 8:10)

"May the God of hope fill you with all joy and peace as you trust in him, so that you may overflow with hope by the power of the Holy Spirit." (Rom. 13:15)

"Where is your heart today? Are you eagerly anticipating the dawn of a new year? Or do the days ahead seem ominous? Is there faith or fear? Joy or dread? Maybe it's "all of the above" for you.

This is why it is extremely important for you to walk every mile of your day with Jesus by your side. As you do, you are comforted and strengthened. More aware of His goodness. Cares are minimized in the light of His glory and grace." David Jeremiah

CHAPTER 5
Managing Stress

"No temptation has overtaken you except what is common to mankind. And God is faithful; he will not let you be tempted beyond what you can bear. But when you are tempted, he will also provide a way out so that you can endure it." (I Corinthians 10:13)

How Our Body Responds to Stress

The most perfect leader who ever lived was crucified. What chance do we have to evade stress. As Jesus said, ""If the world hates you, keep in mind that it hated me first.." (John 15:18)

No matter how pleasing our manner and sincere our motives, there will be some unpleased with our style or leadership. This is inevitable, no matter how faithful we are. As Jesus taught, "Woe to you when everyone speaks well of you, for that is how their ancestors treated the false prophets." (Luke 6:26) Trauma is like a computer virus that changes the way we work from the inside.

Sounding the Alarm

Ashok Gupta, in a book about neuroplasticity, deals with the impact of stress, and how to manage it. (*Retrain Your Brain to Heal from Chronic Illness* © 2007 to 2022)

Our body is hard-wired to protect us against threats from predators and aggressors. To counter a perceived threat, our hypothalamus triggers an alarm system that prompts our adrenal glands to release a surge of hormones, to pump all available energy to physically handle the threat. In the past, threats were more physical, so our natural conditioning is to react with a flight or fight response to fend off the threat or flee to safety. In the quandary between determining the relative benefits of fight or flight, or worse, in desperation, we may freeze while enemies walk over us. This is natural since higher mental functioning and problem solving is not as essential to this immediate physical threat management process, so our brain doesn't receive the same rich hormonal stimulus. Blood flow to the brain may even be restricted. These explain why our mind seems sluggish and brain fogged under stress, even protracted stress so characteristic of the mental and emotional threats to pastors.

So the hormonally driven adrenal response that winds up for fight or flight, tends to leave us mentally incapable to reason through to constructive processes for managing situations. To counteract this, practiced responses for expected scenarios may retrain our mind. Like learning to play an instrument, repetition actually opens new neural pathways for more immediate, more natural, more skilled, less stressed responses to challenges. So, we may improve resilience by rehearsing the tools and templates of this book through our mind so we make them part of our naturalized response to prospective challenges.

Preparation for Stress

Larry Yanch, former American Navy Seal Leader, advises that, 'if we do not prepare mentally and practically for expected stressful situations, our performance will be 180 degrees out of sync with what we hope for.' Without templates for response, pressure will likely prompt missteps that antagonists may use to their advantage, leaving us with a debilitating, demoralizing and incapacitating sense of incompetence. I've been there. I know it – brain fog even over extended periods of perplexity and incapacity when under fire. How frustrating! Just when I needed to be at my best, I was flailing like a victim being restrained, bound powerless not just by assailants but by my own incapacitated mind.

Conditioned response training, like that provided to navy seals, will keep us intellectually capable at just the time we need our intelligence the most. With strategic know-how for managing typical stresses we encounter while pastoring, we won't have to struggle against incapacitation to sort through options, but merely follow and adapt honorable, tried and true plans of action, like a trained navy seal on mission - my mission here.

Stay Ready So You Don't Have to Get Ready.

Winding this through the opposite direction, this type of rehearsing can incapacitate us further if we allow protracted challenges to ruminate like a never ending loop in our mind. This negative mental restructuring locks in detrimental and demeaning self-recriminating dimensions of our life experience. To counteract this we need to discipline ourselves to mentally step outside the problems to rebuild what is breaking, as Philippians 4:8 advises, "Finally, brothers and sisters, whatever is true, whatever is noble, whatever is right, whatever is pure, whatever is lovely, whatever is admirable—if anything is excellent or praiseworthy—think about such things." No Stinkin Thinkin.

In the Greek, the verb translated "think" in Philippians 4:8 is present tense, advising persistence, "keep on thinking". Repeat, repeat, repeat. Repetitive purposeful attentiveness to this higher mental focus can positively renew how our brain works, rewiring it to function more constructively even under stress.

As I assess Philippians 4:8, I find it another example of biblical truth being ahead of the findings of modern science. This solution has been there all the time, not given a fancy name like neoplasticity or conditioning, yet incorporating both. Solid wisdom that works. God knows how we work and how to make us work better. Phil. 4:8-9 — put it into practice, "And the God of peace will be with you."

> It's easy in life to become transfixed on how we've been wronged by others. Yet what good does it bring us to hold onto negative feelings from our interactions? Does it resolve anything? Or does it only make us more miserable? Joshua Philipp

> Every day we will encounter the ungrateful, arrogant, deceitful, angry, envious and antisocial. Expect these annoyances because they are part of what life and ministry with other people naturally brings. It proves that they need a shepherd.

> Rev. Dr. K. Rick Baker

Don't generalize specifics though. Don't let the distorted taint of a few take over the whole color palette of your mind. Too easily we become contaminated by what we let into our spirit. Don't make the congregation or our family pay for the bad attitudes and actions of a few.

The key is not to focus so intently on troubles that we descend into a deep hole of isolation, discouragement and depression. After all, rarely does such mental preoccupation on severely distressing circumstances free us, especially since adrenal response cripples reasoning anyway. So, be kind to yourself, allow for pleasurable distraction and social interaction with trusted friends that restores and heals. If these prove inadequate, seek professional counseling focused on trauma and stress coping strategies. These contribute to peace of mind, less anxiety, enhanced quality of life and greater clarity and creativity for crucial problem solving.

"Despite the things in others that may bother or annoy us there is nothing another person can do to force us to change our own inner nature. Our inner faculties will always be our own to govern." Joshua Philipp

In leadership there will always be those who love us and loath us. Neither of these should be allowed to influence how we lead. We are to lead according to the direction of our Lord and Master. In faithfulness to our calling, we are to keep focused on Whom we are meant to please. Run a clean ship by abstaining not only from evil deeds, but also evil thoughts, especially about those we are called to serve.

We exacerbate problems when, under the spiritual and mental distortions of stress, we make unwise decisions and do inappropriate things. Lack of wisdom, respect does not feed.

Struggling Too Hard; Trusting Too Little

While overwhelmed we may behave like the trapped soldier on the battlefield, screaming for help into his walkie talkie. Problem was, in his desperation, he never released the button to listen for available directions. Likewise, under duress, extreme stress may cause us to behave similarly with our prayer life, crying out to God, and likewise hearing nothing in return. God is there for us but we are not there for Him. With problems bigger and more challenging, God seems farthest away because our desperation and cluttered minds and motivations rob us of balance necessary for attentiveness to hear God's "gentle whisper" (I Kings 19:12).

Enemy Doubt

Then, in our sense of needless isolation, one of our worst enemies seeps in—doubt. How do we instill faith and trust in God when our own is in shambles? To receive, we need to pause peacefully to listen, to receive somehow.

Stress Relief

Where unable to resolve stress-building situations, detrimental consequences of chronic stress can be mitigated by relaxation responses and / or exercises, deep abdominal breathing, focusing on soothing Scriptures, devotions, prayer, tranquil scene visualization, nature walks. My wife and I especially came to appreciate walks by the water with long views across a lake. This is therapeutic because it takes us outside the up-frontness of life – encased in offices, administration, committee meetings, homes, study, sermons – all closed in. Wide open spaces have a way of reassuring us that close up things that stress us are not all there is. Walks in nature can be great places to commune with our Savior as well. Other proven stress relievers are healthful living practices such as adequate sleep, exercise, relaxation, wholesome diet, laughter, emptying mental stress into journal pages, hobbies, time with people who care. Our whole being, spirit, soul and body, needs soothing. Like a spa treatment.

Social Support

Social support is especially therapeutic. The worst thing we can do is to allow managing troublemakers to consume us so much that it distorts our view of everything and everyone. Supportive relations with spouses and people who matter, and whom we enjoy, provides a life-enhancing, balancing social net and stress relief by distraction. If relations with deacons are positive, their focused understanding, empathy, confidence and prayer support are exceptionally beneficial, as they fill their God-ordained supportive role to their pastor. I believe it is always best to give deacons the benefit of the doubt that they will stand forth to meet the challenge. What better way to seal a pastor's relationship to his deacons than to invite them in?

"The more often your body is in a state of peace, tranquility, compassion, love, gratitude and happiness, the faster your body will heal, plain and simple." Nathan Crane

Building on Positive Emotions - From Stress to Excitement

As we have shared, stress research verifies that severe stress incapacitates the thinking part of our brain. Extreme pressure neutralizes our ability to invent wise means of managing the worst. Another means to changing this may be to turn anxiety into excitement. The physical responses are similar, except that excitement animates rather than paralyzes.

I hope that enablement from this book will prepare us to manage whatever comes our way with excitement rather than dread. Excitement releases positive hormones that energize and clear our head. In this book, we have what we need, when we are normally least able to think things through. We have the tools to diagnosis situations to choose which specific templates and tools are appropriate, and instruction for their use. With these in wise synergy, we should be enabled to go forth with holy boldness to serve the Lord with honor, and succeed in almost anything thrown our way.

"Don't ever let your current circumstances bring you down. A great attitude is one of your best assets."—Jonathan Landsman

"If our attitudes are right and expectations teachable, it is in the hardest of times we learn the best lessons and feel the most gratitude." Anon.

Survival

Now, longstanding or chronic stress can indeed be quite detrimental to our health because it is strongly linked to decreased brain health, early aging, decreased immunity, greater susceptibility to disease, and more. If past trauma and / or chronic stress continues to be a breeding ground for anger, bitterness, sadness, or other deeply embedded destructive emotions, it will continue to incapacitate us and compromise our health. But, if we deal with trauma effectively, if we make it through, those tough times may make us more resilient to current and coming stressful challenges. Inner healing is crucial to keep stress from sucking the life out of us.

My daughter is my hero in resilience, despite extended trauma. Out of her darkness has emerged a ministry through photography. In one of her customary Face Book posts, landscape photograph with commentary, Andrea describes her own journey to wholeness in an arresting manner...

> Recently I was reading about the process of a caterpillar becoming a butterfly. We all know the story, Caterpillar - Cocoon - Patience - Butterfly. But then this realization hit me in the gut and ripped me open. The caterpillar turns to liquid inside the cocoon - mush - completely destroyed - unable to hold itself together in any way. It's not just patience that creates the butterfly, it is a complete disintegration of everything it knew to be real and true. Before it could be reformed to thrive in a brighter and more expansive universe, it lost everything right down to its molecular core.

> I know what it feels like to be liquefied on the inside, to no longer be able to hold myself together, to crave the cocoon in which to wrap myself in order to hide my dismantling from the world.

It was only when I finally surrendered to the mush and allowed myself to fully disintegrate that I was able to rebuild into the thriving soul I was always destined to be.

If you are currently being liquefied by life, consider that this might not be the end, but rather the middle - the metamorphosis into something so much better you didn't even have the capacity to imagine it. Get ready to fly.

Andrea Cross Photography

Now, permit me to get personal in my response to my daughter's post. I commented, "I watched you heal, Andrea, but never understood the depth of the reconstruction. You are an inspiration to me concerning my own healing process. Thank you for being understanding and supportive of my journey."

Andrea's Response... "You didn't just watch, you were instrumental in the process and I can't thank you enough for your gentle care during my 'liquid' time. I love you dad!"

"If you're going through hell, keep on going." Winston Churchill

CHAPTER 6
Call – Issued, Accepted, Ended

———

Having received a personal call to ministry and trained for the task, we open ourselves to a specific call for where and who God would have us feed and lead for His glory.

Pastoral Search

Surprisingly, this step can be so complicated and energy consuming as to spread confusion over churches and candidates. It may foment role confusion and misunderstanding sufficient to discourage and disable the ministry it is designed to initiate.

The process begins when a pastor leaves a church. Constitutionally defined procedures set in motion to fill the vacancy. First, the congregation will delegate church members to search for a pastor through participation in a specific task force – a Pastoral Search Committee. Participants are usually solid members of the church who have time to give to the demands of the role. Since the task is so time consuming, Pastoral Search Committee members are rarely those in key church positions, though I think they should be.

In a confidential fashion, so as not to unsettle an existing pastorate by their research, the Pastoral Search Committee will investigate pastors, or Bible College and Seminary graduates, that may be open to a call and those with beliefs and ministry styles that may possibly be appropriate to their church. They will evaluate the effectiveness of existing pastorates. From this research they will narrow their interest and plan ways of personally experiencing pastors they are considering. This may require travel to observe them in their present pastorate, especially service leadership and preaching, and as possible, meeting with the candidate in their present situation.

If the candidate is open to a call, those Search Committee members will report back to the rest of the Committee to assess next steps. The Committee as a whole will likely converse with or meet with one they are considering, to assess relational dimensions and physical issues of possible income and benefits.

Checking Out a Church

There is no better time to assess the available pastoral role that we are considering than when in consultation with the Pastoral Search Committee. It provides greatest prospect to begin a ministry with shared understanding of our role. So, value Pulpit Committee meetings not merely as the church's exclusive domain to assess us, but use them also to investigate the church. We might use questions like, "Where has your church been? Where is your church now? Where are you going?"

Request and carefully read a copy of their church constitution, which sets the structure and lines of authority within which we will work. There can be some real surprises here—making it impossible to effectively serve the Lord in that place. Will you serve from a restrictive cage of control or be permitted to lead?

With friendly inquisitiveness, float trial balloons as a predictor of what is ahead for a pastorate at that church, and whether the atmosphere is conducive to the type of ministry we bring. Ask them about how they see our role. Assess reaction if we share the biblical definition of our role. Probe other important issues. The response of that segment of the congregation could be instructive as to how that congregation, as a whole, views our place and leadership among them. The more clear the understanding we develop with the

Pastoral Search Committee the better the possibilities for our pastorate in that church.

To accept a call without basic agreement as part of the call process leaves us vulnerable to the stress of trying to turn the church to allow us to fulfill our role as we understand it. Churches are like jumbo jets, very resistant to turns, so misunderstanding is not a positive beginning for a functional relationship.

Things we and the Pastoral Search Committee agree to will need to be negotiated with financial and spiritual leadership.

This is all an arduous process, taken with only one candidate at a time that may lead to follow through, or falter so committee members start over again with another. Clearly, Pastoral Search Committees do not attract church leaders because they are so demanding that participants need minimal time pressures to start with.

Call Issued and Accepted

When, finally, the Pastoral Search Committee and church leadership is able to settle on a candidate for presentation to the church, they arrange for the candidate to preach for a call. He will attend a service, be introduced to the congregation as a pastoral possibility.

The candidate will preach the service for the congregation to taste and evaluate whether his style pleases them. Following the service there will usually be a reception during which congregants may mix with the candidate and ask any questions they choose.

After this, without the candidate present, congregants assemble. As its last duty, the Pastoral Search Committee reports, including details of physical and financial considerations, then the congregation votes for or against calling the candidate. Constitutionally, this vote must pass on the basis of a large majority.

A call is extended only on the basis of the vote of the congregation - one vote per member / no respect of persons, no influence or vote by any committee or board. Each vote pursuant to God's will for leadership of the church. So, in a congregational church, as far as human agency is involved, it is only the congregation that is empowered to extend a call to a pastor, and that only by a large majority vote. By this means it is hoped that spiritual church members will tune themselves to God's will concerning their ballot.

With regard to pastoral salary and fringe benefits, the above assumes that the position being offered is the only salaried position in the church, so financial considerations will be provided to all during consideration of a candidate and appear as an individual budget item each year. If the position being considered is one of several paid positions in a church, this opens the possibility of leadership maintaining confidentiality, providing information outside their group only on a need to know basis. So knowledge of pay considerations could be and should be limited to those involved in its determination by blending income for all church employees into one budget item. This removes an unnecessary flash point that some may try to use for congregational control of their pastor through criticism of pastoral compensation. There are still those who may object to pastoral compensation as though a vow of poverty needs to be imposed. As with others, in the congregation, skilled labor is worthy of its compensation. As with others in the congregation, they would not appreciate their income being advertised to all, and subject to their critique. Pastors deserve such equal consideration if it can be provided.

Now, just another matter for consideration - when a pastor meets with a congregation for the first time consequential new dimensions of that pastorate may unwrap. The question is, therefore, "Is a pastor required to accept a call because he receives an overwhelming approval by that congregation?" No. If at any point we sense reserve in our spirit about serving a congregation it is essential that we follow the still small voice of the Savior in pastorates we accept.

There are only two ways that a pastoral call can be justly ended:

By the pastor who accepted the call announcing his intention to end his call to minister there.

By a high majority congregational vote, only one vote per member, to end their present pastor's call and ministry there.

CHAPTER 7
Who Works for Whom?

The Pastor Is Hired By Whom?

The process of finding and calling a pastor is usually so lengthy and exhausting that it can be difficult for congregants to see God active in the process. "We did the research. We did the travel. We asked the questions. We assessed appropriateness. We presented the candidate. We voted to call. Where is God in this process? Did we call him or did God? Through our efforts has God called our pastor, or have we merely hired him? Is he our employee to do as we wish, or the Lord's man to follow God's leading? Are we in charge of the pastor we have called, or is God?" These undercurrents can prove very consequential to pastor, to congregation and to the cause of Christ.

Induction Service

It is probably to help clarify God's involvement in the process that it has become the practice for churches to hold an Induction Service soon after the new pastorate begins. An Induction Worship Service is the usual manner by which a church officially celebrates God's provision of a new minister to serve as pastor of their church. These services are planned by the church in consultation with the new pastor, to give glory to God through public expression of gratitude to God for His provision. During the service, mutual commitments necessary to healthy and constructive ministry of the church and the new pastor provide practical human considerations. So the congregation will be led in expressing its determination to care for, supply for, support and follow their new shepherd. The new pastor will declare his intent to lead with integrity, godliness and love. A guest preacher, chosen by the new pastor, will provide biblical challenge to the fulfillment of what has been pledged. In benediction, God's blessing is declared on the commitments made, maybe even a laying on of hands. Then all enjoy refreshments and fellowship. It is a wonderful way to set the tone for ministry going forward.

Like weddings, Induction Services are feel good times designed as the first step into years of lovingly working to build a life together, but possibly, a rosy hued smoke screen cloaking hidden undercurrents. Some, and hopefully most, will simply receive and commit themselves to honor and follow their new pastor as a man of God. Within the mix, however, will be some with tainted motivations. From their habitual footing these will 'sincerely' speak their vows in a float of ulterior motives. They are sincere to the extent that their character deficiencies permit. Power oriented parishioners may view the new pastor as a competitor to be channeled for control. "We will follow you if you do what we want." Others occupy and own. Their objective is to perpetuate without change. So they tend to distrust the new as a threat. To them, pastors are seen as part of a line that comes and goes, like intruders to be tolerated, resisted, out lasted. From a pastor's perspective, these expectations or requirements give lip service to wanting a pastor who is true to his calling to follow the Lord's lead, yet expect him to operate like a hired hand, doing as he is told. These are so incongruous with God's calling and leading. Awareness of this congregational mix should not jaundice our approach to pastoring, but naivety is not a virtue. Forewarned is forearmed. Preparedness is wise, guards against undue discouragement and provides for astute prayerfulness and planning. With open hands and heart, present yourself to the congregation as a pastor who will serve them in the Savior's love. Set out to win their confidence and support.

Pastoral ministry involves an ambivalence that can twist clergy and congregations. Biblically, it boils down to the difference between an under-shepherd and what the Bible calls a hireling (AV), hired hand (NIV) (John 10:12-13). Are churches and their lay leaders the boss of the clergy they hire, or do clergy have a higher calling of congregational care that they are responsible to respect? Are they to follow or to lead? What does God have to say on the issue? Will churches support what God says?

The temporary Pastoral Search Committee that did the work and presented the candidate to the church, did not make the decision to call. With the call issued, approved by overwhelming vote of the congregation and accepted by the candidate, the Pastoral Search Committee dissolves back into the congregation. Its work over; it ceases to exist.

Standing committees and boards did not hire the pastor. They are not active in the process of finding and calling a pastor.

It is the congregation that votes to call a pastor, and that by overwhelming proportion of the membership. Each member exercises only one vote, so no one has valid claim to act as employer, treating the pastor as though he is their employee. So, mistreating the pastor by those who claim superiority is inappropriate and should not be tolerated by the human employer, the congregation. Only the congregation as a whole can be viewed as the human employer, to adjudicate congregationally disruptive behavior that threatens pastoral tenure.

Since the position sought and accepted is that of being God's man in their midst, whatever the process, hiring is inappropriate terminology or understanding of what has transpired. The man of God is to serve the Lord under His leading and in that manner serve God's church. Why would churches seek and call a servant of God only to resist their being a servant of God? Be clear on who hired you. It is a matter of call.

Employed - Who Does a Pastor Work For?

Picture an orchestra with one or more instrumentalists that refuse to follow the conductor's direction. Would the music be worth listening to? Not at all. A conductor is hired to conduct instrumentalists to follow his direction, all contributing their skills, synchronistically, so that, on the basis of the conductor's reading of the score and his awareness of musicality, the conductor leads all instrumentalists for production of a masterpiece to be enjoyed, as expected.

God means for His church to function similarly, in accordance with God's will communicated through God's man, their pastor. God's word declares defiance of the pastor's leadership destructive of the integrity and effectiveness of their pastor's leadership and its unifying force within the fellowship. This is desperately important. Churches that refuse to be led by godly pastors disintegrate, bringing shame to the cause of Christ.

A faithful pastor, therefore, leads with eyes fixed upon his Leader and Lord to determine how well he is doing. Applause or no, his Lord is the only standard for success or failure. For a godly pastor, he serves others under the guidance of Christ, the Founder and Head of His church, that merits loyalty from all those redeemed by His blood. In this sense, all who defy pastors who are faithful to their calling, defy the Lord Who leads.

It is very disconcerting, therefore, when the untrained and inexperienced, puff themselves up to equal status and authority to that of their pastor, in order to derail his direction. The pastoral role is to be responsive to needs of the flock he leads, under authority of and accountability to the Lord. So, as such, pastoral priority is obedience to the Lord, rather than submission to laypersons. Where there might be reservations about that direction, currency of earned trust from a pastor's character, spirituality, integrity and capability ought to keep things moving according to the pastor's leading.

If the church leadership needle leans toward unspiritual disrepute someone needs to dial Godward. There is no one positioned better for this than a godly pastor, but we have to have the skill to do so effectively.

Priesthood of All

"But you are a chosen people, a royal priesthood, a holy nation, God's special possession, that you may declare the praises of him who called you out" (1 Peter 2:9)

Some claim equal authority on the basis of the priesthood of all believers, kind of like internet surfers who challenge their doctor. They fail to recognize that all believers being enlisted to serve as evangelistic bridges (priests) to the Savior, does not make them equal in authority or responsibility to the position of their pastor. To their trustworthy pastor they are to follow as sheep in his flock. Godly pastors, submissive to their Lord, reach forth in service to His sheep – pleasing God by doing what God knows is right for them.

In ministry, pastors might help to tip the scales with gentle reminders of our inspiration in ministry. When preaching, read the text for our sermons and pronounce, "This is God's Word." Make it plain that we preach God's Word. Insist on prayer before and after church functions and business. Make it plain that, while open to congregational input, we are intent on knowing God's will, and leading accordingly. We are God's man for God's ministry. The authority for our ministry is not derived from people, but from God Himself.

"Obey them that have the rule over you, and submit yourselves: for they watch for your souls, as they that must give account, that they may do it with joy, and not with grief: for that is unprofitable for you." (Hebrews 13:17 AV)

As pastors, it is essential that we be clear about Who we work for, and serve accordingly.

A Whirlpool of Futility.

This is very much the essence of church failure. Pastors want, indeed are called to be God's servants but churches want to be in control. How futile for churches to pursue a man of God that they won't allow to follow the Lord. Is it any wonder that churches find it difficult to acquire and keep pastors? Everybody is disappointed, including the Head of the Church, Jesus!

If the Apostle Paul were still actively overseeing churches, the North American Church would be getting a letter.

Churches in earnest to change their future to one pleasing to their God must bend their knee to the Lord and open their heart to follow His servant pastors. What could be more important than to be on side with the Head of the Church?

Jesus promised to build His Church, not yours.

Let a man of God be a man of God.

CHAPTER 8
Agreed Understanding

Beginning a pastorate with the belief that the church that called us knows what they call us to be and do, may be more delusion than fact. If we assume accord, disagreement may come to bite us. Better to invest in agreement we can stand on together, by leading the congregation to recognize and support the biblical definition of a pastor's role to help them commit to move with us in that role.

With this as background, I will now proceed to analyze the biblical role of clergy in congregational churches with two goals in mind.

Goal # 1 - Knowing who we should be and what we should do.

Goal # 2 - Providing content for explaining pastoring to congregants along the way.

These two goals will be blended together for us to apply as appropriate to situations we face.

Pastoring in some churches can involve different qualities that don't work well together. In some churches, structures or constitutions may be designed that way. We may be given freedom to preach as we feel led, but authority may be curtailed in matters of church administration – sort of like, "The pulpit is your realm. The church is ours. Stay in your lane." This is fine if we have been hired as only a preaching pastor, but if, as is usual, we feel called as shepherd to lead the whole church, it will seem right that oversight of all aspects of the church's life and business should be recognized as our role.

Four Descriptive Titles

In self-governing congregational churches, four titles apply to clergy. The legal designation for ordained clergy, "Reverend" and three descriptive biblical titles that the original New Testament Greek uses interchangeably:

"Poimen" (Pastor, shepherd – feed, lead, guide, protect, discipline the flock) (Acts 20:28, Eph. 4:11-12, I Tim 3:1-13, II Tim. 4:2, Titus 1:5-9, Heb. 13-17, I Pet, 5:2-4).

"Presbuteros" (Elder – by age or spiritual maturity) (Acts 20:17, I Tim. 3:1; Titus 1:5-7; I Pet. 5:1).

"Episkopos" (overseer, bishop, supervisor, superintendent) (Acts 20:28, Phil. 1:1, I Tim. 3:2, Titus 1:7, I Peter 2:25)

"Hedcumenous" (leaders, rulers, in charge) (Heb. 13:17, 24)

With time, these different words to explain the work of pastors, became spread out and applied to several levels of church administration. My experience of congregational churches is that we aspire to be New Testament churches, so the roles originally included in pastoring local congregations should presently be recognized as operative in pastoring today. Post New Testament distinctions should have no place in our churches, but they can rear their head when we least expect, as means to weaken our reach and authority in the church.

Pastor

Perhaps, if awareness of the biblical overseer and superintendent functions adhered properly to our church's understanding of our congregational clergy, those called to lead churches would be given respect necessary to fulfill their biblically defined leadership responsibilities. Instead, congregational churches I have known consistently use only the title, "pastor". Now I love this title. It is my favorite, but it is a word with placement nowhere else in our society, so, actually mostly a title devoid of meaning. It harkens back to bygone years, to shepherding of sheep that we little understand. As I have sensed it, pastor has become more of a cuddle term, without recognition that it requires a flock that follows. Pastoring is disempowered to worthlessness in churches without a following flock that supports and obeys his shepherding leadership - providing, guiding, protecting, nurturing, disciplining.

As a title, Pastor is upfront, on everyone's lips. It's locally relational, shepherd to sheep. Inclusion of awareness of oversight and superintendence dimensions of our role, though important, may be missed. Instilling awareness of and expectation among the congregation of these functions in the pastoral role as a natural part of their pastor's responsibilities is necessary to free a pastor to exercise this authority as an expected part of his service to the congregation.

Set the Table First

Whatever our shared understanding with the Pulpit Committee, we will need to functionally establish our role in our new congregation. It probably won't be exactly as agreed with the Pulpit Committee. No matter what is written or was previously the case, churches morph between pastorates. Leadership vacuums draw opportunists that may change the normal dynamic.

Sitting-In

Since it is appropriate to be uncertain concerning the thinking of a new congregation, to graciously help establish your general oversight function, take initiative early in a pastorate. As we settle in, clearly but gently, generate early recognition of our interest in all aspects of a church's ministries and services. Request opportunity for friendly visits into functioning activities, committees and boards. How they receive this and how they treat us while attending can be diagnostic about how they view us and our role. Express interest in, appreciation and support for what they contribute. In this first, and perhaps only such visit, do not criticize, challenge or advise. Just enjoy experiencing the congregation, and conclude by thanking them for their kindness in letting us attend. By this casual action of showing interest, we demonstrate our intention to be involved in the entire church's functioning. This also provides insight into how ministries operate, how they interrelate, how they might be improved, as well as assessing existing lines and attitudes of and to pastoral authority – any resistance duly noted for future reference.

In assessing how people serve, I found it wise to allow considerable honorable latitude for their approach. Different personalities and giftedness naturally operate differently. I found wisdom in assessing results rather than means to objectives. This permits people to thrive in roles, like artists who paint differently with pleasing results. (For clearer understanding of what I mean, consult my digitally published book entitled, "*Discover the Spiritual Gift in You*".)

Unifying Influence

Like a goose leading the flock through the heavens, it really is not feasible for a pastor to lead the direction of the flock from the sidelines. To lead, the pastor must be central, not only in the pulpit but in the ministries and administration of their church. Not micromanaging everything dictatorially, but coordinating everything functionally. By this means, overseeing involves managing and coordinating for cohesiveness among participants, administrative committees and ministries toward shared goals according to God's will. Without this unifying influence ministries can wander, fragmenting a church. As overseer, a pastor's influence is to stir a unifying current to keep everything flowing with God's purpose. Pastors cannot oversee what they can't oversee. Lead Pastors should be ex officio in all church administration, on all church committees and boards to head off trouble before it has a chance to gain life.

To assist with this, we will find it wise to request delivery of minutes from all meetings transacting church business. By this means, we can manage by awareness more than control. Place these minutes in a binder or portafile, with labeled dividers. Bring this with you to all church meetings so you can quickly bone up on anything for the sake of knowledgeable understanding and input.

Chairing Church Business Meetings

There may be wisdom in reassessing the functionality of the Chair of Deacons chairing church business meetings. If the Deacons Chair is not spiritually and selflessly committed to stand with their pastor and his ministry, they are not qualified to lead. In this circumstance it may be advantageous for the pastor to chair church business meetings. Being led by an unsupportive chairperson positions the pastor in a sidelined position. From a sidelined position, speech from the pastor appears interruptive, stepping out of a structure of expected submissive silence, rather than an expression of leadership.

As shepherd, the Pastor is to set the tone of business meetings, with an introduction of visionary, challenging devotionals. Especially remind members of their responsibility to pursue God's will in all they say, how they say it and in how they vote. In setting agendas for meetings, check the minutes of the previous meeting for unsettled matters, and consult business meeting minutes from a year ago for recurring annual concerns. Include these in the list of issues to be considered.

During church business meetings, heads of activities, committees and boards report and people respond. The purpose is for membership awareness of the ministries of their church for unifying influence for the sake of needed prayer and congregational support, as well as to process business matters that warrant congregational approval, such approving new memberships and congregational concerns that will bind the congregation to major expense for which they will be responsible. During these meetings, as chair, pastors are in position to exert leadership direction as appropriate. At the end of meetings, the Pastor again takes the reins to conclude meetings with a challenging summary and prayer. The pastor's purpose is to keep the church focused on Christ's purpose for His Church.

Support with Latitude

When a church calls a pastor it should be understood that this call is given in recognition of our theological training, our demonstrated close relationship with our Lord and our skill at leading and feeding a church according to God's direction.

For any person, committee or board to set themselves up as the pastoral control agency is to negate all purpose of our calling and coming. We are to serve as God's under shepherd, following God's direction. As a shepherd, of course, we are dependent on our flock following. As long as we lead with Godly wisdom, love and clear concern for the wellbeing of the church and its ministries, we should be given support to do so with latitude that allows for expression of our gifts and talents. No two pastors will be the same, but as long as we are walking in the steps of the Savior, it is for congregants to work with us for God's glory. It's called trust—to follow and discover what God has for them through their pastor's leadership. Flocks that fail to do so hinder and hurt those whom God provides to help church members in their spiritual walk. Sad to say, at times, clergy tread water in a sea of discontent in churches who fail to provide this support and cooperativeness to their ministry.

"Have confidence in your leaders and submit to their authority, because they keep watch over you as those who must give an account. Do this so that their work will be a joy, not a burden, for that would be of no benefit to you." (Hebrews 13:17)

Be Strong

Like Joshua, God's encouragement to clergy is to "Be strong and courageous..." for God. (Dt. 31:7) Backing down for the sake of ease is not an option for men of God. God needs those who will preach and lead with biblical fidelity. The Lord our God is with us.

CHAPTER 9
Setting a Foundation

When candidating for a church, we tend to pull one of our best, favorite sermons to demonstrate our capability. Since, as we begin our pastorate, we do not yet understand the congregation, our tendency may be to continue in this manner, at least for a time, while getting settled. But as our ministry becomes established, one of the first things to lay down is foundational preaching/teaching for biblical understanding for ministry ahead.

What is the Church?

Every church has its own concepts of what a church is and how it should work. Problem is that much of it may be out of tune with the Bible, out of tune with our understanding and out of tune with each other. Such discord may short circuit ministry and set leaders against each other, without their realizing why this is happening. So, while seeking to provide moving gospel preaching in the early months of ministry, that outreach effort is not likely to provide needed foundational structure for our ministry.

Sunday morning service is the crucial opportunity to address structural understanding of what we are about. If we are seeking to establish a biblical church, existing congregational twists in its structure and standards that will likely encumber future ministry need to be addressed through biblical teaching and preaching on the subject. So early in our ministry in a church, initiate a sermon series defining what the church is – rather than a Christian club, a powerhouse targeted on being Christ's Temple and Body, with purpose for evangelism and to glorifying God. Preach sermons exposing the biblical structure and roles of pastor, members and deacons. Get biblical ground rules out front to gird up and guide interactions and responsibilities for the sake of peaceful and creative Godly ministry together.

For congregational churches, perhaps we might make use of a resource like: J. Hammett, *Biblical Foundations for Baptist Churches: A Contemporary Ecclesiology*, 2005, or another that provides thorough biblical insights about ecclesiology we can share, without having to begin from scratch to pull it together.

Laying this down week after week might prove too much pressure. So, perhaps providing one of these sermons each month, with other topics in between, would work best to teach truth to the church, about its purpose, biblical organization and role structure, all designed to lubricate the wheels of a church's ministry in league with their pastor.

As well, you might use a brief resource I wrote to clarify how congregational churches work and group for ministry near and far. In my case aimed at Baptists because I pastored Baptist churches. It could be used to maintain clarity for those who miss our teaching series:

(Appendix #1 "How Baptist Churches Work")

(Appendix #2 "Incorporational Biblical Church Structure")

CHAPTER 10
What's Possible?

———

Jesus: "I will build my church, and the gates of Hades will not overcome it." Matthew 16:18

"Go into all the world and preach the gospel to all creation. Whoever believes and is baptized will be saved,..." (Mark 16:15-16)

Years ago, a friend, who chaired a major evangelistic agency, shared about his son who had recently begun his first pastorate. He glowingly spoke of all the energy his son was putting into his new charge, all the things he was doing, all the improvements he was implementing, the new people that were being drawn to his ministry. I listened attentively, but with cloaked sadness. I could not express to him the future I sensed. I had known typical churches. My friend didn't sense and wouldn't have comprehended. In my spirit, I said, "He won't last long." He didn't.

Awareness

The Church, as Jesus conceived it, is a living organism meant to grow. We are groomed to minister for this, fired up to change the world. Sneaking in from the side, we encounter churches intent on changing us, to extinguish our flame, to morph us into whatever likeness they prefer. That's called resistance.

We need to be aware that what churches give lip service to, may not be true to who they are, or represent their actual values. Pastorates from beginning to end are fraught with such non-intuitive traps.

Change

We, of course, realize that there is no improvement or growth without change. Nonetheless, we encounter sections of church people who:

1. Cling to what is familiar.

2. Out of loyalty to their previous pastor, resist anything out of tune with him.

3. Claim ownership – "We own it, so naturally control what is done here."

4. Cling to the comfort of yesteryear – "We've never done it that way before." "Past is best."

5. Don't like the inconvenience of sharing pews and parking spaces with new people.

6. Then there are ones who will move with change but do not want whiplash.

Growth means change and change means stress.

Resistance

Scientifically, an object moving a certain direction tends to resist any change in direction. Likewise, while a new pastor is exciting for everyone that does not mean that a congregation is enthusiastic about change a pastor might want to implement. Even those expressing enthusiasm for our eagerness, may be selective about improvements we propose. Many don't mind new as long as it doesn't change anything. Anything actually new may be grist for resistance. Since most churches actually tend to be pools of comfort, try to mix in change like cream in a coffee, as enhancements of what they already enjoy.

Misdirected Change

It is important also to be aware that not all change is good or feasible. In my backyard, for example, I assessed that a garden barrel planter was no longer functional. Trees had grown up since its placement, so it was no longer in the sun. It produced stunted, spindly herbs. So I devised a method of moving it where it should be, in the sun. That was a good idea, but it didn't work – not at all. It was a disaster. That was a barrel set in its ways so moving it demolished it. Likewise, great ideas don't always work, especially when not properly adapted to the situation or the sensibilities of those we serve. Sometimes even well intentioned improvements can be ill advised, producing more damage than expected. Be prayerfully discriminating.

Constitutional Challenge

In some cases the status quo may be the best possible for the time being, while we bide our time and prepare the ground. Often means of ministry are restricted by constitutionally enshrined edicts. To defy a church's constitution is often anathema – not easily forgiven, and rightly so. Church constitutions are designed to set the pattern for how things operate in that church. For example, I once pastored an historic church only to find that it had lost its constitution. I couldn't find it. No one knew where it had gone. I couldn't even find a copy in historical archives. Without a church constitution, power rangers were free to ride about doing what they pleased for whatever purpose they chose. These were difficult to dethrone because there was no established administrative standard to challenge them. The possibility of establishing a constitution upset them because it would fence them in, making them accountable to the congregation, by the defined structure and roles established in a constitution.

Not having a constitution defies God's intention for His Church that everything should be done, "decently and in order" (I Cor. 14:40

AV) "in a fitting and orderly way." (NIV), but how, and who decides. So, even though constitutions may prove to be roadblocks, they serve a valued purpose. Moving forward may be encumbered with a need to re-evaluate and re-write a constitution, but the task may prove essential to desired change and growth. It demonstrates respect for the church we serve and willingness to work with them so that pastor and church move into the future together.

Along the way to that juncture, we might propose changes to constitutional policies as one year experiments, to be evaluated at year's end for inclusion or non-inclusion in the constitution. By this means, progress can be accelerated functionally rather than hypothetically by annual approval of appreciated change without threat to the viability of the present constitution or a threatening process for rewriting or replacing the existing constitution.

Church Council

In one church I pastored I discovered that the constitution specified 130 positions in committees and boards of a 45 member church. They were run off their feet filling more than one position each and attending multitudinous meetings. All that time spent sitting and talking meant no time or energy to enjoy their church. I pointed this out to them in a business meeting and asked, "Are we to serve the constitution or is the constitution to serve us?"

So I proposed that all committees meet at the same time one evening per month. That would mean that no one could serve on more than one committee at a time. We would call this our Church Council. We would meet in a plenary session, with each committee reporting what business they aimed to transact that day. Then each committee would separate off to meet in a different part of the building. Since committees were made aware of what other committees were processing, all committees could work in anticipation of each other.

At a chosen time we would all come together again in plenary session for each committee to report what they had decided, and each committee could respond by sharing what they had determined to assist each other in our goals. In this manner, with less effort and time commitment, committees accomplished more per month than they used to achieve in two months.

As a one year experiment the congregation approved this plan, though it was not consistent with the constitution, with the understanding that the change could be added to the constitution only if the members agreed that it improved our ministry together. After a year it was resoundingly integrated into the constitutional structure of the church, not in blind hope that it would be more beneficial than the existing constitution, but with assurance that that was already the case. The result of this was fewer hours spent running the machinery of the church and more time for worship and fellowship.

One church went a step further by structuring the release of time into Christian development priorities by implementing a 1/1/1 format for church involvement – one corporate worship per week, one weekly involvement in a nurturing activity of the church, what they called "intense growth initiative" / small group fellowship, and additionally one commitment to serve in one area of ministry. (1. Instruction 1. Enablement/Application 1. Engagement) This released that church from the tendency to pump people full of Bible facts, without rounding out their social skills and ministry involvement. Well rounded, zealous Christians focused on spiritual growth and ministry are the fruit of such balanced ministry.

How we handle change and constitutional adjustments reminds me of our driving experience recently. Like a cluster of millipedes, we were all caught in a clutch of slow moving traffic, along with a very sleek, hyped up, metallic blue Corvette Stingray. It was trapped along with us and wanted us to know its frustration. Whenever there was a small space between cars it revved up its engine, sped forward, then slammed on its brakes. We pastors also, if we view ourselves as superior, might be tempted to treat our congregation likewise. If we do, we fail to endear the congregation and rally their support for our vision. As a shepherd, our primary role is to feed and lead our flock, not to push or use them for our own goals, and grumble if they fail to catch up with our drive.

We shouldn't be so far ahead of our people that they mistake us for the enemy and shoot us in the back.

Status Quo

Churches can cling to the status quo even if their practices are clearly sealing their demise. "We do what we do the way we done it." As one irate congregant declared, "The Church is the one place where nothing should change." That was a necessary security blanket for her. No recognition that some things do not improve with age. But they are what they are and some pastors are limited to making the best of it, kind of like easing the way toward the funeral. Only an influx of new members may provide new acceptance for change, if the church will allow them to stay.

Haste

Like the first hundred days of a presidency, the early stages of a pastorate can be crucial in setting the tone of what will follow. It can take the wisdom of Solomon to navigate them wisely. New ideas, new programs, new growth, new people, new members are best introduced gradually, after the congregation has come to know, trust and love their pastor. So, first step is to focus on growing these trust necessities. Beware and be aware of the illusion of enthusiasm for change. It does not likely mean change now. Wise pastors exercise self discipline to move slowly in seeking change, especially early in their tenure, before trust has been established. Some have even suggested proposing adjustments in hopes they turn up as the ideas of others. To be honest, this method moves so slow it seems to me that nothing might ever improve significantly.

Seeking Honor

While settling in, a pastor needs wide-eyed awareness of currents that might have alternate intent. Early honor may be genuine or manipulative. We need to be careful to balance our time from the beginning to set the tone that we intend to pastor all equally.

Seeking Favor

One congregational current might involve efforts to seek favor to lay groundwork for control. These may offer attentiveness and hospitality almost as though they want us beholding to them. It is important that all realize that we have come to pastor all in the church, so while we are appreciative for their support and encouragement, we are involved with the concerns of others in the congregation as well. Reserved interest wrapped in ministry concerns is probably wisest, and may prove diagnostic of intent. If they act as though monopolizing us is their right, we know what we are dealing with and should expect problems from them.

"Dorothys" - (Greek - "gifts of God" – self- assessed)

"Dorothys" are self-important people whose tone is that the church needs and depends most on them and their contributions. They run the show, rule the roost and own the church. So, they feel that they deserve special consideration. Faithful pastors need to be careful of commitments these may seek as they flex their muscle to get or keep what they want. Indeed, church growth expert, Lyle Schaller, assessed that churches will not grow until the "Dorothy(s)" leave. (Dorothys may be either gender.).

For one pastor, battling his Dorothys was so tough that it broke his health, but the church resisted and persisted to remove them, succeeded and launched forward with new vigor, led by a pastor encouraged by a congregation eager to follow.

Perspective to Wind Disrupters

A key to backing off determined, disrespectful disrupters is reminding them that they contributed only one vote to our call. It was the congregation as a whole that called us, so it is only by action of the congregation that our call can be removed. Therefore, if they persist, the matter will need to be taken to a congregational meeting for its adjudication. Not something most people of this type want to chance, because if they lose they lose everything.

Threat to Power

People who hold positions of power may be threatened by new people who may become qualified to replace them, so they are against anything or anyone that they can't control, new people especially, because they tend to align with the pastor who won them to faith or whose ministry probably attracted them to this fellowship.

Compromise Convenience

People don't appreciate losing their parking space or usual pew. Lots more children means lots more turmoil. New people are unknowns, like the deacon that complained, "I don't know anybody in our church anymore."

Rapid Growth

In one church I pastored, evangelism swelled their ranks so much that long term members, tired of carrying the load of committee involvement for so long, began refusing to serve. "Let the new people do it." Seemed OK, but I sensed an undercurrent that would rise up to disable later. So, because the church was small and because many of the new people were not ready for the responsibilities being foisted on them, I stepped in to buffer the transition and learn the inner workings that did not seem to be operating well. I took on key positions that were left vacant. It was a one year assignment I figured I could manage for the sake of structural integrity research. In this manner, I softened the stress for a time and decreased pressure against the new, who were being accepted but forced forward too quickly. As well, I learned how to repair what was holding the church back from what it could be. (It was during this time that I designed the Church Council.) A step back provided a leap forward.

Since growth was the cause of the stress, what was needed, as I felt led, was accelerated growth. I prayed for God's answer to our circumstance. The vacuum in leadership needed to be filled. We needed more people becoming members, with increased maturity to be willing to assume responsibilities in the church, and with votes to outnumber resistance. It worked. It was an exceptional circumstance where rapid growth in a small, young church ultimately won the day.

Grumping Up to Growth

Other churches grump up in response to new people, and squeeze them out so they are unable to settle. Who'd have expected that some Christians consider pushing people away from Christ and His Church as their ministry? In fact, several churches I attended that advertised themselves as "seeker sensitive" have likewise been oriented away from the growth that was touted. In one, we attended as visitors. We were asked to stand in the congregation so they could welcome us and give us gifts in a small bag with handles and "VISITOR" printed in large shiny gold lettering. After the service no one came over to welcome us. Since I have always been curious about church growth, we explored through the church for a time after the service, carrying our small bag with large letters, "VISITOR". Not one person welcomed us, spoke with us, or even recognized our presence. It can be disheartening how little of our pastoral drive is picked up by those we think are kindred spirits. It is a challenge for sure.

Stay Determined

Stepping into pastoring is like Peter stepping out of the boat. There will be calm times and stormy times. Sometimes, like Peter, we are out in the tempest alone, other times some stand with us. Whatever the state of affairs, whether we sink or swim, depends on the quality of our determination and spiritual strength.

Gossip

On another level, I was once almost convinced that the whole church stood against me. A lady reported to me that everyone in the church agreed with her upset with a specific aspect of my ministry. It shocked and unsettled me because I did not sense that was true. But she had the proof. She had gone about in the congregation and she said that everyone agreed with her. To clarify the issue, I inserted an "Attitudes Survey" into the bulletin that dealt with a variety of opinions clustered about the specific issue. By this means, I and the lady with the issue, found out, in the privacy of our reading, that the Survey indicated that she was alone in her opinion. Again, the media equation proved true, "One complaint equals one person. One compliment equals a thousand."

Jam the Waterwheel of Gossip

As I assessed how this false impression was created, since the lady really believed the congregation agreed with her, I studied how we communicate. As we listen to people talking, we tend to nod our head. We may not nod to agree; but rather nod to indicate we are listening. It seems this is how gossip gains traction, even unintentionally. Perhaps it is best that congregants learn how to deflate gossipers by not nodding as though agreeing when being probed for support. We might also make them accountable by asking, "Do you mind if I quote you when I check this out with _______ (the person being defamed)?" Speaking out of turn, secretly, can be irresponsible and very damaging. Best nipped in the bud by imposing responsibility.

Seven Year Itch

We may reside in a certain church for enough years to build what we feel is a secure base for dynamic development in ministry. Don't rely on this assurance. Even after years under the ministry of a pastor, tolerating changes and growth his ministry has brought to their church, some will yearn for the coziness of the good old days, so much so that they may orchestrate a coup to get things back to the way they were. This is kind of like the seven year itch. Like a marriage getting stale, their appreciation for their pastor begins to run thin. Not because he is doing anything wrong, just because he is who he is. They yearn for a new voice, new face, just new. Like wanting a new suit, dress or car. These churches are like hamster wheels, turning but going nowhere. On and on and back to where they started. To be aware of what may be stirring is to beware. Since the active thrust for such resistance will generally be a small sector of the congregation, it is not wise to leave it simmering. Expose it to the light of day. Ask them if they would be more happy elsewhere. "We want you to be happy. If you are not happy here, please go where you can more happily serve your Lord."

Breaking News – This church is not begging for the continuance of complainers. Re-evaluation time. How important are they? They don't need to stay. The church will get along just fine with or without them. This might be a non-combative means with a confidential invitation rather than forthright confrontation. It allows them to discreetly leave, removing their taint and stress from the fellowship. If, after an invitation to leave, they stay to continue on with their subversion, there is a base for others who might be aware, rather than being drawn into discussion of their issues, to reiterate the invitation to go where they will be happy,.

This last suggestion raises to the fore a general attitude that should be behind all the challenges in this chapter. Most of these characteristics and challenges are common to any group, so don't get bent out of shape. Take them in our stride. Don't approach ministry with a clenched fist. Keep open handed and hearted, seeking the best for all. Maneuver as discreetly as possible behind the scenes to keep the ship moving and stable in whatever seas being faced. Be genuinely loving, kind, considerate, open, supportive with all and in all. Clamp down discreetly and only as necessary. Being careful to deal with challenges surgically so as not to discourage the innocent.

CHAPTER 11
Volunteer Army

Lead pastors of professional ministry teams are able to assess, vet, select, groom, train, hire and fire pastoral team members. The lead pastor has the recognized authority to groom these staff members into a supporting team, creating, among other things, a circle of protection around his ministry. This gives him a control advantage most pastors do not share. Most church people who freely contribute their time and talents are exactly that, free. Left to themselves, volunteers may be resistant to strong leadership and a pastor cannot fire them. Far better to realize our need to court good relations with the congregation – if they do not like us, they will not cooperate.

Teamwork Can Be Dream Work

When we are young and new to ministry, we may start with the illusion that we can do it all, and everyone will love it and follow us on the basis of our charisma. As we grow in experience, we learn that lasting ministry requires the support and involvement of others. So it is important that we learn the value of teamwork. Teamwork is wonderfully productive because it coordinates gifts, and weds the strengths of some with the weakness of others.

Teamwork, however, does present special challenges to pastors because we usually work almost exclusively with volunteers. Pastors work with what they get. Accumulation of attendees and members is random. Pastors exercise little control or supervision of their allocation to church ministries and positions. It means that a congregation that moves as a team can, over time, lose that characteristic. No matter how good and capable a pastor's ministry, change in congregational composition and allocation over time can disturb, even destroy, its rhythm.

So, even when everything falls into place, just one wrong person in there and all can fall apart. As Jesus warns, "A little yeast works through the whole batch of dough." Gal. 5:9 A bad apple can rot the whole basket. Perpetuation of previous congregational conditions should not therefore be assumed. A pastor must be constantly vigilant to be aware of what is happening and what might be needed to keep teams groomed for functionality.

While reviewing this book, The Rev. Dr. K Rick Baker amazingly, turned all of this on its biblical head. What an eye opener!

> You may cover this later but the whole point of pastoring is because people need a pastor. They aren't dream work - they are works in progress and that's the point. People don't exist to enable pastors; pastors exist to mend people nets with gaping holes that don't catch fish unless attended to. (Eph.4:10f) Pastors must take charge of this assignment and expect the broken nets to be a challenge suited perfectly for net-menders. As I remind our team, the challenging parishioners prove pastors are needed. So many young pastors want "whine and cheers" conferences to commiserate on how tough the ministry is - yes - sheep bite and net mending is tedious! That's the job. If you wish to do ministry light and easy, remain a layperson. The Rev. Dr. K. Rick Baker

That's a ministry challenge to ignite the heart of a man of God to men of God. Go for it!

CHAPTER 12
Staying Afloat

L ike a tuning fork, Romans 12:12 encourages us to, "Be joyful in hope, patient in affliction, faithful in prayer." What a wonderful way to begin each day, and to carry us through each day. Doing so requires our relationship to our Savior to be fresh every morning and refreshing each day. We are not alone. We are in the hands of the Savior, who loves us and wants us to honor Him and bring praise to His name. We represent Him more than ourselves.

It is like a romance – close to the One we love and able to carry on a conversation with Him about everything as we go through our days. To maintain this we have to manage distractions so they don't throw us off balance.

Like the picture we received years ago, days may pan out to be like the irate screaming toddler with a bowl upside down on his head, spaghetti all over everything, with the caption: "This is the day the Lord hath made...Rejoice and be glad in it." (Psalms 118:24) The way I scheduled days, I used to resent distractions that interrupted, until I came to recognize that a big part of my ministry is interruptions – opportunities to infuse God's love and wisdom into the lives of others. Messy perhaps, but meaningful, because purpose-filled.

It seems to me that certain sections of the Scriptures are either unknown to the lay leaders of our churches, or these laymen are so steeped in the spirit of the age that they are either blinded to Scriptural truth or willfully defiant of biblical teaching. For perspective, though, this section of Scripture is difficult for pastors to teach to deacons and congregations because the response tends to be defensive rather than responsive to this aspect of what their relationship to their pastor should be. Our age is steeped in distrust for leadership. Obedience has become a bad word.

In this manner, the ministry of godly pastors is resisted, inhibited and frustrated. Years of training and experience is derailed by deacons and other church leaders who behave as though they are in charge rather than the pastor they called to shepherd and to whom they pledged to follow during the induction service they planned for the launch of their new pastor's ministry in their church.

For our role we need practical optimism, much like The Serenity prayer:

> God, grant me the Serenity
>
> To accept the things I cannot change...
>
> Courage to change the things I can,
>
> And Wisdom to know the difference.
>
> Living one day at a time,
>
> Enjoying one moment at a time,
>
> Accepting hardship as the pathway to peace.
>
> Taking, as He did, this sinful world as it is,
>
> Not as I would have it.
>
> Trusting that He will make all things right
>
> if I surrender to His will.
>
> That I may be reasonably happy in this life,

And supremely happy with Him forever in the next..

Amen

Without being phony, we need to discipline ourselves to set our selfishness aside, to weather storms like a palm tree, bend and bounce but don't break. Keep the Lord, our marriage and our family first, before ministry. If we lose these our ministry won't carry much respect anyway, and will be out of step with biblical standards for our role.

In personal devotions, we should start our day with the goodness of God and His love for us so we can walk on the waters with the Savior, no matter what the waves.

Charge our spirit up with recognition that...

1. We are worth more than what we do.

2. We are worth more than what we achieve.

3. Life is meant to be enjoyed not merely endured.

4. Unreserved love is more important than manipulative control.

5. God is more concerned about our well being than our output.

6. People are more important than things or achievements.

7. A life focused on pleasing and building loved ones is a worthwhile life. Proven by the fact that life without this is not worth living or remembering.

8. God loves people most

> May the God who gives endurance and encouragement
> give you the same attitude of mind toward each other that

Christ Jesus had, so that with one mind and one voice you
may glorify the God and Father of our Lord Jesus Christ.
(Romans 15:5-6)

In the 1960s, our family owned a Renault. It was an interesting,
unibody car, kind of like a box with rounded corners, no bumpers.
Rear wheel drive meant the spare tire was mounted in a slot, under
the trunk at the front. One day, my brother had a head on collision
with a heavily chromed Buick Special. Both cars took the full impact
of the collision. All the Buick's brittle chrome fell to pieces all over
the road. The Renault merely bounced back, almost unscathed,
propelled by the spare tire, securely mounted against the body. That's
the type of resilience we need, keeping our shape under pressure
because our relationship with our Lord is steady, strong. We do His
work. We are His servant. We are His special concern. Keeping close
to Him is our greatest protection.

Be tender, but tough. Keep our personal balance. Remain
appropriate. Express emotion appropriately to ministry needs. In
loving support, reciprocate, don't antagonize. Respond to the heart
of people, not to their personalities. The most excellent
representation of this was a university student who stopped to listen
to a fellow student pontificating hatefully on his soap box in an open,
outside area of a secular university. The speaker was encouraged by
her absorption in his speech. Expecting her affirmation for his topic,
he asked her, "What do you think?" Her quizzical response, based on
her Christian faith, demolished him with its depth of perception—"I
think it must be terrible not to be loved."

Diversify

Pastoral ministry is so demanding that it can be all consuming, with
the weakening possibility of our putting all of our eggs in one basket,
leaving us vulnerable to someone or something stepping on our

basket, leveling us by destroying everything our ministry is accomplishing. To mitigate this vulnerability, some may develop interest in hobbies. I also sought other avenues for ministry outside of pastoring. In the process of pastoring I developed special expertise, and traveled to other churches teaching spiritual gifts, cults, family life and biblical creationism. By these means, when things in pastoring became disheartening, I enjoyed the fulfillment and encouragement of travelling to other places, to work with other individuals and pastors who appreciated my input. Offering to serve in denominational, para-church or community involvement can also provide worthwhile outlet. All of these must be on our own time, so to speak, so as not to aggravate congregants and feed claims of unavailability or denial of ministry by their pastor.

> Will your anchor hold in the storms of life,
>
> when the clouds unfold their wings of strife?
>
> When the strong tides lift, and the cables strain,
>
> will your anchor drift, or firm remain?
>
> Will your anchor hold in the straits of fear,
>
> when the breakers roar and the reef is near?
>
> While the surges rage, and the wild winds blow,
>
> shall the angry waves then your bark o'erflow?
>
> We have an anchor that keeps the soul
>
> steadfast and sure while the billows roll;
>
> fastened to the Rock which cannot move,
>
> grounded firm and deep in the Savior's love!

TOUGH STUFF

Priscilla J. Owens

CHAPTER 13
Where Does Time Go?

I found time management a major challenge in pastoring. There are no clocks to punch, no specific start nor end times for a pastor's work day and work week. Priorities in ministry can be difficult to assess. Interruptions and the tyranny of the urgent can rob us of energy for what is important.

Life is more than ministry. Important aspects of quality of life are outside the confines of pastoring. In fact, in the broader scheme of things, congregational issues might turn out not to be nearly as important as they seem. Being too close to things often makes them seem bigger that they are. Stepping back from pastoring periodically can provide health-infusing grounding and perspective.

Because of my ministry drive, pastoring involved more hours than I expected. I wondered why I felt so tired. Along the way, I set a governor by marking work hours. By this means, I discovered I had often completed forty hours of ministry by midweek, and I still had the later part of the week to complete, including preparing and preaching two different sermons. Marking my hours enabled me to judiciously break away, without guilt, to periodically enjoy life beyond ministry. Pastors burn out often. If we don't develop a means of monitoring and controlling our output, our output will end our ministry, our marriage, our family, our spiritual life, perhaps our life. We and our ministry will only be as good as the care we provide ourselves and our family.

Many pastors, though desperately in need of holidays, dread them due to fear that their absence allows the underhanded to pull strings of discord and dissention. (When the cat's away, the rats will play.) What a heartache it is to return from holidays and sense an arctic vortex atmospheric change in the church toward their pastor. Almost every pastor has had to mop up messes stirred while away. Yet, I found holidays to be essential time away for sanity and family life. It was bonding time that helped keep love and respect alive in our family. Success in ministry at the expense of family is too costly, and condemned in Scripture. (I Tim. 5:8) The risk of mutiny is worth it, for the sake of spiritual and family health. As this book describes, the actions of trouble makers can be managed.

CHAPTER 14
Funding

I went straight out of college and into the pastorate, so had little sense of incomes people earned. Only after retiring did I come to recognize how low my salary had been compared to persons with my education in the business world around me. Nonetheless, I was not hard done by. Housing was either provided or financially subsidized and, like a businessman, transportation cost for ministry (car allowance) was either provided by the church or a tax write off. I was provided a book allowance and continuing education at church expense. What I earned tended to go a long way.

From the beginning, churches consistently allowed me a month of holiday. What career do you know that provides that from the beginning? We used the four weeks to take our grade school children out of class to enjoy out of season, reduced cost travel. Florida beach vacations together were the norm. Diane taught our children along the way to keep up with their school work. Those were rich bonding times, swimming, shelling, exploring together. Such sweet memories, not to be sacrificed for the stake of being engulfed by ministry.

In the Induction Service for one of my pastorates, a speaker referenced what he called, The Deacon's Prayer: "Lord, you keep him humble and we'll keep him poor." This can develop into a problem that needs action. The leadership of one church I pastored, failed in this regard by fixating on setting my salary each year with only a cost of living allowance. It meant that as my family was growing I was falling more and more behind. So one year, I shocked the deacons by rejecting the salary they offered. I followed up by explaining how my expenses were increasing, my family was growing and the church was growing in numbers and finances. I asked them how many of them had received a raise in the last five years; they all raised their hands. I asked how many of them had been given a promotion in the last five years. Most had. I asked what I would need to do to get a raise or promotion? Leave? The shock woke them up to recognize my needs and their responsibility to provide for them. They had not been trying to squeeze me out. Like many pastors, I just hadn't expressed my needs.

They gave me a raise and implemented an every- five-year raise policy. The point is, we need not be backward about being forward about our needs, especially if our ongoing pastorate is desired. Ministry is not about money, but it is hard to provide well when under needless strain. Besides, an important component to our ministry is providing for our spouse and children in a manner that contributes to dignity. There is no special benefit in our family living unnecessarily destitute. It can embitter them. "Anyone who does not provide for their relatives, and especially for their own household, has denied the faith and is worse than an unbeliever." (I Timothy 5:8)

CHAPTER 15
Together Forever

Should We Marry?

The writings of Paul raise issues concerning the advisability of marriage for clergy. As Paul expresses it:

1. Now for the matters you wrote about: "It is good for a man not to have sexual relations with a woman." 2. But since sexual immorality is occurring, each man should have sexual relations with his own wife, and each woman with her own husband. ... 7. I wish that all of you were as I am. But each of you has your own gift from God; one has this gift, another has that. 8. Now to the unmarried and the widows I say: It is good for them to stay unmarried, as I do. 9. But if they cannot control themselves, they should marry, for it is better to marry than to burn with passion.

17. Nevertheless, each person should live as a believer in whatever situation the Lord has assigned to them, just as God has called them. This is the rule I lay down in all the churches....32. I would like you to be free from concern. An unmarried man is concerned about the Lord's affairs—how he can please the Lord. 33. But a married man is concerned about the affairs of this world—how he can please his wife— 34. and his interests are divided. An unmarried woman or virgin is concerned about the Lord's affairs: Her aim is to be devoted to the Lord in both body and spirit. But a married woman is concerned about the affairs of this world—how she can please her husband. 35.

I am saying this for your own good, not to restrict you, but that you may live in a right way in undivided devotion to the Lord. (I Corinthians 7:1-2, 7-9, 17, 32-35 ESV)

Note that Paul makes it plain that this advice is not intended to "restrict" but as guidance toward possible more attentive attention to ministry concerns, only if one can fulfill this without overwhelming temptation to sin. He recognizes the largeness of the drives involved, Vs. 9. "But if they cannot control themselves, they should marry, for it is better to marry than to burn with passion." (I Cor. 7:9 ESV)

Perhaps, due to this, Paul writes elsewhere about the role of clergy with firmer expectation: Vs.2 "Now the overseer is to be above reproach, faithful to his wife, temper ate, self-controlled, respectable, hospitable, able to teach, 4. He must manage his own family well and see that his children obey him, and he must do so in a manner worthy of full respect. 5. (If anyone does not know how to manage his own family, how can he take care of God's church?) (I Timothy 3: 2, 4, 5 NIV)

Having begun pastoral ministry single and walked this path married for so many years, I see the wisdom of Paul's guidance. There may be some who can handle the pressures of pastoring while single, but the temptations are huge. Comforting hurting ladies, attracting attention by walking tall in leadership, harboring hurts with no one to share with can be almost overwhelming to any normal human. So a properly managed marriage can be a great protection, but not one that should be pursued merely for that advantage. Marriage is primarily intended for personal devoted endearment and comfort, not as a qualification for employment. I did find, for the time I pastored single, focus on the Lord and His glory was sufficient to maintain my purity, along with guarded awareness of drives that can consume, if fed. As Jesus taught, discipline your eyes not to pursue what you should not have. Before marriage and in marriage porn is lethal to integrity in ministry. (Matt. 5:28; Rom. 8:6; I Cor. 6:13; Gal. 5:16; II Tim, 2:22; Jas. 1:14-15)

Who We Marry

"An excellent wife is the crown of her husband, but she who brings shame is like rottenness in his bones." (Proverbs 12:4 ESV)

Who we marry and if we marry has great impact on who we become and what we accomplish. There are few decisions we make that have greater impact on us.

This issue is dealt with way back in Genesis 2:18, 24.. Vs.18. "The Lord God said, 'It is not good for the man to be alone. I will make a helper suitable for him.... Vs. 24.That is why a man leaves his father and mother and is united to his wife, and they become one flesh."

That began man's search, (after Adam, of course) to find the right mate for him, the one who is fit to be his helper.

That's the yearning expressed by Solomon in Proverbs 31:10-12 ESV "An excellent wife who can find? She is far more precious than jewels. The heart of her husband trusts in her, and he will have no lack of gain. She does him good, and not harm, all the days of her life." That's the treasure God intends in the lives of His servants.

I remember so well the perplexity of that search – a search that drove me to my knees for God's guidance. I was very aware that my wife and I would face the challenges and rigors of ministry together. It would challenge the best in us spiritually, mentally and physically. I would need a mate fit for the task, and well matched for my nature. The search would be complicated by the role ahead, and only God sees the heart.

Criteria for Clergy Mates

Unequivocally, the Scriptures set a clear standard for all Christians seeking marriage, a standard more essential in those who feel called to represent the Lord in pastoral service:...

> Do not be yoked together with unbelievers. For what do righteousness and wickedness have in common? Or what fellowship can light have with darkness? 15 What harmony is there between Christ and Belial? Or what does a believer have in common with an unbeliever? 16 What agreement is there between the temple of God and idols? For we are the temple of the living God. As God has said: "I will live with them and walk among them, and I will be their God, and they will be my people." 17 Therefore, "Come out from them and be separate, says the Lord. Touch no unclean thing, and I will receive you." 18 And, "I will be a Father to you, and you will be my sons and daughters, says the Lord Almighty." (2 Corinthians 6:14-18)

Then the Scriptures provide standards to assess our partner for pastoral ministry. Bending these with the hope that we can change their character after marriage is a trap. There is far more motivation to change during courtship, though it also may prove to be more manipulation for the sake of entrapment. Best to assess who we are considering for who they naturally are and respond on that basis. Demonstrated genuineness is essential. Marriage is a life commitment with desperate need for pure honest bonding in the Lord. In the context of pastoral qualification, therefore, God's Word states: "In the same way, their wives are to be women worthy of respect, not malicious talkers but temperate [self-controlled] and trustworthy in everything." (I Timothy 3:11 ESV)

Notice the segue, "In the same way." It's a bridge that ties this to what comes before. In other words, pastoral qualifications that preceded have accord with a pastor's mate....

> 2. above reproach, faithful..., temperate, self-controlled, respectable, hospitable, able to teach, 3. not given to drunkenness, not violent but gentle, not quarrelsome, not a lover of money. 4. ...manage...family well...children obey...in a manner worthy of full respect.... 6.... not be a recent convert, or... may become conceited and fall under the same judgment as the devil. 7....must also have a good reputation with outsiders, so ...not fall into disgrace and into the devil's trap. 11. In the same way, their wives are to be worthy of respect, not malicious talkers but temperate and trustworthy in everything. (I Timothy 3:2-4, 6-7, 11 ESV)

As my wife and I dated we visualized together what life in pastoral ministry might be like – the best and the worst. We didn't know what all of that might be like, but I wanted to be sure that we were open to the challenges. How might we manage everything together? Ideally, pastor and wife should join so as to live and serve as a synergistic team.

The final phrase, "trustworthy in everything", pulls a whole lot together. Are we in this together for each other, or selfishly for ourselves? Do we look to support each other or to upstage? Does our union create a team with the goal to win shared objectives? Are we mates? Can we trust each other to support us "for better, for worse, for richer, for poorer, in sickness and in health, to love and to cherish til death"? Are we suited to "love and to cherish each other throughout our life"? With these deeply meaningful commitments firmly in place, we will be able to trust our mate to contribute to our life and ministry. (Proverbs 31:11) Miss the mark on any of these and our ministry may come crashing down by factors beyond our management. Don't just follow our heart or our hormones. Life decisions require long-sighted wisdom primed by our Leader and Lord.

Dating Our Mate

But success by wise choice is not a given. It is my observation that the fairer sex tends to be a responder. We need to give her something positive to respond to. After we find her, court her and win her.... That process should not end. What brought us together is what will keep us together – "to get her". Don't marry a spouse, marry a sweetheart and keep that as the focus of our relationship.

To be honest, when I asked for Diane's hand, I was fearful. Neither of us had been raised in secure homes that patterned ideal family life. We were going to be cutting new territory if we were to achieve what we never experienced, but determination was there. So I committed myself not to lose my date, when I gained my mate. I committed myself to keep dating Diane, within our means, of course. If she would wait for me, I would honor her by opening doors for her (not a put down as though she couldn't do it for herself). I wanted to treat her like a queen, and be her servant-king. She took me at my word, so one day, when eager to catch a favorite television program, I parked the car in the driveway, rushed into the house, turned on the TV, and settled into my easy chair. But, after a while, in the distance I heard a persistent car horn. When I went to investigate, I found Diane sitting in the car, leaning on the horn in rollicks of laughter. I never again forgot, though we did maintain flexibility, according to need. In dating mode, I also committed myself to stand between Diane and danger, so when we walk, hand in hand, as much as possible, I walk on the traffic side. I want my actions to consistently demonstrate the treasure she is. I want to remind myself of this.

Don't allow ourselves to become presumptuous. Don't allow the pressures of life to come between us. Rather, maneuver them in partnership to push us closer together. Work together to resolve challenges. Keep alive the thrill and privilege that we want each other. Continue to date our mate, and while we do, communicate person to person, not just issue to issue.

The Scriptures Say It This Way:

"Likewise, husbands, live with your wives in an understanding way, showing honor to the woman as the weaker vessel [physically], since they are heirs with you of the grace of life, so that your prayers may not be hindered." (I Peter 3:7 ESV)

"Husbands, love your wives, and do not be harsh with them." (Colossians 3:19)

"Husbands, love your wives, as Christ loved the church and gave himself up for her." (Ephesians 5:25)

Priorities for Married Pastors

As Paul pointed out, when married, majoring on ministry as the only priority is misplaced priorities. Fullness of divine blessing on and through our lives is a matter of relationships, with God, our mate, our children, then ministry and others. We are now a team and a well oiled team can do more than an individual. Sacrificing health of the team for the sake of individual ministry is misplaced priorities. It will come back to bite us, painfully undermining what ministry we may have. In marriage, don't let the challenges of life, parenting and ministry come between us. Shoulder them together as a couple. For each other, focus on kindness, courtesy and adoration.

TOUGH STUFF

Guard Your Marriage

I often struggle with my inadequacies as a husband. I know only too well that I could do better, but my wife encourages me because she knows my heart is in the right place. When we married, I warned my wife that our life might not be easy. Neither of us really knew what that meant. She and I took on the challenge together. We determined that, whatever the pressures we experienced, we would not let them get between us, to push us apart. We would keep them around us, pushing us together. So, we have determined to help each other in our weaknesses, to encourage each other in our disappointments, to live the agape love described in the Scriptures – love that is a commitment of the will, a determination to nurture the best in each other, no matter what. It is a love that lives for the best of others, and in so doing stimulates other forms of love, like friendship and romance. Agape is the glue that holds us together.

> This (agape) love of which I speak is slow to lose patience—
>
> it looks for a way of being constructive.
>
> It is not possessive: it is neither anxious to impress
>
> nor does it cherish inflated ideas of its own importance.
>
> Love has good manners and does not pursue selfish advantage.
>
> It is not touchy. It does not keep account of evil
>
> or gloat over the wickedness of other people.
>
> On the contrary, it is glad with all good men when truth prevails.

Love knows no limit to its endurance, no end to its trust,

no fading of its hope; it can outlast anything.

It is, in fact, the one thing that still stands when all else has
fallen.

(I Corinthians 13:4-8 Phillips)

This was a passage I studied long and hard. I even made it a checklist
to evaluate my behavior on dates. I needed to learn how to love
because my upbringing left love skewed. I knew from personal
experience that marriages didn't just naturally turn out happily ever
after. We would have to work at it if our marriage was to survive,
better yet, thrive.

"I, Ray, take you, Diane, to be my lawfully wedded wife, to have and
to hold from this day forward, for better for worse, for richer or
poorer, in sickness and in health, to love and to cherish so long as
we both shall live." – fifty years, and counting, we delight in every
moment we have been privileged to share.

The first challenge flowed out of my insecurity, which drove me to
over-work, long hours away. Sometimes I was irritable and distant.
Finances were always tight. Housing was adequate, but we could
afford little. To save money I learned a lot of maintenance skills.
When the children arrived, I didn't fully appreciate the pressures my
wife bore. Communication and willing adjustment to each other was
essential. Such was our home-work environment.

Protecting Our Wife

Pastor's wives can be misused and abused by congregants. For me,
any treatment of my wife that is inappropriate is not tolerable. I want
Diane to be assured that she is not part of that part of my package as

pastor. Based on my trust in her integrity and discretion, I grant her freedom to advocate for herself and I will stand with her always.

I determined to be appreciative of Diane's efforts as a homemaker, thanking her often for what she does that could easily be taken for granted, and appreciating every meal she provides. I realized also that Diane's beauty has always been precious to me, so I decided to invest into it with generous encouragement and appreciation for her efforts. I'm certain recognition makes wives more beautiful as it invests in her sense of inner beauty that shines forth from their outward appearance.

The spinoff of all of this proved interesting and valuable. Not only did it enrich our marriage and home life, it protected my ministry. Along the way, for every pastor, there will be persons of the opposite gender that yearn for special attention. It is a danger for those who are leaders, upfront, well groomed and well dressed. I sensed them occasionally along the way. None, however, gained much traction because the demonstrated devotion Diane and I expressed for each other was blatantly evident – open courtesy and deference. Many pastorates fall due to sexual indiscretions. Through mutual admiration, I thank God that He helped Diane and I to minimize the danger and avoid failure.

I grew very aware as well of dangers that have tripped up many in ministry. After all, a large segment of pastoring relates to the opposite gender. To protect myself I set some policies to guard my integrity. I determined not to counsel ladies alone in their home.. When counseling them in my study I kept a desk between us. The distance was good to keep us on topic and the guard against any urge I might feel to reach out to touch or embrace them for comfort. As well, to minimize misunderstanding I determined not to initiate a hug or embrace with a lady.

I would accept an embrace but not initiate it - not cool but conditioned not to be drawn in by my emotions or those of another. Whatever attractiveness God had given me I wanted it used to God's glory, not for ego or for evil.

"What do you have that you did not receive? And if you did receive it, why do you boast as though you did not?" (I Corinthians 4:7)

On one occasion I was asked to meet a young lady in my office at the church after hours. In the circumstance I did not feel that I should refuse so I asked my wife to come with me. I left the study door ajar with my wife Diane, sitting nearby in the next room. Not surprising, when the young lady that was setting the trap I expected realized that I was not vulnerable to allegations, her need for counsel disappeared never to rear its head again. The issue here is very crucial, since it is not what we do but what we are thought to do that determines our credibility in ministry. Even, as I discovered that a colleague endured a false allegation of impropriety, later retracted as a lie by the young lady involved. Despite his innocence, the situation left the pastor's career in shambles due to residual distrust. His reputation had been besmirched and the stigma stuck. He was shut out of returning to his pastorate. Other near-by churches rejected him. I lost track of him but I hope that perhaps he was able to pastor again, maybe at adequate distance from his hurtful betrayal.

Loneliness is a surprising spin off of pastoring. Being in the press of ministry to so many can actually pull at a marriage. Church gatherings could spread me thin, connecting with everyone, isolating Diane. As well, a lot of things have to be kept in confidence. Long hours in church concerns may mean little time together. And loneliness is a temptation zone. So, though it is normal for couples to differ in their natural scheduling, great comfort can be gleaned from going to bed together. Just being in each other's arms at the end of a day brings rich comfort, with or without more intimate sharing. God wants us to be there for each other – physical contact is essential to that.

> 3. The husband should fulfill his marital duty to his wife, and likewise the wife to her husband. 4. The wife does not have authority over her own body but yields it to her husband. In the same way, the husband does not have authority over his own body but yields it to his wife. 5. Do not deprive each other except perhaps by mutual consent and for a time, so that you may devote yourselves to prayer. Then come together again so that Satan will not tempt you because of your lack of self-control. (I Corinthians 7:3-5)

Family Awareness through Social Media

Church members encounter their pastor most often in church settings. He's official. Up front or in gatherings, dealing with many people. As well, because some do not have a worship and ministry team to manage pre-sermon activities, they almost never have opportunity to sit with their wife and children during church services. Circumstances like these can leave a skewed taste as to who the pastor really is. What's he really like? What kind of a husband and parent is he really? This is where social media can provide an invaluable bridge to understanding and appreciation for those who choose to connect with their pastor on that level. Pictures of the pastor in relaxed settings, enjoying his wife and family members can be invaluable in filling the void. Pictures with his arm around his wife, with endearing descriptions of their relationship. Honoring family members on their special days. Hugging grandchildren. Pictures of family enjoying recreational activities together - caring colors with gentle relationship hues and exciting colors of enjoying

God's creation with family fill out appreciation of the wholeness of a church leader.

As well, social media can provide another channel for ministry running beside other mediums provided in church life. Through it the pastor can season the core of his congregation with needed instruction for essential church values that are not easily included often in worship services. Services are intended for worship of God and instruction from God's Word. How often does this allow for pointed instruction about the importance of church attendance, abstinence from alcohol and illicit drugs, commentary about local and world events that require illumination by a man of God steeped in God's mind and truth. All of this can be provided in a flowing manner though social media, interspersed of course with wholesome family life promotion and devotion.

Restorative Family Memories

At one juncture, when I had succumbed to the pressures and descended into a deep dismal dungeon of despair, I was unable to see anything good in my life and ministry. As I fumbled around in my darkness, crying out to God for release, He brought to my mind the fact that families take photos almost exclusively of the good times, photos, in our case, stored in many albums on a shelf. I removed them from the rarely viewed albums and scanned them into my computer. They became my screen saver, randomly displaying hundreds of happy visions of loving occasions at home and in our travels. As they rolled before my eyes and soaked into my soul, I began to smile, even laugh. Sunshine seeped in to heal me. The revelation of how much good I had been part of opened my eyes to goodness, and ways I had contributed to the happiness of others.

> Finally, brothers and sisters, whatever is true, whatever
> is noble, whatever is right, whatever is pure, whatever is

lovely, whatever is admirable—if anything is excellent or praiseworthy—think about such things. Whatever you have learned or received or heard from me, or seen in me—put it into practice. And the God of peace will be with you. (Philippians 4:8-9)

Sometimes reliving this needs a little help. I thank God I was led to a door of uplift by the prompting of sweet family memories.

CHAPTER 16
Our Turf

―――

"Anyone who does not provide for their relatives, and especially for their own household, has denied the faith and is worse than an unbeliever." (1 Timothy 5:8)

Guard Our Children

An unexpected spin off, from Diane and my caring love and respect for each other, was our children learning, by example, how healthy marriages work, how to treat each other. They grew up polite and honorable, expecting their dates and mates to be likewise. It's good to recognize that we have established a new trajectory for marital care in our family.

Abuse of Clergy Kids

Clergy kids are exposed to inordinate abuses for inappropriate expectations. Some church members expect them to be perfect, castigating them for minor infractions. It can be enough to spur them to hate who they and their parents are. We needed to reassure them that it was OK to be themselves. They weren't bad kids, just kids. Many issues are merely immaturity. So we didn't take up the mantra that our children had to be showcases for our ministry. It was enough that they were learning and, as all parents hope, being their best selves, as able. If anyone sought to inappropriately hurt or demean one of our children we stood firmly in their defense, most often by encouragement of them, since open confrontation is rarely productive with negative people. Raising our children to mature and stable Christian adulthood was our highest calling. I was determined to sacrifice my ministry to protect them, and I told them so.

An interesting interchange between my teenage son and another adult pastor's kid revealed something I hadn't expected. The adult pastor's kid who exhibited disappointment with her clergy parents, asked my son if he had ever rebelled against his father. His surprising response, "No." "Why not?" "Because my father wasn't a pastor at home. He was my dad." That spoke volumes. It did not mean that I had exhibited perfection. It meant that my son had got to know me as a real person. We had been family. We had been friends. It brought to my mind a day when he was very small. He had been misbehaving and I had disciplined him severely. With the pressures I was under, it was not one of my better days. My son looked at me and said, "You are a bad daddy!" He was right. I broke down in tears, asked his forgiveness and asked him to pray for me because I was having a very hard time due to ministry concerns. We ended our time together in sweet, caring prayer and loving embrace. We bonded. There is no substitute for undefensive honesty with our children.

Discipline

As parents, we realized it was our role to train our children toward responsible adulthood. This involved more teaching than discipline. We mentored them by who we were and how we treated each other. When they stepped out of line we assessed whether it was because of defiance or immaturity. Immaturity invoked teaching and guidance. Defiance was a disciplinary issue.

To be honest, I never heard my wife yell until we had children. Children can squeeze the worst out of us if we are not careful. To guard against overreaction, we set the procedure that, when one of our kids really offended family standards, we would send them to their room. This was not a punishment. It was designed to give me time to cool down so that I did not discipline in anger.

Discipline should always be for the sake of the child, not to vent our frustration. After cooling down, I would go into their room and sit on the bed beside them. I would ask them to describe what they did wrong. If their action bordered on illegality, I would describe to them the heartache I would feel if they did this as an adult, and we had to deal with police and the courts. I would then ask what they thought would be an appropriate punishment. I would abide by that, or less. After the consequences were applied, I would ask them again what they did. They would tell me. At that point I would state that that was sin not merely against us or another, but against God. So, in prayer, they would confess their sin to God and ask His forgiveness. I would then pray that God would help them not to do it again, I would thank God for his love and the sacrifice of Jesus that makes forgiveness possible and I would thank God for the lovely child He had given us to love and care for. Amen. Then we would hug and express together the emotions we felt. After that, if there was offense to their mom or another I would send them out to ask forgiveness. More hugs. After all of this quality time it was amazing to see how exhilarated and happy our children were. Discipline was important in our family, so important that we rarely had to do it to this level. Our children grew to know right from wrong and how to treat others, as they practice to this day.

Provoke Thought

Our children were not encouraged to defy, but efforts to reason were rewarded. We did not want our children to grow up with blind faith. We were convinced in the factual accuracy of Christianity, so freely discussed what we believed and the substance behind it. Communication is not enhanced by suppression. As an example, one day our daughter and her mom were arguing about something she wanted to do, but her mom was refusing to comply. I was on the sidelines with no part in the discussion. As it proceeded my daughter caught me smirking from the corner. She reeled around and asked what I found so amusing. I commented that she had really learned to argue very effectively. She loved it, and glowed with satisfaction, while her mom responded, "Yes, you argue well, but you're still not going!" The fascination was that our daughter had earned respect, and that was enough. She relinquished all claim to the reward she sought. She had something more valuable, the respect of her parents. To this day, in discussions my daughter proves herself a thorough thinker worthy of attention and consideration, virtually whatever the topic. She is a thought provoker. She spurs reconsideration.

Guard Our Home

On another front, even if we are living in church-owned housing, that house is our home. Church members were not allowed unannounced, unrestricted access. They we not permitted to demand that our home be an exhibit of orderly perfection. That is overstepping. As long as not offensively unkempt, we are not accountable to them for the quality of our home, furnishings or environment.

In a sociological study I investigated years back, a sociologist set out to evaluate the best home situations for healthy families. Her conclusion was that very tidy homes are not positive to families. They may mean that no one actually lives there. Healthy homes will be somewhat messy because they allow latitude for family members to live, to enjoy each other and themselves, without having to stuff everything under the couch every time someone visits.

A pastor's home should be real. We should be real. Not for show. Our home is not part of the church's domain. Our home is our refuge from intrusion or rude assessment. As long as we are living to please the Lord, our private space is just that – a place to live and grow as a family without interference. A pastor's home is for the pastor and his family, not turf parishioners have a right to mow. Our children will thank us for the protection that allows them to develop normally, outside the hothouse of ministry. Keep our family a protected circle kept together by God, founded on faith, joined by love.

CHAPTER 17
Deacons

In those days when the number of disciples was increasing, the Hellenistic Jews among them complained against the Hebraic Jews because their widows were being overlooked in the daily distribution of food. So the Twelve gathered all the disciples together and said, "It would not be right for us to neglect the ministry of the word of God in order to wait on tables. Brothers and sisters, choose seven men from among you who are known to be full of the Spirit and wisdom. We will turn this responsibility over to them and will give our attention to prayer and the ministry of the word." This proposal pleased the whole group. They chose Stephen, a man full of faith and of the Holy Spirit; also Philip, Procorus, Nicanor, Timon, Parmenas, and Nicolas from Antioch, a convert to Judaism. They presented these men to the apostles, who prayed and laid their hands on them. So the word of God spread. The number of disciples in Jerusalem increased rapidly, and a large number of priests became obedient to the faith. (Acts 6:1-7)

Acts 6 provides a role description for deacons, with generalized, spiritual qualifications that are to be spelled out in more detail and specificity later.

According to Acts 6, the role of deacons is to lift burdens from pastors so they are relieved to spend more time prayerfully studying the Scriptures for preparation of quality preaching and teaching to feed the flock. So deacons are to be a ministering team to assist pastors.

How then has it morphed into administrative boards that assess and control pastors rather than helping them and working alongside them? Is it the pursuit of personal honor, pride and power, rather than service that honors God?

Pride Can Be a Ministry Killer

"God resists the proud but gives grace to the humble." (James 4:6}

Through my years of ministry one of the greatest dangers has been the intrusion of values from the culture around bleeding into church ministries. One such counter-productive attitude is the "climb the ladder" mentality. If positions in the church are viewed as means to increase personal power, they short circuit ministry as God views it and foster challenges to pastoral leadership. Biblically we are to view positions as roles in ministry that are one shelf below another. It is as we bend in humility that we qualify ourselves for greater responsibility.

It has seemed to me that it is better to speak not of positions but of roles in church structure. The word "position" garners a sense of achievement and pride, whereas roles focus on responsibility. So speak of roles and provide specifics of what roles involve, Keep the focus on involvement rather than achievement and rising through the ranks.

This is very important because the world around the church is focused on pursuing positions that merit greater power, prestige and remuneration. None of these factors are spiritually productive in church life. God would have us serve Him, His people and the lost with a humble heart and a spirit of helpfulness. So structure with roles not positions so the focus is on what we are to do, how we are to approach our roles and with what spirit, rather than what status we may achieve..

This may show up most markedly with regard to deacons. If deaconship comes to be viewed as the apex of lay leadership steps within churches, it may inflate its members to perceive themselves as controllers rather than the servants prescribed in Scripture. There should be no deacon position, just the biblically established role.

Roles call for functional structure - what qualities deem one to be appropriate to a role, what are the responsibilities, who do we answer to and who answers to us. Much of this will not be adequately addressed in a church constitution so it will need to be fleshed out in more detail for each role within the church. As functional means to smooth running structure, role descriptions are always open to adjustment and improvement,

The Most Important Church Partnership

The pastor-deacon collaboration is so essential to healthy churches that any crack in the union is a crack in the foundation. Left unattended and the whole structure is a risk. Since this is so important to us, we need to develop strategies to wisely and continuously enhance pastor-deacon communication and caring. Due to the many twists related to deaconship, this can be a real challenge, but one very much worth the extra effort.

Complexities related to deaconship that go back to the Middle Ages, and ongoing from there, have skewed deaconship in ways for which all have paid. So as I pursue amending these distortions, we must keep in mind that being trapped in cages created by others should not necessarily be construed as the responsibility of deacons themselves. By dismantling the bars it is my hope that the relationship between pastors and deacons may experience new freedom and fruitfulness for the cause of Christ.

With this as a backdrop, let's jump now into the potential twists of deaconship, in hopes of unravelling the tangle to expose what God intended by the service of deacons in churches, and, to do so, so that the knots will not reconfigure any more to the detriment of ministry.

I picture this as a road trip. As my wife and I age we become more aware of our blind spots, so we value the second perspective in the passenger's seat. It seems that, for us, blind spots are proliferating to pandemic proportions. We don't create them. Nobody planted that shrub or erected that fence with the purpose of obstructing our view. Nobody ordered a grey car in order to make it more difficult to see. Things are just that way, and we need help to negotiate all the variables around us. That is what it is like with deaconship. There are blind spots. We need another perspective to help us see and negotiate our positioning accordingly. So, together, we will probe blind spots concerning deaconship to improve our perception, understanding and application of deaconship in our churches.

DEACON BLINDSPOT #1— Distorted Deacon Definition

The purpose of translation is to reveal, in another language, what the original writer and reader understood by what was written in their language. So, the word "diaconos" appears more than one hundred times in the New Testament. Where we read "serve" in the New Testament it is a form of the Greek word "deaconos". So, to Greek readers this was not vague. Everybody knew what "deaconos" was. The word was in general use – with meaning clearly understood by all. It no more needed a description of duties than does the English word, "custodian".

Yet, contributing to the present confusion in English churches is the woefully inadequate practice of selective translation. In I Timothy 3:2 the Greek word "presbuteros" is translated into English, "overseer", whereas, in this passage, verse 8, the Greek word "deaconos", rather than being translated, is merely transliterated, letter for letter, into English – "deacon". So we know, the role of "presbuteros" is oversight, but for English readers the role of "deaconos" is left blurred, untranslated, described by a list of character qualifications but lacking a list of duties. This lack of clarity is a source of great misconception about who deacons are supposed to be in a church.

1 Timothy 3

1. Here is a trustworthy saying: If anyone sets his heart on being an overseer, he desires a noble task.

2. Now the overseer must be above reproach, the husband of but one wife, temperate, self-controlled, respectable, hospitable, able to teach,

3. not given to drunkenness, not violent but gentle, not quarrelsome, not a lover of money.

4. He must manage his own family well and see that his children obey him with proper respect.

5. (If anyone does not know how to manage his own family, how can he take care of God's church?)

6. He must not be a recent convert, or he may become conceited and fall under the same judgment as the devil.

7. He must also have a good reputation with outsiders, so that he will not fall into disgrace and into the devil's trap.

8. Deacons, likewise, are to be men worthy of respect, sincere, not indulging in much wine, and not pursuing dishonest gain.

9. They must keep hold of the deep truths of the faith with a clear conscience.

10. They must first be tested; and then if there is nothing against them, let them serve as deacons.

11. In the same way, their wives are to be women worthy of respect, not malicious talkers but temperate and trustworthy in everything.

12. A deacon must be the husband of but one wife and must manage his children and his household well.

13. Those who have served well gain an excellent standing and great assurance in their faith in Christ Jesus.

For some reason, only where the word refers to a role within the structure of the Christian Church (I Timothy 3:8-13) is "deaconos" not translated. Not translating this Greek word in this context provides no clarification to meaning for English readers, except the name for a position in a church.

Untranslated Words Collect Inappropriate Meanings

The problem with an untranslated word is that it is an empty vessel, a vacuum capable of drawing anything into itself, collecting meaning along the way or being stuffed intentionally. Untranslated words rarely fill themselves appropriately or accurately. So, untranslated biblical words can be the devil's playground. All of this is true of the Greek word, "deaconos", and ministries are paying dearly for the distortions. A support structure for clergy has morphed unjustly into an administrative, supervisory position, over the church and over pastors.

A pastor friend encountered this in a reaction to his attempt to instruct his deacons concerning their biblical role. One deacon recoiled at his pastor's insistence on describing deacons as servants, even though his pastor had taught clearly that that is the meaning of the Greek word, "deaconos". The offended deacon declared, "I am not a servant. I am a deacon." He refused to accept that his purpose was to be of service to his pastor. "Deacon" had morphed into a title of honor, representing an administrative, supervisory position in the structure of the church. Rather than being a group of humble servants, as it was in the beginning, deacons transformed into a board of superiors.

My knee jerk reaction is to get rid of the title "deacon" altogether, but I confess it is so ingrained into church culture that this is unrealistic. I doubt that re-naming "deacon" as "servant", "helper" or "supporter" will sell either. Nonetheless, something needs to be done to take the unwarranted, prideful shine off the title. I Timothy 3:13 makes it plain that honor connected to deaconship does not attach to the title but to faithful fulfillment of character and ministries involved – "13. Those who have served well gain an excellent standing and great assurance in their faith in Christ Jesus."

It's time Bible translations practiced the basic principle of translation – to translate the Greek word "deaconos" for what it means. Yet, it seems to me that the title, "deacon", has an appropriate place in church governance, so maybe best to keep the transliteration "deacon" but clarify it with translation - "servant" in brackets. That is specific enough. Deacons are servants to assist pastors, and it is for the pastor to share how he can best be helped, kind of similar to the specific need they addressed as originally described in Acts 6. Deacons serve to help as needed to free pastors to major on ministry to spiritual needs. Biblically, deacons work under pastors as extenders of their pastor's ministry. Nowhere does the Bible support the view that deacons are governors and controllers. Let's get this clarification into the text, rather than in margin notes no one reads.

This is so important, because deacons too easily settle into old boys clubs that operate like corporate boards, with little consideration for the Bible's description of their support role for pastors. Sometimes their selection doesn't even give due consideration to the biblically defined spiritual and character qualifications, which align closely with those of pastors, with whom they are to serve. Deaconship has become an unbiblical position of unearned honor and power. They have become like Pharisees who delighted in special titles, the best seats or parking places and ostentatious displays of spiritual superiority. (Mt. 12:40)

One barometer for this triggered in a church when the pastor, during a healthy growth period, pointed out to the congregation that the parking lot filled to capacity for Sunday School so that no places were available for the church service that followed. The pastor asked regular attendees to Sunday School to park in another nearby parking lot so there would be convenient parking available prior to the morning service, especially for visitors. Utterly amazing! No deacon was willing to sacrifice his privileged parking spot next to the building. They didn't even adjust their seating, as requested, to make it easier for visitors to slip in inconspicuously. "This is our church. We paid for this spot. No one is telling us what we need to do for anyone else, not even the pastor."

God deliver us from such pompous piety, territorialism and inhospitableness, especially from those who give lip service to wanting to reach others for Christ. For people to come to the Savior, they must know that they are welcome and that, especially church leadership, are prepared to welcome them. Self-sacrificing hospitality ought to come naturally to genuine Christians. How can we expect church people to see the importance of this if their leaders fail to demonstrate it, even if in accordance with their pastor's public request?

Deacon Origin and Role Description

From New Testament times the Christian Church faced challenges of leadership and loyalty, but it seems these challenges were met more constructively in New Testament times. The solution they discovered has much to teach about how to work together to keep the church strong and growing, as it should – effective enough to 'turn the world upside down ' (Acts 17:6)

The passage describing the formation of deacons as a ministering team with pastors so richly defines the original architecture of the arrangement that I will point it out step by step as we read **Acts 6:1-7—**

> 1. In those days when the number of disciples was increasing, the Hellenistic Jews among them complained against the Hebraic Jews because their widows were being overlooked in the daily distribution of food.

Pastors Create Deacons

> 2. So the Twelve gathered all the disciples together and said, "It would not be right for us to neglect the ministry of the word of God in order to wait on tables.

Tasked Servants – to ease stress on pastors

- serve so people's complaints about their pastors are dissolved

- encouragers of pastors

- people for peace and power through unity

- serve the church on behalf of pastors

- tasked to serve under their pastors for their pastors to pastor and serve people

- mitigate complaints against

- tasked by pastors on behalf of congregational needs to mitigate complaints

Pastors Set Qualifications and Responsibilities for Deacons According To Ministry Priorities

3. "Brothers and sisters, choose seven men from among you who are known to be full of the Spirit and wisdom. We will turn this responsibility over to them

4. and we will give our attention to prayer and the ministry of the word."

The New Testament Congregation Selects Deacons

5. This proposal pleased the whole group. They chose Stephen, a man full of faith and of the Holy Spirit; also Philip, Procorus, Nicanor, Timon, Parmenas, and Nicolas from Antioch, a convert to Judaism.

Pastors Set Apart Deacon Ministry Under Pastors

6. They presented these men to the apostles, who prayed and laid their hands on them.

God Blesses the Church as Pastors and Deacons Serve Together

7. So the word of God spread. The number of disciples in Jerusalem increased rapidly, and a large number of priests became obedient to the faith.

This record of pastoral leadership in working with their congregation to resolve a first century internal church challenge led to the calling of deacons whose service was to free apostle / pastors to focus on the priorities and activities for which they were most skilled and needed - those relating to insightful prayer and teaching of the Word of God. Deacons were enlisted and set aside to strengthen the ministry of the church by ensuring that their pastors were not worn out by church duties that would interfere with their ability to faithfully fulfill their essential function for spiritual leadership of the church.

The Essence of Pastoral Ministry

While here I think it important to emphasize an essential point expressed in Acts 6:4, where the apostle/pastors set the priority for Christian ministry when they said, we "will give our attention to prayer and the ministry of the word."

The point is that, biblically, nothing, neither physical ministry concerns, nor visitation or administration should be allowed to interfere with time for a lead pastor to draw close to God for spiritual health and for preparation and presentation of life-changing biblical teaching and preaching. Other concerns were not to interfere with that priority. As much as possible other ministry duties were to be delegated to others, as they were to deacons here.

For any organization to grow and continue to do so effectively requires leadership delegating to others more duties they previously did themselves, especially through delegators capable and inclined to enlist others to participate with them. Biblically, this is essential to ensure that we, as lead pastors, are not throttled by increasing workload from the demands of more members.

Further, as a church grows it may be beneficial to add paid staff to lead more demanding aspects of the ministry. There can be advantages to draw staff from the congregation, a pool of persons who understand the required role and are submissive to the lead pastor's oversight.

To facilitate this, Calvary Baptist Church, Oshawa, Ontario, Canada, implemented an eldership track to channel persons who demonstrate inclination toward full-time ministry into expanding responsibility under instructive supervision. As they progress, their character and spiritual depth are assessed. After a specific period, the congregation is asked to submit their evaluation of the candidate's performance. If reports are favorable, the person is presented to the church for acceptance into an associate pastoral position. The congregation calls them into official pastoral service. As part of the program candidates pursue theological and pastoral training. Some have even moved through the program and on into pastorates further afield.

DEACON BLINDSPOT #2 – Deacons on the Wrong Side

From Acts 6, which doesn't use the word "deaconos", but is recognized as the beginning of this delegated role originally instituted to resolve a church complaint. The setting aside of deacons was deemed so important that they were required to exhibit highest levels of character and spirituality, and they were set aside for it by solemn laying on of hands. Procedures on a level of pastoral installation. All of this, at the time, to take the role of arranging charitable dinners and serving tables. Yet, because their ministry cleared discontent, it resulted in congregational happiness and rapid growth. As a deacon, what a privilege to launch the church into dynamic growth by ending complaints against the apostle/pastors! (Acts 6:7)

Clearly, if we look at taking sides, deacons are to be on the side of pastors, to protect, enable and expand their ministry. (Acts 6:3) Brothers and sisters, choose seven men from among you who are known to be full of the Spirit and wisdom. We will turn this responsibility over to them...

4. and will give our attention to prayer and the ministry of the word.")

What a constructive solution! So sad that, in many cases, this wisdom has been lost to current deacons!

Clearly, **Biblical Deacons Are On The Side Of Pastors, Not On The Side Of Congregational Complaints Against Pastors**.

DEACON BLIND SPOT # 3 – Wrong Deacon Purpose

Consequence of Distortion

Imagine what would have happened to the Jerusalem Christian Church if the deacons had taken it as their role to represent the church in collecting their complaints against their pastors (the Apostles). These actions by the deacons would have destroyed the very purpose for which they were commissioned by the church. Their actions would have kept the pastor-apostles impossibly burdened and under attack. Those deacons would have amplified the complaints they were enlisted to solve, discouraged the pastor-apostles, destroyed the leadership of the pastor-apostles, weakened the church's ministries, damaged the reputation of the church, hindered, maybe even destroyed the growth of the church — kind of like deacons are doing today when they undermine and discourage their pastors rather than standing with them to protect them, to ease their load and broaden their reach for the sake of ministry and the cause of Christ.

Biblically Church Deacons were established to be a Team of Pastor Protectors, Not Complaint Collectors.

Referring back to Acts 6:5 and I Timothy 3:8-13, deacons are to be characterized by a servant's heart of deep spirituality, wisdom and superlative character and morality. These virtues keep deacons properly focused on the purposes of God, and, therefore, secure in their non-competitive support of their godly pastors. In accordance with their role, as described in Acts 6, they ease stress on pastors by providing meaningful ministry supportive of pastors, thereby minimizing congregational dissatisfactions based on unrealistic expectations. Their godliness and wisdom, and proven trustworthiness establishes them firmly so they are not easily turned aside from their biblical role of encouraging and protecting their pastor from complaints.

Positive Results of Properly Focused Biblical Deacons

Clearly, this structural decision for the New Testament Church worked well. This was the beginning of deacons' ministry as practical assistants on behalf of pastors. If the church of our day is to regain any of its New Testament effectiveness and vigor, it must get back to these priorities, releasing their pastors from the clutter of duties that bog them down, to free them to better feed and lead as God directs. Properly activated and energized deacons, to serve and lead in rallying help for the pastor, are God's asset to activate and enable powerful leadership and ministry in the Church.

DEACON BLINDSPOT # 4 – Inadequate Deacon Relationship

Partners in Ministry

Biblically, the position of deacon was established to be partners in ministry with pastors to ease stress on them, by providing for ministries that often consume a pastor's time and energy but don't need a pastor's expertise. (Over worked and under challenged.) As deacons fulfill these functions they stand with their pastors, not to undermine them. Criticism fosters cracks of distrust the devil will most certainly exacerbate. This should not be promoted or supported by deacons. If they have a problem, they should exercise their maturity to discuss it with their pastor privately. (Matt. 18:15-)

Deacon Team

Deacons are designed to be a team, along with their pastor. Good is not achieved if team members work against each other. It is not their role to defy God by setting themselves above or against their pastor. They represent their pastor, not the church or themselves. The biblical intent for deacons is that they be the inner circle for pastoral support and protection.

Somehow deacons misconstrue their role. Somehow they lose track of the fact that deacons are the pastor's helpers to extend the reach of ministry. Instead they assume the role of congregational police, collecting clues to lay charges to prosecute their pastor. Such deacons are a segment of governance in congregational churches that needs to be reined in biblically.

Vulnerability

Pastoring involves many responsibilities behind the scenes that none see, but would be noticed if they were neglected. Even deacons, who need to be our closest supporters, rarely appreciate what pastors do.

For them to offer support they need to be made aware of our needs. To be honest, I found it difficult to be honest and open with my deacons, and I paid for that privacy very dearly.

At one point, the number of responsibilities that I had accumulated became overwhelming, so I broke my inappropriate silence with a printed list of my duties so they could see what ministry duties were occupying my time and effort. After talking them through with my deacons, I stated that I was too busy. I needed their help. Would they please assume some of these responsibilities? Expressing my vulnerability endeared me to them, and their response endeared them to me. They stepped in, took over what they could, and freed me to focus on duties more important to the spiritual life of the congregation – exactly in accord with the foundational beginning of deacons as described in Acts 6. By expressing my vulnerability, we became partners more profoundly than ever before. We needed each other. I came to sense that people actively working together for the good of the church rarely step out of line to trip each other.

So, it is essential that we be vulnerable and open with deacons about our needs so that they know what to be and do to minister to and for us. We need to share open communication and partnership personally and in ministry to hold our church and ministry together in the face of all challenges that come our way. We need partnership, for shared involvement in all that can make our church great for God, and any threat to that. The ideal - whatever we are and do, we, as pastors and deacons, aim to shoulder it together as one. So it is essential that pastors nurture the trusted friendship of deacons.

In Christian ministry, "It takes humility and grace to serve others, but it also takes humility and grace to allow others to serve us." Warren Wiersbe

Helping others reveals the best version of ourselves and accepting other's help gives others the chance to be their best.

Deacons are Crucial

Few things are more important to the health of a church than strong and spiritually unified clergy-deacon leadership.

To operate with biblical power, church leadership must serve biblically under pastoral leadership. So, as key supporters of pastors, according to Acts 6, properly functioning deacons are essential to the strength of our leadership and the wellbeing of our church.

Deacon and Pastor Unity

Deacon division is lethal. Is it any wonder, therefore, that the devil works overtime to break up deacon–pastor relations? The closer our relationship of trust and appreciation the more God will be able to do through us and our churches. .

Some churches are characterized by factions set on their own way, and no other. Pastors in this circumstance are courted and cajoled into siding with one rather than the other. Failing this, both are likely to turn on the pastor and court the deacons to do likewise. Likely the most promising way to survive such a pressured environment is to build strongly loyal deacons who follow the pastor's leadership rather than support one faction or another. This allows the pastor latitude to choose aspects of either faction that may prove good for the church, as well as to venture more from his own leading from the Lord.

Deacons Retreat

A problem in pastor-deacon relations is the possibility of absorption almost exclusively in church matters. How can we possibly get to really know one another when our interactions are all focused through the ministry lens? Where feasible, therefore, it can prove immensely beneficial to deacon-pastor relations to break the rhythm and repertoire of our interactions to something more recreational – where we can just be people with people. We can laugh, joke, tease, hike, fish, boat, water ski, snow ski, and share kitchen duties to prepare perhaps questionable fare. Getting away to a cottage location for a weekend, mostly to enjoy time together, to love the Lord and to pray for each other, could be a wonderful bonding time and memory builder. If schedules do not permit this investment of time, plan an evening or afternoon together just enjoying one another – enjoy a sporting event or activity all appreciate. The key to this is that there be diversion of attention away from church concerns and ministry and toward friendship and appreciation with each other.

Phalanx

The way our churches are organized, nothing is accomplished without deacon support. Pastor and deacons need to move in lock-step, working together in ministry and as a phalanx for God, against influences aimed at division, against the forces of darkness. For effectiveness, wise pastors invest in this accord. Any break in that unity offers opportunity for subversive forces to undermine and destroy.

Leadership that moves together instills security and peace in the fellowship. It moves by example, cooperatively like jets in "V" formation—the Lord, pastor, deacons and congregation helping and supporting each other as they move forward in ministry to people for their Lord.

DEACON BLINDSPOT # 5 – Diminished Deacon Qualifications

Biblical Deacon Qualifications

As in Acts 6, with deacons selected for their fullness of the Spirit, faith and wisdom, so also, in the writings of the Apostle Paul, in I Timothy 3, the qualifications of deacons are clustered with those of "overseers". In this passage, the category of "overseer" applies to all who provide directional leadership to churches or, with regard to specific churches, pastors. Inexplicably, "deaconos" is left untranslated in I Timothy 3. What we do encounter is very high standards for deacons – respected, sincere, disciplined, honest, true to the faith, clear conscience and reputation, good husband and father. These declared high standards for deacons accentuate the importance of their role, as church exemplars of godly living in partnership with their pastor, capable of trustworthy spiritual counsel and practical support.

Concerning Pastors

Here is a trustworthy saying: Whoever aspires to be an overseer desires a noble task. 2. Now the overseer is to be above reproach, faithful to his wife, temperate, self-controlled, respectable, hospitable, able to teach,

3. not given to drunkenness, not violent but gentle, not quarrelsome, not a lover of money.

4. He must manage his own family well and see that his children obey him, and he must do so in a manner worthy of full respect.

5. (If anyone does not know how to manage his own family, how can he take care of God's church?)

6. He must not be a recent convert, or he may become conceited and fall under the same judgment as the devil.

7. He must also have a good reputation with outsiders, so that he will not fall into disgrace and into the devil's trap. (I Timothy 3:1-7)

Concerning Deacons

8. In the same way, deacons are to be worthy of respect, sincere, not indulging in much wine, and not pursuing dishonest gain.

9. They must keep hold of the deep truths of the faith with a clear conscience.

10. They must first be tested; and then if there is nothing against them, let them serve as deacons.

11. In the same way, the women are to be worthy of respect, not malicious talkers but temperate and trustworthy in everything.

12. A deacon must be faithful to his wife and must manage his children and his household well.

13. Those who have served well gain an excellent standing and great assurance in their faith in Christ Jesus. (I Timothy 3:8-13)

DEACON BLINDSPOT #6 – Inadequate Deacon Activism

Some churches have come to treat deacons as an honorary gallery for church patriarchs – an honor conferred on those who have been faithful to the church for a long time - a group of the oldest men in the congregation. This defies Acts 6, where the first deacons were chosen due to their spirituality and ability to be active in church ministry. Stocking deacons with the aged who are no longer able to be active in ministries may weaken the wisdom of their contributions, as yesteryear becomes the theme of counsel and decision making. It can be very disheartening for pastors to discover that the opinions of their deacons are more in tune with past circumstances than with present concerns. Deacons who are active in serving church ministries will be far more aware and sensitive to needs to provide wise counsel and spiritual support.

So, biblically, deaconship was not offered to spectators who live by the adage, "Lord, use me in any way you choose, in an advisory capacity." According to Acts 6, they were to be full of the Holy Spirit, faith and wisdom and willing to work, even in menial tasks. So, no active ministry involvement disqualifies consideration for deaconship.

Part of the Leadership "V"

Deacons are to fly closest to the apex of leadership "V", closest to the pastor. Deacons are meant to be exemplars of faithful support and working alongside their godly and faithful pastor. This sacred partnership is meant to beckon parishioners toward Christian activism. Their role thereby serves to enlist others to live for and serve the Lord and his church. Failing this, they compromise their leadership role and that of their pastor. This can have dire consequences on churches. When the strength and quality of leadership declines, standards are lowered, toleration for biblical exposition declines and congregational life and ministry droops. We can end up with churches that are an ethical embarrassment to our Lord, and to the definition of what a Christian church should be –

more social club than Christian church, without zeal to reach out with the gospel to win the lost and serve needs of humanity.

DEACON BLINDSPOT #7 – Unwise Deacon Selection

The most essential qualification of deacons is not that they have been in the church for many years or have been deacons previously, or they contribute heavily financially, or they have high education or career position or other outwardly impressive accoutrements. No. God looks much deeper, into the hearts of those He approves for service in His ministry.

But the LORD said to Samuel, "Do not consider his appearance or his height, for I have rejected him. The LORD does not look at the things man looks at. Man looks at the outward appearance, but the LORD looks at the heart." (I Samuel 16:7) As Dr. Jack Hyles expressed it, while pastor of one of the largest churches, First Baptist Church, Hammond Indiana, "I'd sooner have a spiritual garbage man for a deacon, than an unspiritual bank manager." This was not to inflate or deflate anyone. He sought godly service-oriented individuals wherever they were to be found, no respect of persons due to their positions of power or wealth.

Careful selection can help head off deacon division by starting out right. Most essential here is the quality of candidates. Far better to have fewer deacons of the right type, than, for the sake of filling constitutionally defined quotas, to swell the ranks with persons biblically unqualified.

A means of pastors protecting deacon selection might be to have serving deacons, under pastoral supervision, select candidates for deaconship.

1. Post deacon candidate names on a white or black board.

2. To begin with, at each session to select deacon candidates, the pastor reads the biblical qualifications for deaconship – Acts 6:1-7; I Timothy 3:8-13; Hebrews 13:17. This should never be abbreviated. Setting and re-establishing the high standard of deacon leadership is crucial to maintaining recognition of biblical standards for this leadership position in the church. Hebrews 13:17, though not specifically directed at deacons, is foundational to the leadership deacons must biblically provide.

3. After prayer, the pastor directs all deacons to bow their heads and close their eyes.

4. As the pastor pronounces names of deacon candidates, one by one, without opening their eyes, deacons are directed to raise their hand if they have reservations about the appropriateness of a candidate for deaconship.

5. If one deacon raises his hand, that candidate is erased from the list.

6. Only the pastor has his eyes open to observe whether a deacon raises his hand. Only the pastor knows whether he, as pastor, removes a candidate's name, as he has the same right as each deacon to do.

If none qualify by this method, do not lower the standard. Pray together that God will raise up high quality leadership within the congregation and work together to that end. Better to wait than to pay.

The goal is to establish a solid core of spiritual leaders, ethical, faithful to their Lord, their families, the wellbeing of their church and, most importantly, as biblically designed, protective and supportive of their godly pastor. Without this core of leadership, faithful to their pastor, churches slide into disunity, ungodliness, social club mentality and divisiveness. Deacons were defined as pastor protectors from the beginning of Acts (6:1-7). To loosen or weaken this dooms churches to the devil's divide-and-spoil destructiveness.

DEACON BLINDSPOT #8—Corporate Confusion

No matter how carefully and prayerfully church leaders, and specifically deacons, are chosen, current trends in church administration lean more and more to a non-biblical corporate structure which pits lay leadership against ordained clergy, sort of like the loyal opposition in government. This is not to demonize anyone, but it seems to me that something is amiss in our minds if so many churches are being ripped apart by these types of tensions.

Where is this new definition of the deacon's role coming from—the idea that deacons are to represent the congregation against pastors? Not from the Scriptures. Not from God. Not for the good of and for the effectiveness of pastoral and church ministries. NO! It is a subversive force that is destroying pastors and churches. What then do I think is the source of this distortion that deacons seem so inclined toward? That's right—if it contradicts God's Word, if it destroys Godly pastors and weakens ministries, it's not from God—it's from the deceiver himself—the devil.

No More "Deacons Board"

A further factor that makes it difficult to keep the role of deacon-supporters clear relates to unbiblical content in the structure of churches. In every church I pastored and in every constitution I read in my extensive collection, those constitutions listed and described the formation and structure of a "deacons board", soft on their function and orientation, heavy on their election and duration.

What is unbiblical here is the word, "board". Never is this word connected to deacons in the Bible. It isn't even a biblical word.

Somewhere down through history it was attached to "deacons" and it stuck.

According to Webster's Dictionary, a "board" is "a group of persons having managerial, supervisory, investigatory, or advisory powers". Tied to the nebulous understanding of "deacon" it adds just the twist not needed, suggesting that deacons are sitting and judging rather than supporting and serving.

Here I propose removing this unbiblical component. Time to do away with the confusion and destruction created by the distortion of "Deacons Board". Let's build our churches with leadership easily understood and accurately labeled. I have noticed that the church I presently attend never uses the phrase, "deacons board". They just refer to "deacons". It's a clean and gentle removal of the offending word.

Other solutions I had considered are more intrusive, less likely to work, such as renaming Deacons Boards as, "Pastoral Support Team" or "Pastor Helper Team" or "Helper Team". I especially like the word "team" because it sums up so accurately the functional dimensions of constructive pastor-deacon relations. Whatever works to rid ourselves of "board", we need to get it right, with a clear connection of name to action. As the passage states, honor for those who serve in this fashion comes not from a title but from the quality of their service – "Those who have served well gain an excellent standing and great assurance in their faith in Christ Jesus." (I Tim. 3:13) Biblical deaconship wears coveralls ... laurels later.

Since the word 'board" is so incorrect, it is probably best to extend the ban to all uses of the word- no more Board of Management, Christian Education Board, Board of Directors etc. So how else do we name these? In larger churches this issue bears little impact, since paid staff members are entrusted with church concerns and ministries, and their enlistment of teams to assist them. In smaller churches, where lay people are needed to manage segments of church life, committees are necessary. What else can we call them? The word committee is actually appropriate, bearing none of the detrimental tone of "board". Oxford dictionary defines a "committee" as "a group of people appointed for a specific function, typically consisting of members of a larger group". So, the word "committee" is not biblical, but is accurate to the delegated responsibility.

No Deacon Chair

As stated previously, concerning church business meetings, in my opinion, to lead properly, the pastor should chair business meetings. Likewise in deacons meetings, deacons do not need a chairperson to be in charge of deacon meetings. This leaves them and their chair to prioritize, set agendas, determine scheduling and meeting termination on their own rather than in accordance with priorities of the pastor. This puts the pastor under the chair, to the side, as a submissive follower, speaking as interruption rather than direction. The result? Pastor's serve deacons rather than deacons biblically serving pastors.

There can be real value in pastors setting agendas and leading deacons meetings. At the beginning of deacons meetings pastors should provide a report of matters important to their understanding of the state of the church's health, ministries and concerns weighing on their pastor. In this way, deacons meetings are directed toward what is important and toward their biblical role of being there for their pastor and his needs. Following this, pastor and deacons should pray together for the needs of their church and pastor. In this manner, the focus of deacons is adjusted to the biblical level of what their ministry in the church should be. Only after this should other issues be considered. In proceedings, consensus rather than proportional voting should be sought to decide issues. Lacking consensus, reconsideration is in order, more prayer, more insightful discussion, maybe delay.

DEACON BLINDSPOT #9—Deacons Without Training

With all the confusion surrounding deaconship, it is not wise to assume that our deacons, no matter how sincere or how long they have been deacons, will understand what the Bible says they are and to know how to serve their deaconship biblically. It behoves pastors to allocate time and attention to the training of new deacons as they assume their duties and, during the early months of a new pastorate to train all deacons in their biblical identity and role.

TRAINING DEACONS

Training New Deacons

It's apparent that trying to correct entrenched distortions built around deacons, may be challenging, even if we prove it from the Bible. Such resistance to correction is a symptom to diagnose who is or isn't appropriate to the position – something that can be used to adjust deacon election procedures for introducing new candidates to the role. New deacons are more likely to be receptive to biblical instruction – more teachable. In fact one pastor has implemented a "Deacon in Training" position and program for new deacons who have never served as a deacon before. So, the expectation is established that the first year of their deaconship they will be Deacons in Training, being instructed in the biblical role. In this manner, like a row of dominoes, deaconship in and to that church can be incrementally adjusted to the original God-honoring, New Testament, pastor supporting and church building model.

DEACON HANDBOOK

Since teaching efforts diminish in their effectiveness over time, a valuable method for establishing and holding a proper sense of deaconship is to create a Deacon Handbook gleaned from the selected descriptions of deaconship we have looked at in this section.

Whenever one is considered for deaconship, give them a copy of the Deacon Handbook before their presentation for enlistment. If, in discussing the Handbook with them, they exhibit resistance to the biblical description of deacons drawn from earlier in this section, they should be filtered out of serving by removing their name from the blackboard during a deacons meeting.

(Appendix #4 Deacon Handbook)

DEACON BLINDSPOT # 10 – Evident Deacon Spirituality

Deacon Prayer

"I would rather teach ten men to pray, than one man to preach." Charles Spurgeon

We have looked at the wisdom of God in requiring of deacons standards of spiritual maturity and morality almost equal to those expected of pastors. This certainly elevates deaconship to a function involving counsel for church needs, planning and problems, along with pastors. They are to support pastors with their ministry efforts, spiritual wisdom and prayer.

In the Fray to Pray

For deacons to know how to pray, deacons must be in the fray. It is only as they experience the spiritual headwinds that they will know how to set the sails of their prayers and their church to provide helpful support and counsel to their pastor and their church. No fans in the stands mocking those on the field. No sedentary saints who know how to do it better than the ones who are trained, totally committed, called to the task and actually doing it. Biblically, all deacons must get down and dirty with the rest of us in order to know and advise on the basis of what the ministry really means and needs.

Prayer Supporters

One of the crucial spiritual functions of deacons is to empower their pastor through prayer and to do so personally, publically, and congregationally. In Matt. 6:1, Jesus did teach that prayer is best performed privately, rather than as ostentatious demonstrations of pseudo-spirituality. For deacons who lead in the spiritual life of congregations, however, saying they are praying for their pastor without openly doing so is lame. Refusal to pray along with others in the congregation demonstrates that person's inappropriateness to deaconship. For example, one prayer meeting group expressed concern that deacons never attended. When this concern from the prayer group was expressed to the deacons in meeting, the deacons raged with anger. Those who will not pray for us will usually come to prey on us. These deacons did exactly that.

Prayer Meeting Attendance

Deacons need to be part of the prayer community of the church they serve, or not be deacons. Regular prayer meeting attendance helps keep deacons in contact with the realities of ministry and their role as biblically defined humble servers of pastor and people to God's glory. What we serve is a Christian church, not a social club. Prayer is not optional, but essential. This is Christ's Church so we must keep in touch with our Head for power and accurate purpose. Setting private prayer as equal to community prayer is to set oneself outside the fellowship of the congregation and apart from conformity to its objectives and direction. Those who set their alleged private prayer ahead of group prayer set themselves apart, superior and inclined toward preying more than praying. Spiritual leaders who will not lead in necessary spiritual disciplines, shouldn't hold positions of leadership. So, crucial to a deacon's exemplary role must include regular attendance in congregational prayer meetings. If candidates were unwilling or unable to put in the time, they shouldn't be deacons. Spiritual qualification far exceeds worldly position in the realm of Christian ministry.

Along with their pastors, deacons need to lead spiritually as well as physically. Sad to say, in more than thirty years of ministry, few deacons attended mid-week prayer meetings. The only time we prayed together was briefly at the beginning and end of our monthly meetings. In one church, I grieved for lack of deacon prayer. I sensed inadequate prayer support as a supply line for our aggressive evangelistic incursions into the enemy's territory. As we grew, deacons became more and more distanced from deep spiritual concerns of the church. Deacons became unfeeling concerning the essence of pastoring in their church. As such their counsel and decisions bore little accord with spiritual concerns of the ministry we shared. It was generally a downward trek toward dissolution.

Since the media has assessed that people are a thousand times more likely to complain than to compliment, deacons are entrusted by God with the important role of defending the honor of their pastor and encouraging their pastor whatever way they can. If deacons are faithful in praying with and for their pastor, publicly and privately, it is much less likely that they will be duped into acting against the fulfillment of their prayers.

What I have labored on here may be one of the most difficult adjustments to enact in a church, but, without it, a lot of power and opportunity in ministry will be missed and pastoring will likely be a lonely, disappointing experience.

Deacon Visitation

For a church to be healthy and able to grow, it is essential that deacon-supporters recognize that their role is to work with their pastor, under his leadership, to provide for and help direct the matters of the church. Scripturally, though voted in by the church, they do not represent the church; deacons represent the pastor. As long as the pastor is leading responsibly as a man of God, it is the role of deacon-supporters to protect their pastor, assist him with wisdom and help to implement the plans and programs developed under the pastor's guidance.

This awareness needs to be foundational beneath all deacon interactions with congregants. Each time a deacon rubs shoulders with church attendees some of their attitudes rub off. By the fact they are recognized as leaders, those attitudes, positive or negative, have a contagion. The effect of this is enhanced according to the intensity of the interactions, such as when deacons are involved in visitation of church members. In the comfortable home settings hosts tend to open up. Since people are more inclined to complain than compliment, it is not unusual for conversation to settle here in exaggerated fashion. All a deacon has to ask is to target the negative with a leading question like, "Do you have any concerns?", and down the rabbit hole they go. Deacons with cracks in their support of their pastor find it almost impossible to resist the draw toward representing the congregant rather than as an extension of the pastor's ministry. Such visitation twists to weaken their pastor by collecting complaints rather than managing complaints on behalf of their pastor as their role is set up in Acts 6—to protect their pastors from criticism and helping to bear the weight of ministry.

Being on the Inner Circle with the Pastor Must Not Be Misconstrued

Deacons need to recognize that their pastor has invested years of his life in preparation for his role and pursues that role. For deacons, therefore, to set themselves on an equal footing with the pastor, or set themselves as supervisors of the pastor or as the loyal opposition to the pastor, neutralizes his leadership and training, thereby damaging the church, its health and its future prospects, as well as discouraging the pastor in his pursuit of ministry. As one doctor stated on a wall plaque: "The success of your treatment depends on which one of us is the doctor." Likewise, the success of a church ministry depends on which one of us is the pastor—the one trained and called of God and the congregation, or unqualified laypersons.

"Have confidence in your leaders and submit to their authority, because they keep watch over you as those who must give an account. Do this so that their work will be a joy, not a burden, for that would be of no benefit to you." (Hebrews 13:17)

Priesthood of All

Let's clear some confusion about Scriptural guidance as well. The New Testament declares that all born again Christians are priests. (I Peter 2:9, Eph. 3:12; Heb. 10:19, 22, 13:15; I Pet. 2:5) This is not a position in church organization. It is the privilege for all believers to enjoy direct access to God, without the mediation of a human priest. It also sets all believers in the role of representing their Lord as a bridge to intercede with and bring others to the Savior. The "priesthood of all" does not elevate them to the status of competent competitors to the pastor. Pastors are to lead churches, with all saved Christian layperson priests fulfilling their evangelistic role of faithfully representing their Lord to the lost and to their fellow believers.

The "V" of Victory

There's a wonder to observing geese in flight. First, from a distance, they herald their approach, honking across the heavens. Then, the expansive "V". One goose leads them all. He cuts the air for all that follow, and each follower, in precision, adds to the flow. By following the leader, as part of the "V", each guides and helps the flight of those that follow. Only the leader peers into clear air, no bird in front. Without honking from behind he could perceive himself as all alone. Only the noise behind confirms that he leads those that follow.

Like a goose that is flying lead needs assurance from those honking from behind, pastors need to know that they are not alone in leadership. Rightfully, pastors value affirmation and prayer support most from those administratively closest. Most pastoral ministry requires steady arms of support. To enable victory, pastors need deacons serving like leaders who held up the tired arms of Moses (Ex. 17:11-13). It is as we serve faithfully together that victories are won.

It brings to mind the way Christ structured His Church to function for the sake of its health and vitality. He has chosen to call pastors to lead His local flocks. Congregations ratify that structure by confirming God's pastoral call. In the process of doing so, churches affirm their agreement for active and prayerful support for godly pastors they call to serve among them for the great mission to expand their gospel ministry to their community and to their world, as commanded by Jesus. So churches are structured to perform like the "V" of a flock of geese – following Christ-honoring ministry behind the leadership of the godly pastor(s) they have selected and affirmed by solemn vows spoken during their Induction Services.

No Ambivalence Concerning Loyalty

One pastor asked a deacons board, "When it comes to complaints from congregants concerning a pastor, should a pastor be given the benefit of the doubt?" They felt it wisest to remain neutral, treating every complaint as a valid issue for deacon meeting consideration. They saw no reason to stand with their pastor to lead the church, rather they saw their role as mediatorial, a kind of wishy-washy uncommittedness which proved discouraging, damaging and destructive to ministry. Based on the wisdom of the age they could see no inadequacy to their approach. They consistently treated their pastor as guilty until he could prove otherwise.

Obey Your Pastor – Deacons Heel Yourselves

7. Remember your leaders, who spoke the word of God to you. Consider the outcome of their way of life and imitate their faith. 8. Jesus Christ is the same yesterday and today and forever. 9. Do not be carried away by all kinds of strange teachings. It is good for our hearts to be strengthened by grace,... 17. Obey your leaders and submit to their authority. They keep watch over you as men who must give an account. Obey them so that their work will be a joy, not a burden, for that would be of no advantage to you. 18. Pray for us. We are sure that we have a clear conscience and desire to live honorably in every way.... 20. May the God of peace, who through the blood of the eternal covenant brought back from the dead our Lord Jesus, that great Shepherd of the sheep, 21. equip you with everything good for doing his will, and may he work in us what is pleasing to him, through Jesus Christ, to whom be glory for ever and ever. Amen. (Hebrews 13:7-21)

It seems to me that certain sections of the Scriptures are either unknown to the spiritual leaders of our churches, or these leaders are so steeped in the spirit of the age that they are blinded to Scriptural truth or willfully defiant of biblical teaching. For perspective, though, this section of Scripture is difficult for pastors to teach to deacons and congregations because the response tends to be defensive rather than responsive to this aspect of what their relationship to their pastor should be. Our age is steeped in distrust for leadership. Obedience has become a bad word.

In this manner, the ministry of many godly pastors is resisted, inhibited and frustrated. Years of training and experience is derailed by deacons and other church leaders who behave as though they are in charge rather than the pastor they called to shepherd and to whom they pledged to follow.

If churches are going to honor their Lord in life and ministry, they need to get with the Lord's program of honoring the spiritual leadership God has ordained, pastors trained and committed to obediently follow the Lord and lead His flock to worship, fellowship and service honoring to the Lord and His goals for His Body and His world.

It's time that lay people grow to appreciate the call of God on the life of their pastor and apply themselves to their proper place in pursuing goals God lays on his heart for the glory of God alone.

Hebrews 13 describes very well the results of the present rampant disrespect and disregard for pastors God sends to us and who speak the Word of God to us when it states that this discouraging behavior "would be of no advantage to you." (vs. 7) It's time that Hebrews 13 was sewn back into our Bibles and back into the minds and hearts of our churches and its lay leadership...

> Remember your leaders, who spoke the word of God to you. Consider the outcome of their way of life and imitate their faith....Obey your leaders and submit to their authority. They keep watch over you as men who must

give an account. Obey then so their work will be a joy, not a burden, for that would be of no advantage to you. (Heb. 13:7, 17)

Those who protest the dangers of such "blind" obedience, miss the point. These are godly leaders who provide godly example that backs up their message – "Consider the outcome of their life, and imitate their faith." (vs. 7)

Most defiance of pastors that I have observed has not been rooted in the godlessness or unfaithfulness of pastors, but in a stubborn adherence to an agenda at variance with the leadership of the pastor, who thereby is unable to fulfill his role to lead the flock as God intended.

So, deacons especially should not collect complaints and look for flaws to pick apart pastors. That is not their biblical role, not their biblical ministry.

Deacons need to be instructed in their biblically defined role. To encourage, not discourage their pastors, or his ministry will be ineffectual and they will put God's ministry and their church to shame. It happens too often, and those who foster it rarely take responsibility for the damage that they cause. But, the judgment is coming, when all the secrets of hearts will be disclosed by He who knows all and judges all.

As a first step to increase the possibility of achieving this biblical working relationship between pastor and deacons in every church, do not assume our deacons know their biblical position and purpose. Whether pioneering a new church or beginning to pastor a more established church, fit in teaching concerning what a biblical deacon is and how he serves. As well, before approving one's candidacy for deaconship, be sure they understand biblical deaconship. They may question for the sake of understanding but any indication of challenging and not accepting the biblical role should be grounds for refusing to present their name to the church for candidacy to serve as a deacon.

DEACON BLINDSPOT # 11 – Deacon Incompetence

Deacons may not only impede progress by disregarding or defying the pastor, they may also do so by knowingly or unknowingly failing to fulfill their role with godly wisdom and discretion.

Deacon Lack of Confidentiality

Along with realizing the position and purpose of deacons, peaceful church functioning depends on deacons realizing that deliberations in deacons meetings are confidential. This is not secrecy but respect for the deliberation process.

Sometimes deacons are unable to make decisions on their own, so one deacons meeting will expose the need for a decision, which they will defer until the next meeting, perhaps due to a felt need for more information. Between that meeting and the next, they go home and discuss the matter with their spouse or some other person(s), then return to the next meeting to express the opinion of non-deacon contributors. In this manner, deacon decision making can become almost completely controlled by their spouses and others in the congregation who had not been elected to the Deacons.

If a deacon shares with others what deacons say in the process of discussing issues that were grist for the decision-making process but were not approved and adopted, they betray the confidence of that deacon and undermine free discussion in future meetings. A deacon may even be exposed to anger from some who disagreed with an opinion expressed in the confidence of a meeting, in other words, something they had no business knowing. By doing this, confidence breakers create upset in the congregation for things that never were the policy of the Deacons or of the Church, and put specific deacons on the spot for a mere opinion they thought had been expressed during confidential discussion among the Deacons. As well, confidence breakers aggravate listeners who had no opportunity to contribute to deacon discussion. They foment needless and irresponsible hurt, betrayal and loss of trust. What should come from Deacons Meetings is one voice of spiritual guidance and decision-making. Discussing Deacons Meeting proceedings outside these meetings destroys this, disturbs churches and damages the people with whom it is shared.

Consultation beyond deacons meetings for the sake of decision making is to be implemented by any deacon only by the prior approval of the Deacons.

As a corollary of this, I discovered that it was not wise to have a deacon whose wife is a minute-taking clerk in Deacons meetings, lest they stir themselves up between meetings, even discussing matters in the presence of their children, damaging their children's spiritual wellbeing and relationship to the church.

Many of these problems may be reduced if deacons keep in confidence the proceedings of Deacons meetings. Surprisingly, it cannot be assumed that they are aware of the need for this. For this reason I created the following Deacon Confidentiality document Appendix #4 that I required all deacons to subscribe to, and to which I held them accountable. Confidentiality concerning Deacons Meeting proceedings is not required to keep secrets but because Deacon meeting discussion is often at the cutting edge of policy and of sensitive issues. If a person will not responsibly keep confidences as necessary, he should not be in a leadership position.

(Appendix #5 Discussing Deacons Meeting Proceedings with Non-Deacons)

Deacon Lack of Decisiveness

Deacons tend to be in the middle of all major stressors of a church. Sometimes deacons back off from tough decisions or push them forward in the hopes that the need will go away on its own. Such cowardice is rarely rewarded. Usually it wears down a pastor or exposes him to unnecessary dangers and abuse.

DEACON BLINDSPOT #12 – Pastor Removal Procedure

Deacons Too Easily Become Conduits of Group Action to Remove Pastors

Generally, if there is group action to remove a pastor, it will come through the Deacons. Others may exert influence on the Deacons, but it will be the Deacons that move against the pastor officially as a deacon function during a regular or specially called deacons meetings. In this manner they may seek to force a pastor to resign without prior report to the congregation.

When this happens in a Deacons meeting, stand up and move to the apex of the gathering for them to present their case. Standing is the posture of prominence and governance, require them to deal with us on these terms, as the pastor. Listen to what they have to say. Inquire about the source of the issue. Ask questions to clarify what is going on. Even go deacon by deacon inquiring their position in the matter, and why.

It is interesting how often this action comes on the basis of a person or persons who convince deacons that the issues they espouse are hugely important in the church. Like the other complainer mentioned sooner who actually believed their opinion represented widespread discontent, but was far from the truth. So the weight deacons give to concerns can be misplaced and therefore their actions in response exaggerated, to the shock and division of the congregation and the deacons themselves.

If the deacons are slanted toward complaint collecting, they are sitting ducks for manipulation by such nefarious efforts against the pastor. I feel sorry for deacons in this regard. They are pushed forward to act, take the strain and the responsibility while those who instigated it sit it out, with arms crossed, judging their performance against the pastor.

Before challenging deacon authority, and to protect them from the consequences of ill advised action, perhaps, if the deacons are still reasonable, so as not to exaggerate anything, you might ask whether they have assessed the actual size and intensity of disagreement with the pastor. Media principles are that one complaint represents one person, whereas one compliment represents one thousand people. People are far more motivated to complain than to compliment. This tried and true maxim demonstrates the exaggeration created by a few aggressive complainers, while most may be quite indemonstrably happy. This gives Deacons opportunity to lead wisely, before possibly making a mistake they may regret. Hold them to awareness of what really is, to keep them from firing off on the basis of exaggeration.

This could be the perfect pill to wizen deacons up for handling this matter and with relation to similar efforts in the future. If they realize that they have been duped, they may be more vigilant not to be duped again. In so doing, it could turn the tide for the perpetuation of wiser leadership and protective care of pastors by these deacons and this church.

Pastors Standing Against Invalid Deacon Action

Failing this, enforce the basis of our call and its implications for the validity of their action. Effectively dealing with deacon action to unilaterally end a pastor's ministry is covered with relation to the means of a pastoral call, which demonstrates such action by deacons against their pastor to be unjustified. (I have never seen the power of deacons to end a pastor's ministry enshrined in a church constitution, so they have no right to claim it.) Any such action must be taken to the assembled congregation for their adjudication.

Since no standing committees or boards have any official function in the calling of a pastor, declare to the Deacons that they have no authority to rescind the congregation's call. They had no part in our call except as individual members, so they have no authority as a group to maneuver the end of our pastorate. It is the congregation that called us and only they are empowered to withdraw that call.

Being challenged behind the scenes to leave, therefore, is time to stand our ground. Don't be like so many pastors, unable to keep our ministry drive going in the presence of official obstruction. Do not adjust our normal pastoral gait to run from or chase attackers. Pick up our Goliath stones and prepare for battle. Surprise them by insisting that the matter be taken to the assembled membership. Detractors will be granted opportunity to state their views and the pastor's perspective concerning their complaint and their actions that have brought us to this place.

Because they are at greater risk from a congregational vote, the prospect of this will likely send a shiver down their spine. As with congregational votes to call a pastor, votes against a pastor must pass by a large majority. As well, from experience, those who seek to pre-empt pastoral ministry mid-stream, usually stoop to devious methods to do so:

1. Secret meetings to transact church business without taking minutes.

2. Secret meetings behind the back of the pastor while he is on holidays.

3. Meeting with select troublemakers.

4. Holding deacons meetings behind the back of other deacons, who might not support their actions, in order to plan how they can manipulate the other deacons to acquiescence, perhaps by couching it in a garb of what is best for the pastor.

They defy their pastor, disobey the Scriptures and the church, constitution and covenant, lead by deceit and frame it as following the Lord.

They expect to get away with these maneuvers because it has been their experience of previous pastors folding and leaving when pressured behind the scenes. Mr. Nice Guys naturally choose to lose because they choose not to fight. Ultimately they are victims, neither liked nor respected. Sharing our determination to state to the congregation the facts concerning their actions and our truth concerning their complaints will likely cause them to step back. Legally and justly, without personal attack, without stooping to their level, we snatch from them power they had no right to claim. We stand our ground on the basis of who we are and always have been, a man of God determined to stand for truth, integrity and congregational authority to decide what type of pastoral or lay leadership they want for their church.

The circumstance of dealing with such challenges appropriately and honorably will be completely unexpected, since most pastors seem groomed to acquiesce to the desires of deacons as a Mr. Nice Guy and as though deacon power is absolute—to take "the high road", protecting the place of deacons in their church, bowing out gracefully, laying no blame, pointing no fingers, solving no problems, providing no possibility for improvement, just allowing troublesome people to learn to do what they do better for next time. But since when was it a pastor's role to bow out of leadership in deference to the disrespectful, dishonorable and unspiritual, and leave the church in their hands rather than that of an honorable servant of God.

So make sure it is taken to a vote. Our detractors have everything to lose. If they lose, their leadership in the church is over. For us as pastor, a showdown provides opportunity to clean house of disruptors by exposing truth and their under-handed actions. If we lose the vote, we lose nothing, because we don't want to pastor a congregation that sides with such disrepute anyway.

If we have been honorable and God honoring, as we have always done, stand for what is right, godly and good against what is dishonoring and disreputable. Thereby fulfill our calling by demonstrating to our sheep how they should honorably do likewise. Plan to stay on leading the flock for God and for good until God moves us or the congregation does. Determine to survive to revive through godly leadership with renewed mandate to lead, unless directed otherwise.

CHAPTER 18
Vote Tampering

At the beginning of every church business meeting, instruct the members about the essence of congregational government. "We gather in session to seek the Lord's will. For this, each is to seek accord with the Lord and His will. When issues are presented, each is expected to look to God to express His will in the opinions shared, and in votes cast. We are not to look around, to allow the opinions of others to influence our decisions or voting. By this means, congregational government aims to seek, find and follow the leading of the Lord."

So that they prioritize attendance to church business meetings, instill recognition of their importance to the church in regular business meetings as well as any special meetings that may be required from time to time - no church board or committee may, or should be allowed, to overrule what they decide.

Church Membership

Every church constitution I have read contained standards of membership – how people become members, their responsibilities and privileges as members, and a standard to evaluate whether they are remaining active. Usually "active" is determined by a standard related to the regularity of their church attendance.

When members drift, it is important to determine what is happening. Have they backslid? Are they experiencing problems that need ministry? Have they become upset with someone or something in the church? Are they upset with the pastor? Anything that can be resolved without compromise of church and ministry integrity ought to be addressed.

Trustworthy deacons might be entrusted with this responsibility, but only if they do not slip into complaint collection rather than faithful support of their pastor as peacemakers. If the slope is too slippery for them, a pastor is best for this effort to re-establish the absentees for active involvement, or not.

If, after a period of time, usually defined in the constitution, the distant member makes no effort to begin active attendance, a letter should be sent to inform them that, with no change in their attendance, their status will be adjusted to "inactive member, with no voting privileges". "No voting privileges" is most important.

If they continue to remain inactive, constitutions provide a standard by which they can be removed from the membership rolls and informed accordingly. The process is not without ripples, as some unjustly consider church membership their right, with no responsibility.

The process of keeping church membership rolls accurate may prove exceedingly important if it becomes necessary to expose a mutiny for congregational adjudication. The key to this is the issue, "no voting privileges" for inactive members. In a mutiny situation, expect under miners to pull out all the stops:

1. Be prepared for the challenge that the membership has declined under our ministry if greater accuracy is presented as decline. Answer this firmly, factually and constitutionally. Our unperturbed validation sets the stage for who is in charge.

2. Benefit from the fact that voting members are actually active members.

3. Troublemakers are notorious for dredging uninvolved members to swell the vote to support their agenda at business meetings. These members with voting privileges, despite being inactive, are easily stirred up to contribute to trouble, based on whatever dissatisfactions they might hold and whatever they are told. As well, these tend to be most outspoken about things they know nothing, since they have not been attending. These are often enlisted for votes against pastors, since these votes require a large majority to pass. The only way to head off such underhanded action is to keep a clean house so that only truly active members have a vote about the direction of their church and decisions related to the ministry of their pastor.

Membership Hesitancy

Another issue in this regard relates to church growth, especially by means of evangelism. New believers, who are appreciative of the pastor who brought them to Christ, may be hesitant to become members of their local church. More than once I have heard them bemoaning that they lost the pastor they loved, the pastor who brought them to faith, because they had no vote. So they lose their pastor and in disillusionment, probably their church. And the old guard celebrate that their comfortable little club is once again secure.

It is important that new believers realize a sense of responsibility for the quality of their church. Implications of this are best communicated by the pastor as he works to blend them into the fellowship. They need to be aware that their membership and voting responsibility must be established prior to a challenge, as it cannot be implemented quickly to meet a challenge.

As well, we will encounter those who resist membership because they were deeply hurt previously by involvement in a power struggle that went wrong. So they attend but refuse to be involved as members in the politics of the church. They need to be nudged that this irresponsible position is detrimental to their interests, their pastor and their church. They leave the door wide open for the rug to be pulled out from under them once again. If good people do nothing, evil runs rampant and wins.

CHAPTER 19
Dojo for Demons

L ife involves challenges and dangers, but to live is to face them. So let's get into the inner workings of pastoral ministry in churches.

A friend of mine described his experience of learning karate – "I went to the dojo every week, and was beat up every week." This can be, but should not be, our experience concerning pastoral and church dealings with the demonic. The Apostle Paul, the biblically renowned pastor to pastors, writer of two-thirds of our New Testament, much of which targeted helping pastors to pastor, wrote, " For our struggle is not against flesh and blood, but against the rulers, against the authorities, against the powers of this dark world and against the spiritual forces of evil in the heavenly realms." (Eph. 6:12) "It's true, the source is "powers", but the agency is flesh and blood and packs a physical wallop." Dr. K. Rick Baker

Awareness

The Apostle Paul's description of Christian ministry flies in the face of mere successful career expectations. Time to set aside expectations of cuddle Christian ministry. There is a reason why everybody will not love us, no matter how likeable and loving we are. We are targeted. Paul presents Christian ministry in terms of fighting invisible foes. In thirty-three years of pastoral experience, I found this awareness essential to surviving and thriving in God's call.

Notice that Paul is saying whatever Christians experience on the surface may not be all that is really happening. Dealing with the demonic is described as the true battlefront of Christian ministry.

Even if you are delivered from frontal attack by demons you need to be prayerfully aware of forces the Bible says are at work behind the scenes. Indeed, if we take Paul's words literally, his view, as enshrined in God's Word, is that if we never encounter the demonic in the process of Christian ministry, it's valid to question whether we are doing what Christ would do. Is what we are doing actually Christian ministry? Paul declares demonic forces to be behind the scenes of virtually every problem and every problematic person we encounter in ministry, yet, so many of us, in my experience, graduate for ministry with no practical dojo training for the demonic.

Throughout the New Testament, Jesus deals with demons. He sends his disciples out to command control, yet we graduate from Bible College with little awareness of these battle lines of Christian ministry. Unaware of the warfare ahead, we are sent out with what spiritual weaponry we know about sheathed—unskilled to recognize the demonic and weaponry available for the battle before us, nor are we skilled in its use. I realized this early. I was set off balance, beaten but not broken. I set out to understand and wrestle with what I encountered along the way – shadows of control over churches, unentreatable disrupters, individuals seeking the Savior but inwardly blocked from responding. To be effective, I had to learn how to deal with invisible forces, wrestling against evil spirits. Not what I expected, but where the real battle for the Kingdom had to be fought.

My experience was very much as described in Frank Peretti's novels, beginning with *This Present Darkness*. Surprisingly, Peretti's first novel was incredibly popular. Surprising to me because it depicted, in graphic and danger-filled fashion, the activity of demons behind the scenes as I had experienced them. The fact so many gobbled up his books about the demonic, causes me to question my inclination to keep spiritual warfare as a hidden realm for the few. My concern was always awareness that the more we look toward the devil the more he can instigate fear for increased influence. So, my preference has been to deal with the demonic only as necessary for the health and safety of those I serve.

Satan

Newton's Third Law, "For every action there is an equal and opposite reaction.", does not apply to the battle between good and evil. Biblically, God is the creator of the Universe. The devil is merely a disruptive created being, so much less than God that he is unworthy of attention except as needed to push him out of the way.

In ministry and personal Christian living, my goal has been to keep, "Looking unto Jesus the author and finisher of our faith; who for the joy that was set before him endured the cross, despising the shame, and is set down at the right hand of the throne of God." (Heb. 12:2 AV) For most, this focus on Jesus provides proper perspective for fulfilling Christian living that thwarts wily maneuvers of the evil one.

There is no need for paranoia. There is no need to be looking over our shoulder all the time, but then again, at times, being Mister Nice Guy may prove inadequate in dealing with invisible satanic forces active in defiance of the Lord's work.

So, let's get to know our adversary, the devil. What's Satan like? Is he a scary red being with ferocious face, horns and a long tail? Not according to the Bible.

Satan was a resplendent archangel named Lucifer ("light bearer") who, in pride, rebelled and continues to rebel against God. That rebellion did not change the essence of Lucifer's beautiful being, just his humiliated prideful, defiant, rebellious, hateful heart toward God, everything He represents and everyone who represents Him. Though Lucifer/Satan is evil, he is not repulsively ugly. In fact, Satan is beautiful, winsome, charming to manipulate our desires, our weakness and our strengths for the sake of his evil ends.

When Lucifer was cast down for his rebellion a third of all angels, angels that were under his command, went with him and continue to serve him as demons in opposition to God and His servants. (Is. 14:4-17; Rev.12:7-9) These demons are of different levels and capabilities (Eph 6:12) and can and do influence and inhabit receptive people. When they do inhabit, demons do not necessarily fill the entirety of the individual, but any part of the individual that the individual surrenders to them due to evil, bad attitudes or hatred. These demons may come and go, which means, the person you meet today may not be exactly the same as you encounter tomorrow. In fact, some demons move about from person to person – you will sense this when the MO of attack is the same from several sources

Keep in mind the beauty of Lucifer. He is a charmer who loves to enlist beautiful, charming people to do his bidding. He woos people under his sway by redirecting their strengths and weaknesses toward his desired ends. If you keep this in mind, you will tune your spider sense to wise awareness of Satan's maneuverings. Don't expect his attacks to be blatantly evil. Why a frontal attack when slipping in surreptitiously, stirring up support, would work, maybe better? The devil is strategic. He and his demons will catch you off guard if they can, or deceive others to take their side against you, thinking they are doing God's will. (Is. 14:12–15; Lk. 10:18; Job 1:12–19; 2:7; 2 Cor. 11:14; Eph. 6:12-18)

So, as the Apostle Paul declared, there is a deeper, invisible layer to Christian ministry, a warfare layer. The devil is set against the success and growth of Christian churches and godly servants who lead them. Without scruples, Satan will use anyone and anything available to achieve his ends. So we who lead must be prepared. This is a book for this battle. There will be people that will cherish us, but, as well, we should expect, not merely human disagreements, but also demon-motivated forceful resistance. In fact, if we never tangle with the devil and the devilish, this passage questions whether we are actually in the flow of genuine Christian ministry.

" For our struggle is not against flesh and blood, but against the rulers, against the authorities, against the powers of this dark world and against the spiritual forces of evil in the heavenly realms." (Eph. 6:12)

Primary Target

A corollary of this is recognition of the devil's targeted strategy for churches, as Jesus affirmed it, as revealed in the Old Testament, "Strike the shepherd, and the sheep will be scattered" (Matthew 26:31; Zechariah 13:7) So, we need to be aware that, when persons accept a call to pastor, they enter a realm of strategic risk. When we assume the role of pastor, we put a target on our chest. The devil and his minions are out to get us by whatever devious means they can. As leaders we need supernatural awareness of our foes, and their adeptness in maneuvering information, instigators and naivety to their benefit against us.

It is a far different picture to the one displayed by a teenager who wandered into my study, sat in my swivel chair, leaned back, put his feet up on my desk, cupped the back of his head in his hands and announced, "I think maybe I will become a pastor." He expressed so graphically a delusion shared by many, that pastoring is a sweet spot of armchair ease, outside the struggles faced by others living in the real world. Certainly this needs to be expunged from the mind of churches. Any remnants of it sure were flushed from my mind early in my pastoral experience.

So much of what we do is hidden from sight. Congregants are mostly unaware of what we do, the long hours and heavy weights we carry. A reality check is in order to motivate congregants to pray earnestly for the protection of pastors from stress, loneliness, isolation, vision frustration, lack of respect and support, discouragement, temptation, injury, illness and deterioration of family relationships, all of which weaken and discourage our effectiveness. Faithful pastors cut the darkness with Scriptural truth and spiritual example. Wise congregations and church leaders take seriously their role to strengthen and protect their pastors from harm by extending to them faithful prayer and regular encouragement. A good place to prime this support base is among prayer meeting attendees, and deacons.

Attack from Within

> Do not suppose that I have come to bring peace to the earth. I did not come to bring peace, but a sword. For I have come to turn a man against his father, a daughter against her mother, a daughter-in-law against her mother-in-law—a man's enemies will be the members of his own household. Anyone who loves their father or mother more than me is not worthy of me; anyone who loves their son or daughter more than me is not worthy of me. Whoever does not take up their cross and follow me is not worthy of me. Whoever finds their life will lose it, and whoever loses their life for my sake will find it. (Matthew 10:34-39)

A real eye opener is Jesus' revelation of lines of resistance to ministry, as He sees them – God's view. Even though it is predicted, it is still disorienting to have to deal with antagonists we expect to be our helpers, encouragers and supporters in churches. As with Jesus' ministry, religious leaders may provide most determined opposition.

"Et Tu Brute!"

Such painful betrayal from those closest to us, those we trust, can be so disheartening that it drains our drives for ministry, if we do not take Jesus at His word. This devastating betrayal is predicted so should be anticipated, so that we bring our grief to Jesus, and carry on in the footprints of our Savior.

Resistance from church people is actually most likely because they are most exposed to our ministry. We deliver God's truth to their lives. If their heart is out of tune with the Scriptures, it is they who will most likely react. People outside the church actually encounter little of what we do. Generally there is little for them to react to from our ministry.

So don't expect the primary source of resistance to be from outside of the church. We need to set this unbiblical illusion aside now so that we are not disappointed and disheartened when major resistance comes from those who should, like family, be supporting us and partnering with us. As with Jesus' experience of religious people, even leaders in our churches may provide most determined opposition. They may not even be aware that they are doing the devil's bidding. Clergy graduates need to be aware of and prepared for this reality that lies before them.

As Jesus warned: "... a man's enemies will be the members of his own household." (Matt. 10: 36) Pastors, fellow church members and leaders, need to be aware of this flank. "Remember what I told you: A servant is not greater than his master. If they persecuted me, they will persecute you also. If they obeyed my teaching, they will obey you also." (John 15:20) The battle lines for victory are clear. Win or lose will be decided by how we handle such close-to-our-heart engagements and disappointments. Together we win. Divided we lose.

Genuine Christian ministry can be slippery and tough, but that is our calling. There will be times we need skin like rawhide, when doing what is right will be hurtful to those closest to us. Not to please the Lord, first and foremost, though, is wrong. Read on as we walk through spiritually tough aspects of ministry to help us milk best possibilities for our Lord, for our church, for our parishioners, for us, whatever stance they choose concerning our calling. I target assured confidence for clergy, that they are prepared and skilled to manage whatever, beyond intimidation of antagonists. If spiritual warfare walks our way we will be appropriately armed to win for God.

Since writing the above, it is becoming more evident that resistance is building in society against churches, Christianity and faithful clergy. Our changeless message is becoming more offensive to powers that be, rooted the powers we are discussing.

"For God has not given us a spirit of fear and timidity, but of power, love, and self-discipline." (I Timothy 1:7)

"The dark does not destroy the light, it defines it. It's only our fear of the dark that casts our joy into the darkness." – Brene Brown

For this battle, wielding special weaponry may be needed, as the Bible declares.

Finally, be strong in the Lord and in his mighty power. Put on the full armor of God, so that you can take your stand against the devil's schemes.

For our struggle is not against flesh and blood, but against the rulers, against the authorities, against the powers of this dark world and against the spiritual forces of evil in the heavenly realms.

Therefore, put on the full armor of God, so that when the day of evil comes, you may be able to stand your ground, and after you have done everything, to stand.

Stand firm then, with the belt of truth buckled around your waist, with the breastplate of righteousness in place, and with your feet fitted with the readiness that comes from the gospel of peace. In addition to all this, take up the shield of faith, with which you can extinguish all the flaming arrows of the evil one. Take the helmet of salvation and the sword of the Spirit, which is the word of God.

And pray in the Spirit on all occasions with all kinds of prayers and requests. With this in mind, be alert and always keep on praying for all the Lord's people. (Ephesians 6:10–18)

Along with these, here are some specially designed biblical weapons. Most of these weapons are hidden from most, wielded by the few who are aware, who understand and stand rather than being spooked and fearful. Demons wield power by fear, fear fomented by our ignorance and lack of skill in how to ably confront them. We need to be spiritually prepared and enabled pastors with assurance and boldness necessary to victory.

Spiritual Weaponry Discovered and Used Includes:

Spiritual Weapon #1—Preaching and Teaching

Spiritual Weapon #2—Exorcism

Spiritual Weapon #3—Prayer and Fasting

Spiritual Weapon #4—Disposing of Strongholds

Spiritual Weapon #5—Hedge of Protection

Spiritual Weapon #6—Church Discipline

SPIRITUAL WEAPON #1—Preaching and Teaching

Since most who attend churches are not aware of the demonic dimension and might be distracted from the Savior through fear of it, I felt it wise to keep, in confidence, some of the more specific weapons I used, except for necessary sharing with those I trusted to move with me in warfare.

I may be wrong. Maybe I underestimated people I served, but my sense was that most church people I have ministered to would not handle a lot about the demonic. Revealing it to them might spur them to doubt my sanity. If they accept what they are told, it may unsettle them, threaten them, even scare them, perhaps because most are not spiritually aware enough to realize God will give them what they need to claim the upper hand. For this reason, I have been hesitant to deal with this in public church sessions. Since discretion is the greater part of valor, the demonic has rarely been a public focus, more in the background of Christ honoring ministry, and not confused with psychological disorders deserving of care and counseling. Here we are dealing with spiritual personalities that influence, infiltrate and afflict, but are responsive to the superior spiritual power of God.

My target is never to hurt people who may be afflicted or afflicting. In ministering to such situations, distinguish between the psychological and the spiritual and adjust ministry accordingly.

No need to spook people unnecessarily, though, as led by the Holy Spirit, early in my ministry I did exactly that, to shake a church out of Christian club ineffectiveness. The church went through the actions of worship and ministry with no awareness of spiritual realities, so

God led me to an unusual, daring form for ministry through preaching. An assignment I accepted, but would not recommend without the kind of clear leading that I received.

Satan Series

I preached a biblical series about Satan – who Satan is, how he got that way, what he wants to accomplish and how he seeks to do it. I preached the doctrine of Satan biblically while vigilantly assessing the sermon series' impact on the congregation. There was actually discussion that I had lost it. That they might need to deal with me. But behind the scenes, as I rubbed shoulders with the congregation during the week, I probed for evidence of demonic activity. The devil usually overplays his hand, and I was giving him a platform for expression.

There came a point when congregants complained about systemic misfortune. So, as I began preaching that Sunday, I asked about what was happening – was last week an unusually tough week. There was a wave of affirmation. So I exposed the purpose behind the series – "We don't get serious about spiritual ministry until we become aware of our enemy." So that day I preached the superiority of Christ over Satan, exposing how puny Satan is compared to God – not equal and opposite, not equal evil against God's goodness. The actual situation is Almighty God created a being who chose to defy and challenge God. He was an angel that fell away from God. He hates God and takes his hatred out on His special creation, people, especially those who love the Lord. As believers, "You, dear children, are from God and have overcome them, because the one who is in you is greater than the one who is in the world." (I John 4:4) Firm faith in God makes us out of reach of Satan's most powerful weapon – fear. God in us is the greatest protective care as we serve the Lord.

This resounding revelation of the spiritual reality of the essence of Christian life and ministry, that the sermon series had primed to reveal, changed our church. Prayer became more important. Worship became more earnest and real. The desire to glorify the Lord and defeat the devil took greater importance. We don't prepare for battle until we see the whites of our enemy's eyes.

The Satan series had profound impact, but, along the way, it was scary for people, and this pastor. I wouldn't recommend it as I delivered it. I had a congregation that stuck with me to the end. For that reason, my original Satan series worked, but we went through the valley of the demonic to get where God wanted us to be. If, perhaps, the congregation had mutinied before it reached the turning point, the devil would have won, and my ministry would have probably ended permanently. Since then I have encountered congregants that wouldn't even stay for the completion of a sermon that started in a manner they distrusted. Probably, unless directed otherwise, if I preached such a series again, I would disperse it among other sermons, and complete each Satan sermon with proclamation of the superiority of Christ.

Preaching Purity – the Fruit of the Spirit

When the winds of evil begin to spread through churches that we pastor, another answer could be to preach such topics as godly purity, honesty, love, kindness, forgiveness. By this means we may move detractors to amend their ways, attitudes and actions. Failing this, we will prime the congregation to be sensitive to frosty winds of evil and those that promote them, producing a warm and loving Christian atmosphere that makes evil stand out in stark contrast when it rears its head to attempt its intent.

I confess that when the pressure rose exponentially during demanding periods in my ministry, I found it very difficult to prepare sermons and to know what to preach and how to do it well. Not being adequately prepared for pressured times left me weakened to the point that the quality of my preaching declined when strong preaching was most needed. This played into the hands of those already poking holes in my capability.

Don't do this to yourself and your ministry. Stock a shelf with super sermons on topic to spread the sweet love of God that He wants characterizing His Church. Perhaps make it a series to deflect charges of targeting specific individuals. Be prepared to melt the dry ice of demonic assault with superb sermons that move the heart and spirit of God's people to live and stand for the love and kindness God requires of His people, and their need to resist efforts to quench what is good and godly in church life and ministry.

SPIRITUAL WEAPON #2—Exorcism

There is no biblical justification for viewing exorcism in Hollywood fashion of burning crosses, magical incantations and physical abuse. As Jesus exhibited it, exorcism is simply claiming God's power to cast out demons. In pastoral ministry I have found exorcism necessary concerning individuals and with regard to a former cult building we bought to house our new church.

Concerning the former cult building that our church purchased, the first diagnostic was people who attended our church coming down with headaches that would not go away for days after attending a Sunday service, and then only by prayer. I came to recognize that the building had been dedicated to the cult and the service of its god. That needed to be revoked. A pastor friend and I went through the building during the week while no one was there. We went room by room revoking the previous dedication and commanding all demonic forces to be gone. We threw water at them in symbol of the spiritual cleansing we were commanding. We burned a pulpit that had been left behind because when I encountered it in a closet the Lord showed it to me in flames. Despite no one knowing what we did, the infliction of headaches ceased and peaceful and powerful growth followed.

In researching exorcism I encountered a school of thought that it was important to get a demon to reveal its name so we would be able to cast it out by name. Then I realized that Jesus taught that demons are liars (John 8:44). So we can't trust anything they say. All that was needed to drive out a demon was to claim God's authority over the demon so that it obeys God's command to leave. The degree of authority depends on the quality of our relationship to the Lord, distance from sin and unresolved sin. Indeed, prayer and fasting might be in order in some circumstances.

SPIRITUAL WEAPON #3—Prayer and Fasting

Prayer and fasting involves earnest pursuit of God for cleansing and spiritual power.

There is an interesting interchange between Jesus and His perplexed disciples. They had been entrusted with powerful ministry that included authority over demons, but they failed (Matthew 17:16-21). In response, Jesus explains, "This type comes out only by prayer and fasting." (Matthew 17:21)

"For our struggle is not against flesh and blood, but against the rulers, against the authorities, against the powers of this dark world and against the spiritual forces of evil in the heavenly realms." (Ephesians 6:12)

Jesus describes our battle with demons in terms of levels of authority, which matched my experience. I encountered demons that were dumb, others that were brilliant and powerful. Some were more commanding. Some adhered with a person, then moved to another, taking their characteristics with them. Some, I discovered, ruled over churches, inhibiting ministry and discouraging minister after minister the same way over and over. We need to know how to spiritually clean up church buildings, congregations and ministries. Failing this, our efforts for the Lord may be thwarted.

SPIRITUAL WEAPON #4—Disposing of Strongholds

Individuals and situations exhibit bondage to Satan's power when the penetration and effectiveness of the Word of God is hindered by strongholds (i.e. obsessive desires and habits), by false reasonings and by obstructions to right action and godly outcomes.

The weapons we fight with are not the weapons of the world. On the contrary, they have divine power to demolish strongholds. We demolish arguments and every pretension that sets itself up against the knowledge of God, and we take captive every thought to make it obedient to Christ. (II Corinthians 10:4-5)

In regard to spiritually oppressed individuals or situations, I learned the value of inquiring whether they might possess physical objects related to cults or the occultic. These function like spiritual handles satanic forces are free to use to influence their owners. After all, by choosing to possess objects that belong to the demonic, we invite demons to play devilish games with our soul.

In one church, I encountered a man who seemed to desire the Lord but demonstrated a bondage that made him unreachable. I asked his wife whether they had any cult or occultic materials in their home. She didn't think so but would do a search. She found a collection of cult books she didn't know were there. I directed her to burn them if possible or at least put them in a green garbage bag for pick up at the curb. Soon after these were gone, her husband beautifully committed his life to Christ.

SPIRITUAL WEAPON #5—Hedge of Protection

God's declaration to Hosea concerning his concerns related to his wife:

"Therefore, behold, I will hedge up thy way with thorns,

and make a wall, that she shall not find her paths." (Hosea 2:6 AV)

Why not petition God for something He declares that He will do in a specific circumstance?

When it comes to understanding the Hedge of Protection Prayer I feel like Elisha's servant, as described in II Kings 6.

> ... the king of Aram...sent horses and chariots and a strong force there. They went by night and surrounded the city. When the servant of the man of God got up and went out early the next morning, an army with horses and chariots had surrounded the city. "Oh no, my lord! What shall we do?" the servant asked. "Don't be afraid," the prophet answered. "Those who are with us are more than those who are with them." And Elisha prayed, "Open his eyes, Lord, so that he may see." Then the Lord opened the servant's eyes, and he looked and saw the hills full of horses and chariots of fire all around Elisha. (II Kings 6:11-17)

In like fashion, the thorn hedge is also spiritual, rather than physical, and apparently, I don't have the vision of a prophet. Like the servant who couldn't see God's army, I have not been able to distinguish what the hedge actually is, and I find the biblical context in which it appears perplexing. Though unseen, however, I just cannot deny the hedge's impact in a number of situations I have encountered.

While not a major teaching of the Scriptures, for me the hedge of protection prayer has proven a powerful tool of ministry; one I can recommend with confidence as one of our weapons against the evil one and the activity of his agents. (II Cor. 10:4-5)

My experience began with a spat of vandalism at our church building. I enlisted a pastor from another church to go with me as we walked around the structure asking God to build a hedge around the building as we prayed. After that prayer, vandalism ceased abruptly. Coincidence? While we appreciated the benefit, we were really quite perplexed by the means. Not assured enough to share our prayer behavior and experience. I and my prayer partner shared with no one what we had done.

Soon after that, I met in our church building with a parishioner who was exhibiting demonic influence, of which he was aware and seeking release. This man had battled with demons for a long time, and quite regularly would describe to me the demons he saw. At his request, I was praying over him for God to drive out the demons within. As I prayed the man became agitated. I asked him what was happening. He said that a demon had left him but couldn't get out. It couldn't get out of the church building. When I asked why, he responded, "Because it can't get through the hedge." So I asked the Lord to open the hedge to let the demon out and the man calmly said, "Oh, there he goes."

Apparently he and the demon saw a hedge, a spiritual hedge that was capable of deflecting their influence and surprisingly incarcerating the demon in the church building. He perceived a hedge God had erected in response to our prayer, a hedge of which he should not have been aware for no one knew nor had told him about it. Only we who had prayed, and God to whom we had issued the request, knew about the hedge. I had mentioned it to no one because I was uncertain that it even existed. All I knew was that things changed when we prayed for that hedge of thorns.

Apparently, through prayer we had hedged in the church building, closing it in from demon action. Strange to say the hedge seemed equal on both sides. It deflected demons outward and inward, away from the church and inside the church. Demons could enter within the vehicle of a person, or perhaps an object, but once released from that person or physical object they were trapped by the hedge. What became very certain to me is that whatever the spiritual hedge is, it is real and powerful for the effectiveness of Christian ministry in the spiritual realm.

From there I sought to hone my spiritual sense to perceive when demons were involved with people and issues. After extensive research from many viewpoints and much soul searching and prayer, I became convinced that, in most cases, I was blind and oblivious to most of the devil's activities. Satan is a master of deception, and of using our weakness against us, kind of like sticking a finger into our gaping sores. He is even involved in flipping strengths into weaknesses to gain advantage. Without trying to sort out circumstances and the degree of Satan's participation (because I am not smart enough) I find great impact and effectiveness by adding the hedge of protection prayer-weapon to my prayers for virtually all needs, whether doing well or struggling, whether evidently demonic or not. It's not that I see the devil everywhere; the point is I do not see him at all. The devil and his minions are involved in so many different problems, perplexities, even physical illnesses. The hedge of protection aims at binding Satan's power (Matt. 12:29) and raising up a protective wall that fends off demonic interference. Along with other prayers, praying the hedge around anyone and anything God laid on my heart seems appropriate since God's hedge of protection will not do harm in any circumstance. I pray it often for many, leaving the application and efficacy to God. (II Cor. 10:4-5)

HEDGE OF PROTECTION PRAYER TEMPLATE

Heavenly Father, in the name and through the blood of Jesus, I ask You to rebuke and bind Satan and his influence concerning (person(s) and/or circumstance(s)).

I ask You to raise up a "hedge of protection" around _______________________, which the power of evil cannot penetrate.

Restore a right heart within _______________, Lord, and guide me to actively help rather than hinder Your working.

Release your power to heal and help _________ according to your wisdom and for your glory.

I thank You for hearing and answering this prayer, for it is founded on Your revealed will in Your sacred Word, which states, "I will build My church and the gates of hell shall not prevail against it."

or

"What therefore God hath joined together, let no man put asunder."

or

"Come to me, all you who are weary and burdened, and I will give you rest." (Matt. 11:28)

or...

Jesus—"The Spirit of the Lord is on me, because he has anointed me to proclaim good news to the poor. He has sent me to proclaim freedom for the prisoners and recovery of sight for the blind, to set the oppressed free" (Luke 4:18)

AMEN

(Appendix #5 Hedge of Protection Template with Biblical Backing)

Spiritual Warfare

The spiritual weaponry of this prayer aims at removing Satanic strongholds in lives and situations.

With Eyes Wide Open... Even Christians May Be Demonized

Some object to the idea that Christians might be "demon possessed". After all, how can demons occupy people who are indwelt / filled by the Spirit of God? Though this seems to make sense mathematically, it is not an accurate objection biblically. In actual fact, the Bible does not speak of "demon possession" as though it is absolute and complete. Nor is the indwelling of the Holy Spirit necessarily so complete as to allow no room for individuals to entertain or allow other influences. Christian believers do not lose free will when they become born again. Free will is an essential characteristic of humans that God does not diminish.

Absolute and complete spiritual occupation by demons or the Holy Spirit is not taught in the Bible. The idea of "demon possession" does not accord with biblical terminology. The original Greek of the Bible speaks of being "demonized". The measure of filling or possession is influenced by the exercise of a person's free will, and the degree to which they live in a devoted relationship with God or a demon, and the degree they are open to God's infilling. Holy Spirit infilling is incremental according to the desire and cooperation of the individual. Christians remain free to choose to cooperate with the devil, and allow demonic forces to occupy aspects of their being and influence them accordingly.

Those who come to Christ from societal, ancestral, family or organizational and situational involvements that include the cultic, occultic and demonic may bring these along with them into their new life in Christ. Their spiritual growth may be complicated by residual demonic influences that they will need to repudiate and petition the power of God for release. Like all believers, their spiritual growth involves renewal of their spirit, soul, mind and body by the infusing of biblical truth into their thinking and living – a rewiring of their thinking and drives according to God's perspective and ways.

"Do not conform any longer to the pattern of this world, but be transformed by the renewing of your mind. Then you will be able to test and approve what God's will is–his good, pleasing and perfect will." (Rom. 12:2)

Personal follow-up to the Hedge of Protection Prayer involves sensitive, loving, bridge-building to facilitate communication and the displacing of false reasonings with appropriate Biblical truths.

Prayer for a Hedge of Protection, when effective, removes the weights and blinders of Satanic oppression, freeing individuals and situations from spiritual bondage so their will and vision is released, providing new freedom to choose for good and God. If, however, their heart is set on evil, they will continue to seek it, and, in opposition to Biblical truth, cling to their false reasonings. By poking holes through the hedge they reduce its effectiveness on their behalf considerably. That does not mean that we cease to pray it if you feel so led.

Scriptural support for the Hedge of Protection Prayer, referenced to numbers in the text, can be found in Appendix #5, along with Scriptures concerning divine, natural, church and demonic discipline, all of which are aim to bring sinners to repentance. With these Scriptures, those interested in understanding and learning concerning this prayer may compare its contents with biblical truth. In prayer we humbly talk with the God of the Universe in pursuit of His mercy, favor and provision. The more sensitively we align our prayers with God's mind and values the better our prayers please Him and the more effectively we communicate.

SPIRITUAL WEAPON #6—Church Discipline

Pastors are protectors. This will probably become most evident if a pastor enlists a congregation to adjudicate disciplinary action. This may shock or even repulse them.

Church discipline is in a slightly different category. Though it is appropriate to neutralize the demonic, those demanding church discipline may present different levels of spiritual need representing demonic attitudes and actions, whether motivated by demons or by the fallen nature of individuals or groups themselves – mixtures of pride, immorality, anger, vengeance, dishonesty, disrespect, slander, bullying, betrayal, antagonism, heresy, ...

"Our lives begin to end the day we become silent about things that matter" ~ Martin Luther King Jr.

The Purpose of Church

The need for church discipline relates to what the Christian Church is all about. Jesus declares the purpose of His Church in Matthew 28:16-20 – The Lord's Great Commission:

Then Jesus came to them and said,

"All authority in heaven and on earth has been given to me.

Therefore go and make disciples of all nations,

baptizing them in the name of the Father and of the Son and of the Holy Spirit,

and teaching them to obey everything I have commanded you.

And surely I am with you always, to the very end of the age."

Salvation, Support, Safety

Churches are to deliver from sin's consequences by salvation, support and a safety system. It's like a family with members who take responsibility for each other, to love, lead, feed and discipline toward maturity. Together we lovingly, selflessly, take responsibility for the wellbeing of others, rather than being denigrating, hateful or immoral toward them (Eph.4:15; Hebrews 3:13) "But encourage one another daily, as long as it is called 'Today', so that none of you may be hardened by sin's deceitfulness." So discipline is in tune with all church ministries. It aims to redirect sinners to repentance, thereby redirecting them back to faithfulness to their Lord, protecting the vulnerable, strengthening the fellowship, and venerating God's character and reputation. As in family life, discipline of the immature involves instruction, encouragement and support. Defiance, another dimension that needs to be wrestled with discipline, prompts restriction and, if necessary, rejection in pursuit of restoration. Safety concerns mean we do not cover for threatening people. Like doctors, our love and care for the Body under stress, requires therapies that head off disturbances and intruders and send away invaders that endanger the individual and those around him.

Whereas Jesus was silent before his detractors, Jesus does not require this of his followers. For Jesus, allowing accusers the upper hand, in the end served the purpose of His earthly life which was to die for our sins. Though Jesus was heading this way and paid this price, in his living his backbone was strong for right, especially concerning religious leaders (Matt. 23:23-27). If martyrdom were the purpose of our lives, at that juncture it would be appropriate to allow indiscriminate undefended blows, but we, as pastors, are entrusted with the care and safety of others. Defiantly treacherous people are therefore to be redirected away from our charges. Godly pastors must stand for biblical truth and righteousness from the pulpit and with vigilance for risks to their flock. Firm discipline, even expulsion, must not be optional if the ministry of a church is to achieve what Jesus wants.

It reminds me of Sherman. When my son married a missionary in Ecuador, one of the Ecuadorians gave them an appropriate Ecuadorian wedding gift - a live young ram. (Its purpose, in their culture, is to provide a foundation for personal wealth, as a means of building a flock.) My son and his wife's concern with this gift was its future, since they lived on the campus of an orphanage, with children that might make this ram a pet rather than a functional animal the giver intended. For clarity of purpose, they actually wondered whether they should have named him "Lunch" rather than "Sherman". Their concern turned out to be unfounded, however, because Sherman grew to be an aggressive ram, rather than a cuddly pet. As Sherman moved about ramming everything and everyone in sight, children began campaigning for a Sherman dinner. Sherman was so disruptive that he had to go.

We will meet Shermans in churches as well - people who are obstructive and threatening to godly leadership and to the health and growth of churches and church members. Their defiance may be based on ego, on territoriality, on presumed privilege, on a power struggle, defense of secret sin or direct demonic control. This is where the Bible's depiction of a shepherd's role comes into play to strengthen the role of pastors. David described how he, as a shepherd, battled lions and bears to protect his flocks (I Samuel 17:34-37). Likewise, responsible shepherds provide for and protect their flock's safety and health. They do not fold and flee in the presence of threat. Shepherds who run rather than confronting are labeled by the derogatory title, "hireling" or "hired hand"; i.e., financially focused employees. Since their focus is selfish they are notorious for running from trouble, leaving flocks, for which they are responsible, exposed to threat.

The hired hand is not the shepherd and does not own the sheep. So when he sees the wolf coming, he abandons the sheep and runs away. Then the wolf attacks the flock and scatters it. The man runs away because he is a hired hand and cares nothing for the sheep. (John 10:12-13)

If we are not a hired hand, as described by Jesus, do not act like one. Do not opt out of battles to protect the flock. If we leave churches because they are cruddy (poor quality, offensive) we leave them cruddy, cruddy for the next pastor, and the next, and the next....

If you are standing in the gap, holding back the forces of darkness with which your antagonists surf, don't step out of the way in hopes trouble makers feel the full turbulence of their antagonism to God. Stand firm. Push them out of the way to protect the church from the evil tide. Do right even if it means weathering a storm of abuse from those who defy you.

Someone, sometime needs to stand his ground to purify the church so it is led and serves the way God desires.

When truth and your faithful representation of it is challenged, speak up, back them off.

Exposing evil is part of our job, our calling, especially as it is discovered to be hindering the work of God in His church.

"Cast out the scorner, and contention shall go out; yea, strife and reproach shall cease." (Proverbs 22:10)

"For pride is spiritual cancer: it eats up the very possibility of love, or contentment, or even common sense." C.S. Lewis

I was given no teaching concerning church discipline. Again, it was a learn-as-you-go. Strange how ignorant churches are of this as well, so much so that they can be offended if the exercise of congregational discipline becomes necessary. Such lack of awareness of the biblical function of church discipline may be indicative of a lingering lack of moral purity in a fellowship – akin to never washing one's clothes, even never realizing the importance of doing so.

This raises the issue of conditioning. By conditioning we come to accept as normal the way things have come to be. The worst example of this was expressed by Nazi Doctor Joseph Mengele, "The Angel of Death": "The more we do to you, the less you seem to believe we are doing it." It is so easy to become accustomed to the temperature of the air around us, without anything to alert us to truth or even trouble, leaving us unwittingly committed to the way it is, unawareness leaving us helpless and hopeless for improvement. Churches may even resist what they need.

No church is so pure and honorable that church discipline is never necessary. So when congregational discipline becomes necessary, they should trust in their pastor. Failing this, church discipline descends into political wrangling of factions, and taking sides without reference to right or wrong. Indeed, it is at a juncture when they can cause such damage and division that the demonic may most clearly raise its fists.

My Go To

To understand church discipline, Matthew 18 is my go-to. I appreciate how it deals with all levels of concern. But applying this requires first of all dealing with the Bible's guidance in I Peter 4:8. "Love covers a multitude of sins." does not mean to encourage irresponsibility by turning a blind eye that sacrifices God's honor and ministry. The Bible supports that this, and turning the other cheek, are applicable to personal matters between individuals; i.e. Stage#1 of Matthew 18.

For faithful pastors, called to lead in accord with God's Word and values, these are ultimatums from God, not optional. Pastoral ministry is to serve within the framework of biblical ultimatums. Those who challenge these and their pastor, who is bound by them, should be at loggerheads with church leadership. God wouldn't have it any other way. The one called to lead should be permitted to lead by deference and obedience to the Power and purpose he serves. Pushback against evil is not only permissible but essential to be faithful to the One we serve.

"The hired hand is not the shepherd and does not own the sheep. So when he sees the wolf coming, he abandons the sheep and runs away. Then the wolf attacks the flock and scatters it." (John 10:12)

"All that is required for evil to prosper is for good people to do nothing."

"Not doing or saying anything in the presence of evil is to be part of evil."

"Get sick about being the one who says and does nothing."

"Learn to play hardball, honorably."

Be Decisive

Pastors need to face threats rather than running from them, or avoiding them as though they do not exist or will go away on their own. Offenses dealt with in an appropriate and timely manner minimize risks of severe injury to members, to ministries, to reputation. Not dealing with them, kicking them down the road or burying them, will work no better for our churches than it has for the Roman Catholic Church, trapped now by skeletons from their past.

Offenses that demand discipline must not be covered or deferred. They are offenses that must be exposed by love, love for the offended and for the offender. Love that reaches to concerns of example, guidance, protection, direction, reputation, integrity and godly honor. We must not back off. We should quit leaving churches for which we are responsible in the hands of the disreputable, to perpetuate their defilement.

This does not mean that pastors should ferret around trying to find dirt on people. Threats in the congregation are dealt with as they reveal themselves and those serious enough to threaten the integrity and safety of the congregation extrude unresolved from Matthew 18 preliminary efforts to settle them discreetly and confidentially.

Stages of Matthew 18 Discipline

When persons are out of tune with the biblical direction of a church, they will bump into others, upsetting, tripping them and even endangering them. Most times this is handled confidentially by structural input through preaching, teaching and counsel. So, Matthew 18 provides a biblical template that aims to head off problems while they are small and to keep them that way. So it begins privately, individually, then increases pressure by expanding exposure in hopes of turning offenders toward repentance and restoration. By this means, Jesus' guidance in Matthew 18 is adequate from resolution of small offenses to the toughest of the tough.

The Words of Jesus, The Head of The Church

The Template for Redirection of Errant Parishioners – (Matthew 18:15-18)

> If your brother or sister sins, go and point out their fault, just between the two of you. If they listen to you, you have won them over. But if they will not listen, take one or two others along, so that 'every matter may be established by the testimony of two or three witnesses.' If they still refuse to listen, tell it to the church; and if they refuse to listen even to the church, treat them as you would a pagan or a tax collector. "Truly I tell you, whatever you bind on earth will be bound in heaven, and whatever you loose on earth will be loosed in heaven."

>> DISCIPLINE STAGE #1 (Matthew 18 vs. 15)—IN CONFIDENCE

"If your brother or sister sins, go and point out their fault, just between the two of you. If they listen to you, you have won them over."

Offenses worthy of discipline are listed in I Corinthians 6:9-10–)

„„do you not know that wrongdoers will not inherit the kingdom of God? Do not be deceived: Neither the sexually immoral nor idolaters nor adulterers nor men who have sex with men nor thieves nor the greedy nor drunkards nor slanderers nor swindlers will inherit the kingdom of God.

The incredible wisdom of Matthew 18 resides in its guidance that church discipline begins with intimate conversation, involving upset between only two, and if the Spirit is active in both, it ends there. Usually, never to be known by anyone else. Because it comes from the lips of God Himself, we can implement it with assured confidence of its wisdom to manage the challenge.

So, in the unfortunate case where someone strays outside the biblical norms of the community, every effort should be made to make them aware and solicit their change of direction. Immaturity and unawareness invokes caring confrontation, encouragement, instruction, guidance and restoration. Most offenses can be resolved in this manner. Not only personal confrontation, but also preaching, fulfills Stage #1, as individuals repent privately in response to the truth. Only determined defiance demands more forthright effort, pushing the Matthew 18 strategy to more demanding processes.

>> DISCIPLINE STAGE #2 (Matthew 18 vs. 16)—PRESSURE FROM MORE

"But if they will not listen, take one or two others along, so that 'every matter may be established by the testimony of two or three witnesses.' "(Deut. 19:15; 1 Timothy 5:19; II Cor. 13:1)

When meeting with someone you are trying to motivate to change, after a private meeting, bringing at least one other with you ups the pressure to responsibility. Since they demonstrated resistance already, you should expect the possibility of argumentation in a second encounter. It is wise, therefore, to bring a witness or two with you to confirm everything that is said and done. Without this, your words and motivations may be misconstrued, and we are left with a I-said, he-said. Keeping your position clear, according to this biblical principle of verification, is wise so you provide no fodder for attack.

Deacon Witnesses

If deacons are fulfilling their leadership role along with the pastor, they may function within the "two or three witnesses stage" as a more authoritative message to the offender, to slow down troublemakers or send them on their way with little upset to the congregation. Their acting as witnesses may increase the impact of this stage, helping to deflect trouble makers from their intentions. Deacons could even actively pursue the offender with demands for accountability, challenging them with the seriousness of what is in motion, perhaps curbing their defiance, thereby completing the discipline cycle prior to the next stage, relieving the congregation of having to deal with it.

Documentation

For self protection and effectiveness of discipline, there is also wisdom in documenting events, actions, statements, telephone and internet communications involved with the process of dealing with a troublesome person or group. You may never need this record, but it is virtually impossible to remember in detail when you are under extreme stress. You cannot produce it or consult it if you didn't document it as it happened, or soon after, while memory is fresh.

>> DISCIPLINE STAGE #3 (Matthew 18 vs. 17) EXPOSURE TO THE CHURCH

"If they still refuse to listen, tell it to the church"

A Pastor's Sense of Defeat

A pastor's heart reaches out to bring all to Jesus – who died for all—"whosoever will may come.' It is truly heart-wrenching to reach out to some who insist on defying all our efforts. This is not unique. Lest we fail to understand and castigate ourselves unjustly, God, in His Word, describes the truth behind what most often is behind this. Why some defy our ministry efforts on their behalf. Why some are so determined to push against us, against truth, and against the Scriptures' threat of full congregational exposure in discipline.

The Bible declares that some choose to be unteachable and unreachable:

Prov. 1:7 The fear of the Lord is the beginning of knowledge, but fools despise wisdom and discipline.

Prov. 1:22 How long will mockers delight in mockery and fools hate knowledge?

Prov. 9:7-8 Whoever corrects a mocker invites insult; whoever rebukes a wicked man incurs abuse. Do not rebuke a mocker or he will hate you ; rebuke a wise man and he will love you

Prov. 10:23 The fool finds pleasure in evil conduct, but a man of understanding delights in wisdom.

Prov. 13:1 A wise man heeds his father's instruction, but a mocker does not listen to rebuke.

Prov. 18:6-7 A fool's lips bring him strife, and his mouth invites a beating. A fool's mouth is his undoing, and his lips are a snare to his soul.

Prov. 20:3 It is a man's honor to avoid strife, but every fool is quick to quarrel.

Prov.21:24 The proud and arrogant man—-"Mocker" is his name; he behaves with overwhelming pride.

Prov. 23:9 Do not speak to a fool, for he will scorn the wisdom of your words.

Prov. 24:9 The schemes of folly are sin, and men detest a mocker.

Prov. 29:8 Mockers stir up a city, but wise men turn away anger.

When God says something so many times we can be sure it is something important that He wants us to understand. What may appear as our failure in ministry, what may seep into soul as defeat, may be no such thing. Not at all. The Bible specifies people who will not learn and change; they only learn to do what they do better. In the Bible they are called fools, arrogant, scoffers and mockers. When pastors deal with people like this it becomes evident that no matter how we try they just consume all our efforts, defying everything we do to help them, leaving no resolution feasible except excommunication.

One term for these people is serial bullies. They are died-in-the-wool antagonists. Antagonism goes to the core of their being. They demand to lead because they will not follow. For those they court these can look like attractive wild stallions. They may be beautiful to watch but people should know better than to hitch them up to their wagon. They delight to undermine and sabotage. It's a point of pride for them to play the game. Ephesians 6:16 even goes so far as to describe them as spiritual or social arsonists, flinging "flaming arrows". We will know these by all the spot fires of lies we have to douse with truth, as much as it is possible to do so. So, only one social arsonist in a forest of naivety can spark wildfires of dissent and destruction. These strange people seem to just want to watch the world burn. You cannot negotiate with them or reason with them.

Keeping this type of people in a church compromises peacefulness, safety and ministry credibility, and that without hope of improvement. They refuse to learn and improve so will push ministry to them to the limits of Matthew 18 discipline, to excommunication. Only by excommunication do churches heal from the demeaning and divisive abuse of intractable trouble makers. For these reasons, those determined to sow descent and damage must be removed from the congregation. If not, their contagion will destroy it.

Congregational Shock

For a congregation, the rare event of official congregational discipline usually intrudes like a thunderbolt. To a pastor, this may not be surprising, since they may have never witnessed this before. Most discipline is managed privately according to Matthew 18, so it never sees the light of day. As well, in accordance with the stages of Matthew 18, most times moral failure and subversive defiance is hidden to most congregants until it becomes necessary to publicly expose it. As well, trouble-makers can be winsome to everyone but their target, so it can be threatening to flush them out if we, as pastor, are almost the only one aware of their undermining activities. Pastors and deacons, and those involved in trying to manage trouble, usually keep biblically guarded in the process that brings things to a head. When presenting the needed discipline to the congregation, therefore, it is best to bring it forth in the natural biblical framework of the congregational care that is already being provided in hopes of avoiding what the defiant has made necessary.

If an offender is defiant to all discreet efforts to turn him toward repentance, church members should be instructed about upcoming presentation of the matter and the offender to the church for adjudication, as in line with Matthew 18 biblical guidance and the normal flow of the community. They need to realize that such upsetting public exposure is only made necessary by defiance, and necessitated by the failure of all other attempts. Its primary goal is to warn and restore the sinner as discreetly as possible by incremental exposure of the aberration. So, as the meeting begins the pastor should provide a report of disciplinary efforts this far according to Matthew 18 thus far. The report should demonstrate that this congregational action is necessary due to defiance and the danger of this person's actions toward the pastor, the leadership, the church and its congregants.

Public congregational discipline is meant to be the overwhelming force factor described by Navy Seal Larry Yanch. He described a display of overwhelming force as a battle strategy that encourages enemies to surrender rather than fight. Aside from legal exposure, congregational discipline exposes unrepentant actions that threaten the congregation, to the awareness of their friends, relatives and fellow worshippers, in hope the specter of embarrassment by congregational exposure might motivate repentance. It answers George Orwell's question, "What can you do...against the lunatic who is more intelligent than yourself, who gives your arguments a fair hearing and simply persists in his lunacy?"

In the church, the highest level of overwhelming force is the congregation. The unrepentant's infractions are exposed before the assembled congregation for them to decide what should be done, according to the scriptural guidance of Matthew 18. Such pressure is immense. In my experience, the defiant were not inclined to attend this level of public exposure. They felt they could not handle the threat of such a meeting. Better to express their opinions from the side, which they generally did with considerable vociferous emotion.

Necessary exposure relates to the degree of defiance and the extent of awareness and impact of the infraction. If defiance is determined and involves damage to the church's integrity, congregation or to church leadership, it may require action by the congregation to determine whether removal of their membership is necessary. Even this, as the Scripture declares, is not meant to be punitive, just added pressure to encourage repentance for restoration.

>> DISCIPLINE STAGE #4 Matthew 18 vs. 17 & 18—EXCOMMUNICATION

"and if they refuse to listen even to the church, treat them as you would a pagan or a tax collector."

(Stay away from people ejected from a church by discipline, lest they perpetuate their disruptiveness.)

The purpose of this is to allow no remnant to remain. As Jesus taught, "A little leaven leavens the whole lump." Any residual requires continued resistance which, along with the defiant reactions of the disciplined, keep the problem persisting in the fellowship.

Disruptive Defiance

While travelling, a friend opened his suitcase to find a shocking surprise. He had shut the lid on the button of his shaving cream. Who could believe how much is stored in one of those little cans?! The foam got into every cuff and button hole of every piece of clothing. Likewise, the influence of defiant people seeps into every part of a church. Those that side with their views, amplify them. Those that don't, are upset with what they don't like about what is happening. The settledness of a church is sent spinning. Opinions pro and con set people against each other. So, whereas we might expect that church discipline would primarily deal with moral aberrations, in our "upstage age" more disruptive church issues relate to being defiant to leadership and seeking to undermine them in the performance of their leadership functions. This evil can, in fact, prove more damaging to a church than immorality, in that it seeks to build a ground swell tsunami to overwhelm and destroy trust in and support of godly leadership. When these cannot be brought into line, no matter what the effort, they must be removed for the sake of a church's integrity, health and effectiveness. If they insist on aggravation, their destructive disruption must be sent elsewhere. Church members must not follow or expose themselves to their contamination.

In one situation, it became evident to me, as pastor, that a popular church song leader was soliciting sexual favors from vulnerable ladies in the church. The ladies had said, "No!". Which led him to approach another and another. When this pastor confronted him in privacy to stop, he went ballistic. Within an hour he had appealed to the denomination for action against me, and spread his distorted complaint against this pastor throughout the church. As you might imagine, this degree of defiance escalated disciplinary action from Stage#1 to Stage#4 immediately – disciplinary action needs to extend according to the extent of exposure, which, in this case, the offender had spread far and wide.

Appeal to Denomination

There was a slight delay as denominational representatives arranged to visit. Since they had been drafted by the offender, they arrived evidently slanted in his favor. Denominational officials come in blind. Not knowing the issues involved, they will naturally incline toward siding with congregational power blocks. Their natural bent is to view the pastor as at fault - the Caiaphas Principle ..."better for you that one man die rather than the whole [church]." (John. 11:50; 18:14). Remove the pastor. Problem solved. NOT LIKELY! Godly pastors stand in the gap praying for and working for Godly resolution. Removing pastors usually means problem perpetuated.

Good and godly people lose their pastor and their church. Some victory for God or good that is!

It is rarely advisable to allow denominational personnel into management of such internal church matters. So, our leadership told them to end their efforts and leave the matter to us. They seemed relieved to do so. Of necessity, we had to proceed with congregational discipline against this defiantly unrepentant leader who had blabbed his offence, wrapped in distortion, throughout the church and beyond. No matter how unpleasant, it is an essential responsibility of church leaders to protect the safety of congregants and to protect the integrity of a church's reputation and witness in the community, and that of their pastor of course. At the conclusion of his necessary exclusion from the church it came out that the disciplined church leader had a reputation in the community for the offense we encountered and dealt with – community reputation of our church as a reputable and safe place was re-established.

Prov.21:11 "When a mocker is punished the simple gain wisdom, when a wise man is instructed he gets knowledge."

Prov. 22:10 "Drive out the mocker, and out goes strife; quarrels and insults are ended."

Jas. 3:16 "For where you have envy and selfish ambition, there you find disorder and every evil practice."

Spin Doctors

Just for awareness, we might also encounter spin doctors. These are wizards at turning virtually everything to their advantage, and may even do so with delight, cloaking their evil intent from observers – we get to be the target, others become weapons enlisted against us. One such trouble-maker in my experience was a master. I managed them with the guidance of a good book about *Antagonists in the*

Church, by Kenneth Haugk. Everything I tried to contain them, they skillfully turned to their advantage. It was so difficult to pin them that others in the church, even deacons, naively joined in their enterprise at great expense to my ministry and the church. It's good to be aware. Like any marshal artist, there is always someone who can clean our clock. Since these relished the repartee, duking it out with delight, even when beaten, they refused to quit. It was evident that they were the type that never learns. They only use everything they experience to learn how to do what they do better. For these, a wall of separation provides the best possibility of peace. With such, only the most severe outcome of congregational discipline holds possibility of resolution for a church. There must be absolutely no further contact with them by any connected with that church.

As revealed in Matthew 18, effective congregational discipline requires unified congregational action. The decision of a congregation concerning discipline binds all congregants to abide by the biblical consequences of that congregational decision.

Matthew 18:17 "If they still refuse to listen, tell it to the church; and if they refuse to listen even to the church, treat them as you would a pagan or a tax collector."

Obedient application of biblically decreed excommunication is demanded and necessary. Those excommunicated by congregational decision are to be left to their own devices, outside of congregational support, in hopes this will stir their desire to humbly and repentantly return to the church, under the Lordship of Christ. So, as a follow through to congregational discipline, congregants must break all contact with the disciplined. To keep the disciplined from continuing their divisive endeavors, there is to be no communication, no socializing. Efforts by the disciplined to continue this must be rejected.

So, to seal the conclusion of congregational discipline, near the end of the congregational disciplinary proceeding, it is essential that congregants be informed of the biblical command to treat these disciplined as outsiders. However difficult and disappointing, congregants need to obey God's Word concerning this disciplinary procedure or place themselves under the same disciplinary structure as those removed. In other words, if, in accordance with biblical standards for church discipline, they do not separate themselves from the disciplined, treating them as outsiders, they must remove themselves from the church as well. Either obey the biblical decree and that of the congregation, or go elsewhere. The Bible demands this because continuing contact with the disciplined provides troublemakers with a platform to re-infect a congregation, perpetuating problems church discipline was designed to remove.

This may seem harsh, but the Bible demands the firmest discipline, because the issue is huge. What the Bible is describing is precision surgery by the congregation. A surgeon that winces at the incision and gags at the appearance and touch of vital organs is not suited to the task. As well, for protection, successful surgery requires the team work of post-surgical follow up. In matters of church discipline, the congregation and its leadership must be thorough. There is little value in removing cancer and allowing its tentacles to remain to continue their undermining of the health of ministry and the church. Advocates left in place, determined to reverse the discipline of churches, continue damage the congregation has rejected. They harbor and incubate re-infection.

Proverbs 6:16-19

> 16. There are six things the Lord hates, seven that are detestable to him:

17. haughty eyes, a lying tongue, hands that shed innocent blood,

18. a heart that devises wicked schemes, feet that are quick to rush into evil,

19. a false witness who pours out lies and a person who stirs up conflict in the community.

"Praeis" in Discipline

Important clarification for church discipline is expressed again and again by the Apostle Paul. Again and again he connects biblical church discipline with "praeis". As shared previously, this is not twentieth century dictionary "meekness"; i.e. self-less submissiveness. No! Rather, biblical meekness operates as a deliberate choice, rather than helpless default. It relates to Paul's admonition to people and / or groups involved in administering discipline to erring members (I Cor.4:21, Gal.6:1, II Tim.2:25). In each case, "praeis" is to characterize an attempt to correct or restore a person to faithfulness and to church fellowship. Please note, in no instance is clear offense to be ignored, overlooked or minimized. Offense worthy of discipline is to be confronted plainly, but not arrogantly. The goal, without enjoyment, is not exclusion, but, if possible, restoration.

The Apostle Paul demonstrated this in his challenge to the church in Corinth to exclude an offender from its fellowship. (I Cor. 5) Then, later, Paul encouraged them to restore and welcome the disciplined member back, due to evident repentance (II Cor. 2:5-11). Discipline, though difficult, had done its desired work of cleansing and renewal.

The Danger of Bringing Discipline to the Congregation Alone

To move in congregational discipline as a pastor, alone, may be necessary, if deacons have been conflicted concerning facts of the matter. Realize that moving forward in congregational discipline on our own may be a recipe that ultimately ends our pastorate in that church. Even if the discipline succeeds, congregants inclined to advocate for underdogs tend to undermine and weaken ongoing ministry in that place. For this reason, as a responsible pastor, we may succeed in protecting our flock, but, after things seem to settle, it may be necessary, like David, to leave the ongoing building of the temple to an heir to the peaceful ministry our warfare has created.

Having to Stand Alone to Bring the Need for Discipline to a Congregational Meeting

In my ministry, one circumstance, with deacons divided concerning the offender, dragged on for years making unified action impossible. Nonetheless, despite the risks, I deemed that congregational discipline was essential, even if it was necessary for me alone, as pastor, to initiate the necessary congregational gathering. Concerning support, I merely invited the deacons to sit behind me in support or anywhere else if they chose not to support my action.

As the session began, all deacons sat behind me, in declaration of support.

As I presented well documented facts concerning the defiance behind the disciplinary action, the congregation was moved to two stage discipline I had not anticipated. They felt the couple were so devious that they might seek to turn the discipline to make the church look bad. Their decision, therefore, was to strip them of "membership in good standing" leaving them with "membership not in good standing". After that passed, they moved, seconded and voted that the couple be stripped of their "not-in-good-standing membership".

Be Biblically Thorough in Discipline

As the disciplinary session began to dissolve, and people were leaving, the two deacons who had divided the deacons for two years by being agents for the troublesome couple against the pastor, deacons who, in the meeting, had positioned themselves behind the pastor in expression of support, disclosed that their sitting in the supportive position was a lie. They stated openly, in my hearing, that they disagreed with my actions and with the decisions of the congregation. Though at an inconvenient time, I knew I should have given them a platform to express their disagreement with the church openly. Within myself, I knew this also needed to be adjudicated by the congregation, but I felt so emotionally drained that I let it pass. I let them walk away. Their damaging and divisive attitudes and actions needed to be exposed, but weren't.

The printed materials distributed for the meeting did include a quote from the church constitution, which read:

ARTICLE III.1 (f)

> When the Church has determined upon a course of action by proper vote, it becomes the responsibility of each Member to support that course. If a Member is unable to harmonize with the decisions and beliefs of the Church, they should not seek to disrupt the fellowship, but quietly withdraw by transferring to another church. Refusal to harmonize or withdraw may call for church discipline.

Nonetheless, I failed to provide this direction to all present that those who continued to support and keep contact with the excommunicated, would, according to Matthew 18 and the constitution, have to leave the church as well. I knew full well that the two were determined to reverse the action of the congregation and to destroy me. If leadership or membership is divided, that division must be part of the disciplinary action, or the fragments of factions will be emboldened to retaliate. How can we move together if we are divided? Proper biblical disciplinary thoroughness settles this. Otherwise

Friendship Weakness

In Psalm 55 David lays bare the deep perplexity and anguish with which I also have struggled during thirty plus years of pastoral ministry...

12. If an enemy were insulting me, I could endure it;

if a foe were rising against me, I could hide.

13 But it is you, a man like myself, my companion, my close friend,

14 with whom I once enjoyed sweet fellowship at the house of God,

as we walked about among the worshipers. (Psalm 55:12-14}

Sad to say, valuing friendship may interfere with necessary leadership decisiveness. It can actually be a form of respect of persons (partiality) that the Lord damns throughout the Scriptures, Old Testament and New, (James 2:1-9; 2 Chronicles 19:7; Colossians 3:25 et al.) But it hurts to have to deal harshly with friends who deviate from what is good and wholesome for the Church, for the cause of Christ and for the effectiveness of our leadership as pastor.

My failure to properly adhere to this principle softened my perspective at the time and throughout this disciplinary process. I found it difficult to be firm due to memories of good times I had shared with these antagonists. We had been friends, I thought. Their friendship meant a lot to me., apparently much more than it should have, and much more than it meant to them, for I allowed it to strengthen their hand by weakening my leadership. I was soft-hearted, not wanting to hurt them even when they were out to destroy me. Soft-hearted when I should have been firm. Friendship must never interfere with what we need to do as a leader, responsibly serving the Lord and His Church. To put friendship before responsibility is irresponsibility that may prove very costly for the cause of Christ. Keep in mind the maxim, "True friends take our part when others take us apart." Beware of keeping our Judases in play with power to sway and betray. Strategically weaken and neutralize determined antagonists in a timely fashion. Such action is best implemented in concert with church leadership, but, for the sake of church integrity and ministry continuity, it should not be shirked even if we have to stand alone as a shepherd defending our flock. Turn them if possible, or remove their power or their presence as necessary. We must never put friendship ahead of responsible leadership.

How wrong I was not to be thorough in discipline. The two devious deacons did as expected. Their continuation of collecting and fabricating complaints wore me out. When ministry becomes a Whac-A-Mole world pastors are easily made to appear either incompetent or aggressive in their effort to bring things back under control in a church that is spun not to know which way is up. So, by pure exhaustion these orchestrated the end of my ministry in that church and further division among deacons. Once I was gone these attempted to reverse the church's discipline, to get the couple back, which failed. The deacons and the church fragmented unnecessarily due to my failure in responsible leadership.

If I had only known then what I know now. Hind sight is twenty-twenty, but you can't go back.

"Life has to be lived forward but can only be understood backward." Kierkegaard

Official church discipline needs to be thorough or others will rise up to continue and even exacerbate the problem. So, don't let anyone walk away from a disciplinary session with guns loaded for the cause of the guilty. Make it clear that, according Stage #4, siding with the disciplined, places them under the same biblical command to be removed from the church. They are one and the same. (Matthew 18:17-18 "and if they refuse to listen even to the church, treat them as you would a pagan or a tax collector.")

Thorough in Healing

"For our struggle is not against flesh and blood, but against the rulers, against the authorities, against the powers of this dark world and against the spiritual forces of evil in the heavenly realms." (Ephesians 2:12)

When dealing with divisive forces within a church fellowship, whether I can clearly see it or not, I never discount the probability that demonic forces are involved. Whether regarding an individual or a church fellowship as a whole, as taught by Jesus, the same biblical principles of management apply.

What kept rattling around in my head was the expression, "Swept clean but not safe."

When an impure spirit comes out of a person, it goes through arid places seeking rest and does not find it. Then it says, 'I will return to the house I left.' When it arrives, it finds the house unoccupied, swept clean and put in order. Then it goes and takes with it seven other spirits more wicked than itself, and they go in and live there. And the final condition of that person is worse than the first. That is how it will be with this wicked generation. (Matthew 12:43-45)

It is important to recognize that after the removal of troublemakers by congregational discipline or direct action of the pastor and/or deacons, a church enters into a dangerous juncture. Their action, though right, may backfire, especially if their pastor remains exposed to ongoing abuse due to ongoing misunderstanding within the fellowship. The tattered ends must be trimmed and stitched for the sake of full healing from the hurt.

After discipline there is great need for not only cleaning house but for filling any void created thereby with strength of spirit to ward off worse effects. Ministry by the shepherd and deacons must be focused on healing and filling of the spirit both individually and congregationally.

Neither pastor, nor deacons, nor congregation should underestimate the impact of divisive forces and attacks on a pastor's heart for his congregation and his health, physically, psychologically and spiritually. All of this can have lasting impact on his ministry. That deep hurt, like that of a parent dealing with the burden of a wayward child, must be taken into account for the road ahead.

We are not God; we are Jesus' under shepherds for leadership of His Church. Likely we entered pastoring with our heart on our sleeve, with an earnest to bring blessing to those we seek and serve. It is that tender heartedness that is our great strength and our Achilles heel. We can be hurt and broken by ministry because injury goes deep into those who live unguarded lives of service. That is a pastor's lot. We need to recognize that ours is not a dictatorial position of control. We serve. We hurt. It would be good if deacons and congregations came to appreciate the Achilles heel that makes their pastor of such benefit to them but such risk and pain of vulnerability to themselves.

If the pastor has been injured by the battle, deacons should be enlisted and/or prepared to provide their servant function on his behalf. The pastor should actively seek their support for his healing. Perhaps a public service of support as part of a worship service would be in order. After the intensity of discipline, enlist the deacons to gather around their pastor during a morning service to lay hands on him and pray for God's continued strengthening of the pastor for health and spiritual enablement for the challenge of leading the church wisely in accordance with God's guidance. In so doing pastor and deacons openly declare their intent to stand together for church health and ministry. It would be a healing moment for all, and a reminder of a role of congregants and deacons concerning their pastor.

Imagine the sweet healing essence of such a moment. Wouldn't it be worth the humility of admission of need? Whether provided publicly or in the privacy of a deacons meeting, this would be a moment of caring cohesion, laying aside all misunderstanding to bind together in mutual support for the sake of ongoing spiritual strength in ministry.

Then, with clear concern for the dangers of the situation, the pastor should fill the void of discipline disillusionment with preaching and teaching about unity and spiritual empowerment to be the Christians and the church that honors its Master and Head, Jesus.

If the Lord is on the throne of all hearts we move in mutual consideration, unity and power to His glory.

A Glitch in the Impact of Biblical Excommunication

Sad to say, Step #4 of Matthew 18:17-18 congregational discipline doesn't work as well as it did in Bible times. In New Testament times, being cast out of a church left one without anywhere else to go in that community for Christian fellowship. The Apostle Paul described the expected extreme impact of this in I Corinthians 5:5. "...hand this man over to Satan, so that the sinful nature may be destroyed and his spirit saved on the day of the Lord." That was a very different time. Today, towns and cities have several churches to choose from, so a disciplined believer can move down the road and attend another church. To seal this they will often spread a distorted story of their situation, making them look hard done by, and mistreated by their previous pastor and church.

Godly pastors have wider concern than the health of their own congregation. They are concerned for the health of the Body, as expressed in other adjoining congregations, but struggle about whether they should venture to interfere with another pastor or church. It hurts to experience renewed health at the expense of another congregation.

It saddens pastors who have struggled with discipline, only to see their Stage #4 decision dissolved by a nearby church, so eager to have new member(s) that they welcome them with open arms, even taking up their offense without consulting the pastor in the previous church about the facts, even proceeding despite the facts. In one case, a pastor did check out what had happened but insisted on extending membership to the offender anyway. He was highly intelligent, a former Oxford University professor. He was warned of the danger. He was introducing to his flock, but he insisted. Why might that pastor so naively misconstrue the motivation of the previous pastor? Sad to say, having left the matter to the responsibility of that pastor, that new member he gained from the previous church set himself up to do the same thing there. And he did. He inflicted severe damage to an innocent, recently widowed woman. I do wish that churches and their pastors were less competitive with each other, indiscriminately celebrating problems in other churches, and joyously capitalizing on their "losses". We need to honor our fellow pastors and their integrity, and benefit from their input.

So the disciplinary impact of biblical excommunication is thwarted. Subversives continue unabated. One pastor, at least, after unknowingly receiving troublemakers into its fellowship, sensed something amiss. So he did consult with the original pastor. On the basis of what he learned, he was wise enough to restrict their activities in his church, to give them no latitude to continue previous misbehavior.

My Experience of Congregational Discipline

In my thirty-three years of pastoral ministry, congregational discipline was only necessary twice, and that with regard to belligerent, retaliatory individuals determined to increase damage and disunity to their advantage, unless exposed and appropriately disciplined by the assembled congregation. It is defiance to all efforts for resolution that drives a church toward the necessity for discipline on the congregational level. It is far too painful to everyone for any to desire it.

Who Should Win?

Determined, troublesome people should not be allowed to win, to stay or lead – their contagion is too unhealthy for the Body. As a pastor, to commit to anything less than squelching their activities is irresponsible – the action of a hireling. Repentance or removal is essential, The integrity and health of God's work requires it.

Challenges pastors face should not be dealt with as personal offenses. Personal issues are not the issue. Rather, our primary concern must be for the effectiveness of our faithful ministry for the Lord, our responsibility to Him, our credibility and the reputation and effectiveness of churches we serve.

If We Stay to Fight

We need to recognize, however, if we stay to fight, our opposition is skilled to make our ongoing ministry hellish. For these, show down at high noon may be the only effective resolution. For this, it is unwise to be cornered into personal management of these people. Managing them this way leaves us very vulnerable to debilitating and ministry destroying charges of egoistic roots to our actions. Far better to face these challenges as a corporate phalanx, with leadership as a group, pressuring discordant people to conform with congregational expectations for peaceful relations. In accordance with Matthew 18, most of this can be and should be done confidentially, to protect their dignity and give them the best opportunity for positive change and growth. Only if this fails, should this phalanx move against detractors in accordance with Stage#4 of congregational discipline decreed by Jesus for His Church, in (Matthew 18:17-18).

>>DISCIPLINE STAGE #5 – (Matthew 18 vs. 18)—Binding and Loosing

"Truly I tell you, whatever you bind on earth will be bound in heaven, and whatever you loose on earth will be loosed in heaven."

Restorative Purpose

The restorative purpose of this methodology is demonstrated in the sensitive nature of its approach. (I wish this guidance were applied to issues with clergy as well. Surely clergy deserve biblical treatment by parishioners.)

1. Confidential confrontation

2. Expansion for defiance, as needed, to include witnesses

3. Failing this, defiance persisting, and especially if the matter has become of public concern, next step is exposure to the congregation for their assessment and disciplinary decision.

4. Strategic withdrawal for the disciplined to motivate their repentance and to protect the congregation from perpetuation of problems the disciplined have been causing.

5, Church members distance themselves from the disciplined and excommunicate.

To reiterate, every stage of Matthew 18 church discipline is intended as redemptive and restorative. If the discipline produces repentance, the repentant is to be restored in mercy and forgiveness. (I Cor. 5:5; II Cor. 2:6-8). This is the result we pray and hope to experience.

Wider Responsibility

It is important to recognize that chronic subversives are hard to cure. If they can get away with their evil action they will continue with impunity. If someone, some church, does not stop them, they will keep doing it, if not to us and our church, to others, other pastors, other churches. There is a contagion to their infection – they will infect and train others. It becomes an epidemic.

We need to draw a line in the sand with people addicted to damage. Run a clean ship. Don't leave messes for others to have to tidy. Don't be timid concerning right. As spiritual leader of a church, it is our responsibility to stand against mutinies. Because it is so painful for all, disciplining does not win popularity contests, but since when was that God's criteria for faithfulness. "Woe to you when everyone speaks well of you." Luke 6:26

>>DISCIPLINE STAGE #6—Debrief

After a session of congregational discipline, all kinds of emotions and questions flow through congregations. We need to settle their perplexity, anger, upset, whatever. Take the next Sunday service to open our heart to re-assure our congregation.

Let them know the procedures and struggles that preceded congregational discipline. There is no basis for these disciplined to claim the underdog position that appeals to the defender instinct of some. These demanded discipline by their determined defiance of all efforts to reach out to them for discreet repentance and restoration.

Make them aware that the anguish of disciplining hurts like that of disciplining one of our children.

Assure them that we are not tuned to seek out problems or investigate people. We are not out to get anyone.

Assure them of our drive to protect them, their families, their children.

Express our faithfulness to God, the Bible and the integrity of the church we share and lead.

Pour out our love on the congregation.

End with prayer – rich, anguished pastoral prayer that settles the past and looks thankfully to a peaceful and fruitful future together under God's protection.

In recognition that, "In conflicts, truth is often the first casualty and propaganda the liar's greatest ally.", keep the focus on facts and truth. Settle things and fortify them with a solid wall of truth, steering them away from unsubstantiated speculation and gossip.

>>DISCIPLINE STAGE #7—Reaction

Realize that no matter how biblically pure church discipline is exercised, every church has those who will be repulsed. These may be people who believe church should be a no-upset-zone. To them, whoever exposes a problem is the problem. Their heavenly idealism is so right to them that they will likely move on. Church discipline, though necessary and biblically advised, is always costly to leaders and churches. It is a last option necessity to be avoided but not rejected.

>>DISCIPLINE STAGE #8—Retaliation

In preparation for this latter stage of church discipline we should expect unrepentant offenders to defiantly paw at any means to win – by trying to make the pastor and church out to be the guilty party, by seeking to undermine the authority of the church, by attacking the pastor and/or defaming the church.

Use of Media

One method of doing this is exposing the disciplinary action unfavorably through the internet and the media. This can be very stressful since community standards have moved so far away from biblical norms. Headlines, newscasts, even protests or lawsuits may ensue. Pastoral leadership, in one such circumstance, wisely advised church members to say nothing to the media. This is wise because media loves to misquote, take quotes out of context, twist meaning, exaggerate disputes in order to stir up the community, for the purpose of increasing readership and viewers, thereby lifting ratings and advertising revenues. It is a game wise churches and church goers do not play with secular media that should be assumed to be unsympathetic.

Security

As a further assault, churches may require new security procedures to filter attendees. All of this becomes business as usual, without any vindictiveness to associated combatants. In fact, one church, caught in this circumstance, with picketers carrying placards back and forth across a parking lot entrance one cool night, treated them to hot coffee and donuts before they realized the hated church was the source. Kind of took the venom out of their efforts, exactly as hoped – they never picketed again.

Legal

In the lawsuit category, church membership has become very important. Non-members make no commitment to the constitutional and covenantal standards and disciplines of the church. Non-members who serve in significant church functions, therefore, do so outside of any personal commitment to standards church ethics or discipline. If they fail morally or otherwise, and the church takes exception, the church may be sued and will probably lose. For the sake of legal liability, work within the church's ministries should be limited to members,

To protect itself, church membership and police checks are essential, especially in dealing with children. The old Sunday School rooms with no windows are taboo for liability as well.

Not Too Tender

Congregational discipline has been most painful for me. These are congregants I love, even if they cause difficulty. My role is like that of a parent, parishioners like my children. Having to discipline them is heart wrenching. In fact, I discovered that, in this matter, my pastoral tenderness was a harmful weakness for me. It scarred me within, as though lack of what I hoped from discipline crushed me. If they hated me because of being brought to account, it stuck in the dagger that much more deeply. Discipline, though sometimes made necessary to counteract destructiveness, is so hard, because it is a counter current to our heart for uplifting ministry.

For the wellbeing of our life and ministry, we must learn that it is OK to be both tender and tough. Allow others to choose their direction and bear personal responsibility for their choices. Don't be so tender that we grieve over God's justice. Be sufficiently committed to what is right and good to be firm, without apology, when necessary.

Don't let God's judgment break us, as it did me, both times, due to my exaggerated sensitivity. I was learning as I went, and it cost me. I hope and pray that this will help protect you from harm.

"Be kind, be loving, be caring, be understanding, but never lose yourself in the process." Anon

"The church should not be the only place where good guys never win."

There is a price to pay for godly leadership.

Quit complaining about the state of the church, stand our ground and clean it up, if not for ourselves, for the next pastor and for the Lord, His reputation and His great commission.

> Though much is taken, much abides; and though
>
> We are not now that strength which in old days
>
> Moved earth and heaven, that which we are, we are;

RAYMOND CROSS

One equal temper of heroic hearts,

Made weak by time and fate, but strong in will

To strive, to seek, to find, and not to yield.

—Alfred Lord Tennyson

CHAPTER 20
Vigilance

It's Not What We Do; It's What They Think We Do.

If we recognize that Christian ministry is warfare against the forces of darkness, we will recognize the need for vigilance against the devil's traps. Temptations come in all forms, usually piggybacking on our drives. Setting personal protective policies is wise.

One area of special concern is private times with persons of the opposite gender. Beware of visiting them alone in their homes. Counseling can be emotive and can be connecting time that endangers standards of right and decency. One procedure is to always be sure to have a desk between us and a person of the opposite sex. Door ajar is also crucial.

At one time a woman requested desperate counsel at the church out of hours, when no one else would be there. I felt that it was necessary that I go but was suspicious, so I requested that my wife accompany me to the church, to sit in the room next door, outside the open study door, while I met with the lady. When she arrived and we were together in my study under this arrangement, she suddenly had nothing to share. In these matters, in a "he said she said" situation, men are guilty on allegation, even without evidence. Clearly, I needed the protection of a witness.

In fact, one pastor shared how a young lady had accused him of misdeeds, only to retract her allegation later. It didn't matter. In that case, just the insinuation of inappropriateness ended his ministry without opportunity for appeal. These dark clouds of suspicion can move with us to dim all prospects.

One church has set the limit of three pastoral counseling sessions per lady, If more are needed the pastor's wife is to participate as well.

Where a church does not provide guide rails, in times of spiritual and moral clarity, we should set our own so that, whatever the temptation, we do not allow ourselves time to consider. Rather, in time of weakness we fling ourselves within our guard rails to keep ourselves from ever venturing where we should not go. Never try to excuse what should have been avoided in the first place.

A Bible College friend of mine described to me her slide into questionable activities. She said that the first time that she did it her conscience bothered her, the second time not so much, after a while she felt just fine. What she described was justification and accommodation. She stepped on a slippery slope and it sucked her into dark water deep enough to drown her. It's a process that drowns many.

I was intrigued by an evangelical leader in our area who spoke of martini evangelism. I wondered what he did with:

"It is not for kings, Lemuel — it is not for kings to drink wine, not for rulers to crave beer, lest they drink and forget what has been decreed, and deprive all the oppressed of their rights." (Prov. 34:4-5)

We are leaders (i.e. kings). Leaders of leaders. People depend on our good, unobstructed judgment. Alcohol on any substantial level impairs this, thereby threatening our credibility and integrity.

The ministry of that dynamic preacher carried on with great vigor for years, but his indiscretion caught up with him, and his ministry ended shamefully. It is not wise for leaders to consume something that interferes with discretion and reduces inhibitions.

When we compromise God's guidance for His chosen vessels there is a price to be paid, and God also wears our shame.

But, some object, didn't Jesus make wine, the best wine? Yes, at the wedding in Cana He did exactly that.

> ... Jesus said to the servants, "Fill the jars with water"; so they filled them to the brim. Then he told them, "Now draw some out and take it to the master of the banquet."... Then he called the bridegroom aside and said, "Everyone brings out the choice wine first and then the cheaper wine after the guests have had too much to drink; but you have saved the best till now." (John 2:7-8, 9-10)

Biblically and in the spoken language of Jesus' time on earth the word "wine" was more generic than our present use of the word. It was not limited to an alcoholic beverage as it is today. As well, due to weaknesses in their ability to preserve freshness, in the first century "best wine" had a different meaning than in our culture. For them, as for us, "best wine" referred to the rarest quality wine. In that day and age "best wine" therefore, referred to the new wine of harvest when the fresh juice expressed from the grapes was available. Only at that time could it be enjoyed because methods available to try to preserve it adulterated it.

What Jesus made was not wine as men make wine but wine as God makes it, fresh and pure - "the best wine".

Other factors that can injure our ministry are laziness and slovenliness. Generally pastors do not punch a clock. They work according to their discretion. For some this may offer opportunity to slum it, to start late and leave early, days away and aside. Such behavior tends to be recognized and undermines support of quality people for their pastor.

As well, when on duty, recognize that when people enter our church they enter our place of business, we are the host in that role. We should look the part. At the least, we should dress a little above the average to be appropriate to the occasion and our role in it. In fact, whenever out and about, generally dress sharply because church members love to take pride in their pastor, and would love to feel good about introducing him to others.

As well, beware of the possibility of suspicion of dishonesty. We need to not only keep our distance from church finances but also honor personal confidences. Be careful not to use private information in sermon illustrations or personal conversation with others.

Reputation is fragile – it is built up layer upon layer, but only takes one misstep to collapse.

CHAPTER 21
Swan Song

But Paul said to the officers: "They beat us publicly without a trial, even though we are Roman citizens, and threw us into prison. And now do they want to get rid of us quietly? No! Let them come themselves and escort us out." (Acts 16:37)

There will certainly be times that pastors fail functionally, ethically or spiritually. In these circumstances, for the well-being of a church's ministries and / or reputation it may be necessary to remove a pastor. Where a pastor is at fault, discreet removal is usually wisest, rather than blasting clergy inadequacy unnecessarily beyond the congregational community.

"Darkness cannot drive out darkness, only light can do that." Martin Luther King

Why should a small group impose its will to remove a pastor in defiance of the will of the congregation? So, where unjust action is brought against a godly leader, the pastor should feel justified in bringing the matter out from backroom dealings and pressure. For power brokers to move against the call of God on their pastor is an affront to God that requires public disclosure for congregational adjudication.

In all efforts to dispose of a pastor, whether justified or not, biblical considerations can be lost along the way if strong wills determine to achieve their ends. As Rev. Dr. Les Dennis points out:

"Those intent on ending a pastorate tend to become oblivious to biblical principles such as:

1. Jesus is the Head of the Church. It is His church.

2. The position of pastor is as Jesus' messenger to their church.

3. If an individual or group turns on their pastor, they had better be right, because God will hold them to account for it.

4. They had better use only truth against their pastor because God is truth and does not take kindly to those who lie about His chosen messengers. Less than truth is a lie. The devil is the ultimate source of lies. So trading in lies to allegedly do God's work is extremely insulting to God. It is surreptitiously serving as the devils agents in simulation that their ends are God's will for His church.

5. The essence of congregational government is that Christ's church determines God's will for the congregation by majority vote. Each member determines between himself and God how to vote on an issue, looking to God, not to the perspective of friends or relatives to skew their ballot. If God's will is actually discovered by this means, Christ is Head. If a majority does not discern God's will by this means, Christ is no longer Head.

6. For an individual or small group to displace a congregation's accurate determination of God's will by lies, usurps God's role as the Head of His Church. They do the work of the Father of Lies. Those who dare perpetrate such deception should expect God's most severe righteous judgment.

7. Every member needs to be very sure whose side they are on, for Jesus, for His man, or for the devil.

These principles reside on detractors, and rightly restrict reaction to their action.

8. The attacked must also respond with integrity, honesty and respect under the Headship of Christ. Response should be according to the guidance of their Lord.

Consequence of Pastoral Removal FOR a Church

"...Strike the shepherd, and the sheep will be scattered, ..." (Zechariah 13:7)

Pastor's leaving churches opens up new opportunities but also many stresses exacerbated greatly if the transition is not cordial.

Termination is costly for everyone. For a church, it robs them of pastoral leadership and protection. Churches fail to recognize the ministry of pastors standing in the gap between marauding forces of darkness seeking access to their flock. Take a godly pastor out and demons invade. Things get worse not better. Peace is not the result of bad attitudes and actions. Lay leaders have no idea how to handle the maelstrom of confusion that will reel around them.

Removal of godly pastors leaves churches devoid of truth proclamation targeted to congregational needs. Quality members desert, offerings decline, quality leadership leaves, friendships fracture, ministry momentum falters, honorable church reputation in the community is marred. As well, it dooms the church to onerous hours and financial expense in search of pastoral replacement.

As well, churches that unjustly fire their pastor should not be allowed their usually expected exemption from paying appropriate legal severance. No way should a church be allowed to drop their pastor at the side of the road in this fashion. Severance commensurate to years served will prove very important to that pastor, providing for his needs and the needs of his family. Basic Christian love warrants such consideration.

As well, it is wise to be careful how the reason for our leaving is expressed to governmental employment insurance. Some ways of expressing it could disqualify our claim so that we receive no financial support between positions. Maybe best to consult with the employment insurance office to ensure our report to that office is accurately expressed in a manner that does not prove detrimental. In our case, I found that expressing it as, "irreconcilable differences" worked. Reporting that I had been fired or quit would likely disqualify me. This slip up has harmed many already hurting pastors.

Troublemakers are notorious for fabricating reasons why their pastor's leaving is good for the church and for the exiting pastor, but it remains a shock to the church and its community from which it is not easy to recuperate. Everybody knows it is not as it should be, and the devil laughs.

Would it not be appropriate to wipe the celebrative self-aggrandizing smirk off Satan's face, and that of agents of his injurious will? Would it not be godly for us to serve notice of the implications of what they are doing? Especially for churches that implement pastoral removals like an assembly line, would it not be appropriate for pastoral leadership to pull the rug out from under their sanctimonious stance – to end the pattern with a biblical shock of responsibility to the Lord for what they do? Too often lay leaders pursue their intents without looking up to seek God's will. Time to end the cycle, to re-establish the Lordship of Christ over His Church. Let's look at God's guidance for such depth of ministry.

Meetings designed for the removal of a pastor should follow a regular church business meeting procedure:

Step #1. Welcome—introductory words

Step #2. Declaration of intent for the meeting by those that called it. At this the pastor might choose to declare your intent concerning it as well – "I have no intention of leaving, no divine leading to leave and no sense that anything you are alleging justifies these actions."

Step #3. Prayer – If this looks to be left out, volunteer.

Step #4. Sharing of the troublemakers' case.

Step #5. Without betraying professional confidences, the Pastor shares truth concerning his ministry and his antagonist's misdeeds – no holding back, Not standing in defense of our ministry and therefore of our flock is the spineless behavior of a hireling, unwilling to stand their ground against attack.

Step #6. Opportunity for congregants to ask questions – again, as pastor, do not hold back in accurately expounding truth in response.

Step #7. Declaration of the intent of the vote – either the pastor leaves or his detractors do.

Step #8. Vote by private ballot.

Step #9. Vote result - declaration

If we stand in defense of our pastorate, expect this to be a turbulent meeting. Heated insults will likely be flung about as people vent, and others call them down and push them back. One pastor, describing such a meeting, spoke of men surging down the aisle to physically attack him, and others tackling them to thwart their intention. Such meetings produce violent church splits, so vilified among peace-loving church members, yet so necessary for the cleansing of congregations. Such events splash out evils so they can be washed away, hopefully restoring health to the Body. Churches so cleansed by appropriate church splits generally surge forward in God honoring ministry and growth. We may not like the process, but how can battling for right and good be displeasing to God, so why should it be despised by godly church members or the community?

If we have been obedient servants of God, leading and caring for our flock according to the Good Shepherd's guidance and faithfully preaching and teaching God's Word, it is inappropriate, unjust and dishonoring for the devil to win in Christ's Church. So, if a power group succeeds in achieving their objective to end our ministry, there is no shame in leaving. Even God knows that some "Christian" communities are hopeless. The Bible's guidance is to shake off the dust of that community in judgment on them and in preparation for new doors that may open to us. (Mk. 6:11)

"No amount of regret changes the past, no amount of anxiety changes the future, any amount of grateful joy changes the present." Ann Voskamp

Accountability for Judgment

Let's deal first with the judgment function of this biblical guidance from the mouth of Jesus Himself:

"And if any place will not welcome you or listen to you, leave that place and shake the dust off your feet as a testimony against them." (Mark 6:11)

This passage I had always understood as a private function for the pastor's personal benefit, meaning, in the rare event of a Christian church actually choosing to vote for the removal of their God-honoring pastor, don't carry their dirt with you. Make a clean break so that memories of our past does not ruin our future. While this has merit, it is clearly not the primary intent of Jesus words. Jesus clearly meant this to be a public exercise because it is described "as a testimony against them". It is something to be done in front of them, for them and others to see, as an indictment against what they are up to.

Now this instruction from our Lord is like that of the Year of Jubilee in the Old Testament (Lev. 25:8-28). Like the Year of Jubilee, God gives clear direction as to how it is to be practiced, but there is no description of it actually being implemented in the nation of Israel. Likewise here, the prescription of what and how it is to be done is clear and detailed, but there is no biblical or historical description of it being practiced by any rejected truth-proclaimer. Lack of this may be the cause of it drifting out of our consciousness as something we should do, despite the fact that Jesus commanded it. Surely, the fact that some have failed to obey Jesus is never justification for our failure to obey Jesus. I think it is time that we did what we are told for churches and church leaders to be reminded of their responsibility to their Master Shepherd.

> It is especially important that an innocent pastor recognize the situation as spiritual warfare. He should not fall into the trap of using non spiritual means of defense. He must keep a proper attitude and remain spiritual. I found that i had to spend a long time daily reading Scripture to keep the proper attitude. I had time to read this much because the congregation was backing away from me. Those who oppose the pastor do not want a pastoral visit, counseling, etc. Rev. Dr. Les Dennis

Since Jesus declares it to be a public function, if we can't win by staying, God intends His faithful servants to win for God by the way we leave. In the last moments, before our exit, Jesus intends that we snatch them out of their celebrative comfort zone. Yes, they have won on the short term, but they have brought upon themselves, and the church they claim to serve, the curse of God that the congregation should know about. It's a moment of accountability. Time to unsettle their throne of victory.

As I think of this, as a Bible College student, I witnessed a mutinous church action against a godly pastor, following which a church patriarch rose to his feet, and smacked his hands together as though triumphantly brushing off garden dirt. "Well that's done!" So much evil that it resonates to turn my stomach to this day. I'm certain God also was sickened. How dare this church leader and patriarch gloat over the ministry demise of a man of God? Such should not be the case. God has given us a means of ending this shameful, disgusting attitude and action over the dissolution of what God designed to bless and build the Body of Christ – godly pastoring of the flock.

"Do not touch my anointed ones; do my prophets no harm." (Psalm 105:150)

Too often, terminated pastors leave dejected and demoralized. This should not be. As the vote of a congregation draws down the blind on our ministry, Jesus does not want His faithful servants sitting drooped, dejected and defeated. He has told us what to do and His commands are always right and divinely purposeful. Before anyone declares the meeting completed, therefore, we are to stand up front-and-center with preaching Bible in hand, and, as should be expected from clergy, offer to conclude by reading a Scripture. It would be almost impossible to refuse this and retain any semblance of spirituality, so, at this moment we have the upper hand.

We are speaking the truth of God specific to this situation, over this situation. Announce that we are reading the words of Jesus in Matthew 10, verses 12 to 15:

> 12. As you enter the home, give it your greeting.

> 13. If the home is deserving, let your peace rest on it; if it is not, let your peace return to you.

> 14. If anyone will not welcome you or listen to your words, leave that home or town and shake the dust off your feet.

> 15. Truly I tell you, it will be more bearable for Sodom and Gomorrah on the day of judgment than for that [community] town.

End with—"This is God's Word. These are the words of Jesus, the Head of this church."

(Substituting a more targeted, yet accurate translation for "town", is advisable - use "community". "Community" neutralizes skeptical side-stepping of the point by debating why their actions should curse the whole city.)

Those who turn on their faithful, godly pastors bring God's curse upon themselves.

There is nothing more loving than for a shepherd to warn his flock of impending danger, if they continue on the path they are following in seeking to dismiss him.

Pause, then, demonstrably shake the dust off our shoes. Follow up by picking up our things, and move with purpose down the aisle and out of the church. While doing so, proper attitude is essential. This is a solemn gesture of judgment on offenders, which brings joy to no pastor. As such, it should not be a gesture of defiance – disrespecting the disrespectful makes us no better then they. So, no enjoyment, not celebrative, more a solemn recognition of unsuspected biblical consequences as a last effort to decisively preach repentance for a needed reset of that congregation's direction and spiritual tone.

This biblical manner of handling the event enables a pastor to walk out a winner, no matter what the outcome, knowing that, to the end, we have done exactly as God advised for the best of his ministry to that congregation and for the pastor's own sense of inner wellbeing. Nothing feels better for a pastor than moving in the center of God's will.

So, we complete our unjust termination with a biblical podump-bump reminder of their accountability to God, leaving them to carry their guilt for the part they played – actively and passively. Talking about Jesus advising a super impact methodology. If they haven't paid attention to us before, they will this time. Take the wind out of the devil's sail, and leave as a biblical servant of God, moving forward in the wind of the Spirit. Defeated but not beaten.

Reconsideration?

A few years ago a neighbor asked me to keep starlings from roosting in my trees because they were tearing apart their nests and dumping them in his pool. I took the request seriously, declaring war on the little critters. It was an education of learning how intelligent and resilient these socially connected birds are – knock a nest, and next day six starlings gather to rebuild it; like a barn raising, sneaking to their nesting sight from the side of the tree I could not see, defending the nesting sight by vigilant scouts cackling warnings. Starlings are very intelligent and determined.

One year I had a problem – these starlings choose to nest at the top of trees, and trees grow. One of my trees now exceeds my twenty-foot extension ladder and twenty-foot extendable pole. Beyond my reach. But they are intelligent birds, so that year I just leaned my ladder against the tree they were preparing for nesting. Zip Zap! Look at that – no starlings.

What might God do if, in accordance with His direction, pastors obeyed by leaning God's ladder of divinely described intent against a congregation. Will they be as responsive as starlings? Their depth of character and spiritual integrity will determine the outcome. Let biblical truth fall as it may. Ours is to proclaim truth as God decrees for people to learn and apply, or, for them to seek to escape its effect and scramble about in pursuit of cloaking their evil in hopes of evading its impact.

If we do not win, our pastorate may end, but, from a pastor's heart, it should grieve us to leave our church with troublemakers still comfortably in control. We could hope that the Lord's provision of His way to destabilize the simulated spiritual reputation of the victors, might also leave that church in a state of reassessment of what they are about. Surely, congregants who are spiritually sensitive, should be moved by an awakened awareness and foreboding for God's declaration of judgment on their behavior. Perhaps there might be sufficient spiritual impact to build resistance about ever following this track with a future pastor, maybe sufficient for reassessment of who they are positioning in leadership of the congregation, maybe a stimulus for repentance and renewal in the grief of losing a genuine man of God to lead them. At the least, it will initiate a reassessment whether this is the type of church some would want to attend and support. Who wants to be in a church under the curse of God? – "it will be more bearable for Sodom and Gomorrah on the day of judgment than for that [church]." (Matt. 10:15)

As it has come to me, it doesn't seem that the curse in Matthew 10:15 is presented as an attack but as a prophecy. The fact is true, even if they are unaware of it. So I believe it a kindness for a pastor to declare it to them, so they are made aware. Our final seismic sermonic biblical prophecy tantamount to, "Unconfessed sin will damn you." will undoubtedly penetrate the hearts and souls of spiritually aware people. Especially disturbing is the unusual shotgun nature of the prophecy. It heralds back to divine practice more evident in Old Testament times. The New Testament seems to focus more on individuals, whereas, in Old Testament times sin among a nation is shown to have consequences, perhaps dire, for the group as a whole. As well, leaders bear great responsibility for dreaded consequences they inflict on their followers. Woe to those who follow the ungodly.

So, I have wondered whether such an unexpected, decisive pronouncement of divine judgment might spur reconsideration in the congregation. It has been my observation through the years, that usually congregations, in these situations, abide by the actions of their leaders and view votes to remove their pastor as irreversible, but thus far, these actions have not been accompanied with a specific, targeted, biblical reminder of accountability to and judgment of God for their actions. They might view this a time for decisive response to injustice rather than just acquiescing in the manipulations and consequences of others .

Might a congregation, with a vision of God's storm clouds casting their shadow over their present "warmth and light", reconsider and repent of their actions, and solicit the pastor to reverse what transpired? If the pastor feels so led, might he allow for the congregation to process this with another meeting and vote. The result of this vote should apply in two ways. If the vote is to recall the pastor, those who instigated the mutiny, unless repentant, should be voted out of membership,. The door must be closed to the past in order for a reasonable prospect for fruitful ministry in the future – reconsider, repent, redirect and, to mitigate a slide into previous disunity, remove determined, unrepentant detractors who will continue to taint the fellowship with mutinous emotions and intentions. None so seething with anger as prideful humiliated. They need to be elsewhere.

So, what if a congregation reassesses its action; is it entitled to pursue recourse? If it were to be inclined that way soon after the vote, and wanted to ask their rejected pastor to reconsider staying as their pastor, decisive action would immediately be required. First they would need to approach their former pastor to determine whether he would reconsider staying. They would need to call another congregational meeting in short order. They should invite all members and the terminated pastor to attend. They might perhaps need his guidance for steps required.

Steps in the meeting would be:

Step #1 - Representation of issues related to the pastor by detractors

Step #2 - Pastor again speaks his truth concerning the issues and his detractors

Step #3 - A private ballot vote – A vote for the pastor is a vote against those who have pursued his termination, and express no repentance.

Step #4 – Discipline - Any persons unbendingly defiant of the church's chosen redirection, thereby demonstrate that they have stepped out of the fellowship, so should be asked to leave, with official relinquishment of their membership and involvement.

If the church fails to face this hurtful disciplinary procedure, problems will persist in perpetuity. No matter the pain, those unrepentant who led and those who actively supported action against the pastor must be stripped of their power, removed from their realm of control and influence in the fellowship. In fact, with regard to church discipline, the Bible advises against having any social contact with them whatsoever, lest they seek to twist and control from the sidelines.

"Drive out the mocker, and out goes strife; quarrels and insults are ended." Proverbs 22:10

Matthew 18:17 With regard to church discipline, ...

"If they still refuse to listen, tell it to the church; and if they refuse to listen even to the church, treat them as you would a pagan or a tax collector." i.e. – Stay away from them. This must be complete, not just a dilution of this movement and its impact on the church..

Step #5 - Congregational Confession Since the congregation's sin in acquiescing with action against their pastor has been public, confession and repentance must extend to the level of the sin; i.e., public.

Step #6 - Congregational Repentance expressed

Step #7 - Forgiveness administered by the pastor.

Step #8 - Deliverance from the biblical curse administered by the pastor.

Step #9 – New Call - Once these tough things have been administered, the church would then extend a new call for their pastor to resume his duties as shepherd of the flock.

Step #10 - New Induction Service - This should be followed by a new Induction Service with renewed promises of pastor / congregational relations, under God, and a laying on of hands by congregants.

Step #11 - Words of appreciation and pastoral challenge.

Step #12 - Restoration and Renewal - What should follow is restoration and renewal, perhaps refreshments.

While perhaps this seems farfetched, it is included here so a pastor, in this situation, might be prepared to lead a congregation through the possibility of this process to the glory of God, if the opportunity arises.

"Churches Never Apologize"

For years it was my observation that churches never apologize for their misdeeds. They just muddle along in their unconfessed sin and its consequences, seeking to worship and serve the Lord with a spirit of foulness and rebellion lurking in their midst. Recently, however, I noticed glimmers of hope as a few churches straightened out the evil of their way with humble confession and repentance.

As one pastor explained the situation in his church, as trouble-makers moved in on that pastor, for the sake of the church, he warned them that that church was composed of three factions. As pastor, he had mediated the disunity. Removing their pastor would leave each faction with two-thirds of members opposed to them. No faction would wield sufficient power to get its way. The church would split. No group would be able to implement their views without huge losses. Problem was that, in the present situation, the pastor stood in the way of all factions, so they agreed on one thing—the pastor must go. In the meeting, to decide the fate of his future, rather than looking to the Lord, the pastor noticed members looking each way, conferring with friends and relatives to align their votes.

After being voted out, huge losses spewed from the splits. Over time Sunday attendance declined 90%, from around eighty-five to between six and nine. Leaders of the mutiny drifted away, unsettled by the unexpected, though pastoral predicted, disastrous effects of their actions.

After six years, the Lord began to deal with the conscience of the remaining congregation. They voted unanimously to go to the home of that pastor (still in the area) to apologize to that pastor and his wife, for treating them wrongly and for removing him as pastor on unbiblical grounds. They invited him to preach during a service in which they publicly apologized. As a man of God, he was gracious and forgiving. He preached about dealing with the past, forgiveness, letting go of the past and pressing toward the future. As a man of God, he administered forgiveness: "You have been forgiven; you have dealt with your past; now move on to a biblical future."

More than two years later, they extended a call for him to once more pastor the church he had left under duress years before. Today he describes his experience, "This church has been the worst and the best church to pastor." The congregation has come to trust their godly leader and that trust is producing a sweet worshipful atmosphere so demonstrable of the love of God that it attracts new people to the Lord and to the fellowship of that congregation. Under his leadership, a dying church is being restored, with Sunday attendances more than quadrupling thus far. How wonderful to be part of a church with a clear conscience before God!

In yet another surprising case, a retired pastor joined a church, undermined the founding pastor and led the church to mutiny against him. Years after this crushing end to a dynamic church planter's ministry, his successor, recognizing, after a few years, the curse of ongoing spiritual scars that were hindering his ministry in the church, asked the rejected pastor to visit for a healing service to help resolve the spiritual heaviness. In that service, the former founding pastor was entrusted with the sermon. With the richness of a true spirit-driven pastor, he preached from John 13, which reads:

1. It was just before the Passover Festival. Jesus knew that the hour had come for him to leave this world and go to the Father. Having loved his own who were in the world, he loved them to the end.

2. The evening meal was in progress, and the devil had already prompted Judas, the son of Simon Iscariot, to betray Jesus.

3. Jesus knew that the Father had put all things under his power, and that he had come from God and was returning to God;

4. so he got up from the meal, took off his outer clothing, and wrapped a towel around his waist.

5. After that, he poured water into a basin and began to wash his disciples' feet, drying them with the towel that was wrapped around him.

6. He came to Simon Peter, who said to him, "Lord, are you going to wash my feet?"

7. Jesus replied, "You do not realize now what I am doing, but later you will understand."

8. "No," said Peter, "you shall never wash my feet."

Jesus answered, "Unless I wash you, you have no part with me."

9. "Then, Lord," Simon Peter replied, "not just my feet but my hands and my head as well!"

10. Jesus answered, "Those who have had a bath need only to wash their feet; their whole body is clean. And you are clean, though not every one of you."

11. For he knew who was going to betray him, and that was why he said not every one was clean.

12. When he had finished washing their feet, he put on his clothes and returned to his place. "Do you understand what I have done for you?" he asked them.

13. "You call me 'Teacher' and 'Lord,' and rightly so, for that is what I am.

14. Now that I, your Lord and Teacher, have washed your feet, you also should wash one another's feet.

15. I have set you an example that you should do as I have done for you.

16. Very truly I tell you, no servant is greater than his master, nor is a messenger greater than the one who sent him.

17. Now that you know these things, you will be blessed if you do them.

As he completed his sermon, the guest pastor moved toward the congregation, picked up one of the boxes of wet wipes he had brought. He went directly to those who had been most hurtful to him, bowed down before them and wiped their shoes, as they wept openly. He demonstrated the wholehearted godliness they had spurned and he offered them forgiveness, healing and restoration. The healing was profound.

In this case, the clergyman that ministered in his old church did not return as pastor of that church. From there, he went back to the church he was presently pastoring, a church that actually had some powerful people moving toward a similar mutiny against him. This time, however, that church had such love and loyalty for their pastor, that they locked elbows in his defense and sent the troublemakers packing by means of a turbulent church meeting and overwhelming vote in favor of their pastor.

With their pastor more firmly established in his church, his ministry blossomed, and that church launched into profound spiritual development and growth. There is no better way than God's way of building His Church under the leadership of God's servant pastors.

> Obey your leaders and submit to their authority. They keep watch over you as men who must give an account. Obey them so that their work will be a joy, not a burden, for that would be of no advantage to you. (Hebrews 13:17)

God's curses are not unconditional. They always have an open door to repentance that should be offered to them by their pastor, even if they have voted him out. Only churches that short circuit this possibility, pay as declared. However shocking and disconcerting the biblical method, we, as His servants, should do all we can to direct churches away from God's judgment on their sin and its painful and counterproductive consequences. What could be more loving than shepherds vociferously warning their flocks away from the inevitably of impending danger ahead? Woe to the church, its leaders and its congregation that will not repent.

Starting Again is No Escape

Congregations who remove pastors, likely have considerable time to reassess and reconsider the advisability of their actions, as they seek another pastor from a pool of hesitant candidates aware of how this congregation disposed of their previous pastor(s). Getting a prime pastor will be a reach for them for sure – a reach to find available willing candidates and stressed by the duration of their search. Certainly they will have to fill their pulpit with stand-ins for many months while they cool their heels.

Mutinous churches, with pastors exiting triumphantly, quoting openly God's specific message to churches that reject God honoring ministry, may seek to save face by defaming such godly pastors as irresponsible for leaving churches in disarray, vulnerable to a worse future. Don't fear. If we have been responsible and non-retaliatory, it won't stick. Honorable people and churches assess the quality of sources of criticism. What we have actually achieved is to leave them with a renewed awareness of Who is the Head of their church—Who they are responsible to, accountable to and Who is watching. We have fulfilled the role God expects of His under-shepherds in such circumstances - to expose the undercurrents of defiance to God and to the pastors He sends to guide His Church. No irresponsible hired hand here. Caring pastor to the end.

Biblically, as we look at the book of Revelation, it is apparent that God does not bleed for sick churches. Jesus views spiritually sick churches as repugnant. In Revelation 2, Jesus threatens to shut down the Church of Ephesus because they are playing church rather than worshipping Him devotedly (vs. 5). Likewise, due to lukewarmness, Laodicea's church nauseates Jesus (3:16). Sardis pretends to be alive but is dead (3:1). If unrepentant, guess their predicted future? Apparently Jesus has little patience with bolstering sick churches that distort who He is by their hypocrisy or abuse. Such are detrimental and disposable to Him. It is appropriate and even necessary, in the specter of deep damage, to take dramatic and decisive action, whatever the potential for reaction. The attitudes and actions of the mutinous leadership and the congregation cooperating with their endeavor have brought the whole community under God's curse with God's surety that payday for their deeds is coming, unless they confess and repent.

The Parable of the Tenants, in Matthew 21:33-44 likewise warns the unrepentant of the consequences of rejecting the servants God sends to represent Him.

> 40. Therefore, when the owner of the vineyard comes, what will he do to those tenants?

> 41. He will bring those wretches to a wretched end,...

> 43. Therefore I tell you that the kingdom of God will be taken away from you...

It is a woeful state to defy the living God and the servants He sends to us.

Church Splits

God is not concerned for the perpetuation of churches that don't honor and please Him. So, God is not nearly as concerned about church splits that we dread if they may bring a significant step up in genuine godliness, humility, congregational unity, ministry clarity and effectiveness among those who remain. A pastor's biblical swan song, while shocking, may be used by God like a rolling boil in maple sap, exposing the impurities so they can be removed to purify the sweet syrup. Without the contaminants, a purified congregation might be released to do what is right. It is what we can hope for, but only they can decide the future of their lives and church, and whether God is their partner.

Service of Repentance and Confession

In my years of ministry I have come to recognize the perplexing difficulty and struggle pastors encounter seeking to build purity and power in ministry in churches with faulty foundations. They step in with the purest of motives, unaware of the malaise that lurks in the background due to unconfessed sin. Such maladies grant the devil license to thwart ministries. I know because I have struggled with this in churches that had been so bad that their reputation in the community was damaged. So, due to previous unconfessed sin in churches, I wonder whether there may be wisdom in pastors leading a Service of Confession and Repentance for churches soon after initiating a pastorate. There may be foul stuff in their past that has never been dealt with. It can be dealt with corporately, with congregational confession and humble petition for forgiveness for cleansing, leaving individuals to apply the process to their own guilt as appropriate. Cleansing is good for the soul, and for the church, for the sake of renewed purity and vigor in the things of God. Cleansing is warranted and required for God to once again work mightily among us.

Consequence of Pastoral Removal FOR the Pastor

Both Mark 6:11 and Matthew 10:14-15 advise a rejected man of God to "shake the dust off your feet," We have seen how this works as a testimony against offenders. This gesture also serves the psyche of the pastor as he disposes of all physical remnants of his being in that place. This can serve a very important function, to remind that pastor to move on, unencumbered by the depth of hurt churches are able to inflict. As we brush the dirt off our body, we should flush away the disgust, disappointment, injustice. We set the stage for release from harboring hurts, thereby extending forgiveness and healing. It is an action designed to peel off the hold of our past so that our past hurts do not destroy our future. We dynamically rest in the Word of God that declares:

> 14. If anyone will not welcome you or listen to your words, leave that home or town and shake the dust off your feet.

> 15. Truly I tell you, it will be more bearable for Sodom and Gomorrah on the day of judgment than for that [community]. (Matthew 10:14-15)

"Father forgive them for they know not what they do." (Luke 23:34)

The past is good to learn from, not to dwell in.

Whatever our past, our future is spotless. Don't let disappointments and hurt from our past cling to taint our future. Prayerfully let it go and move on afresh. Termination is painful and complicated enough without carrying within our spirit deep and dirty clouds of hurt and self-doubt. Apply ourselves in the exercise of forgiveness. God is a God of justice. Remind ourselves how serious God has declared their infraction to be. They have much to fear and need our intercession. We walk forward in freedom to serve the Lord fully, with open hands and heart, wherever and however He chooses.

"For His anger lasts only a moment, but His favor lasts a lifetime, weeping may stay for the night, but rejoicing comes in the morning." (Ps. 30:5)

If we don't leave our past in the past, it will destroy our future.

Live for what today has to offer, not for what yesterday has taken away. Whatever our past our future in the Lord is pure promise.

Realize that forgiveness may not come easily. It can prove challenging as aspects of our hurt disturb our waking and sleeping hours. While sleeping, our dreams will likely spin around what we have experienced, "If onlys?" "What ifs?" Frustration because it's too late to bring change. We may need counseling to release trauma that has been locked into our gray matter. Don't diminish the challenge. Face it squarely. Don't leave pieces of ourself attached to people or places tied to bad memories. Drain off emotional attachment of those memories. Walk away whole. Wherever we are, be all there for God. Be whole. Be godly. Be open handed, not clenched in fear of recurrence. Be a better pastor as we implement what we have learned to who we are. Trust God to protect and be with us for effective ongoing ministry. God is not just interested in what we can produce for Him. He is much more concerned for us, who we become through what we go through. He is reaching out to us in love. Take His hand. Accept His embrace. Live and serve in the arms of our Best Friend, Jesus. He paid much that we might be much. All our hurts, failings and disappointments are in the past; keep them there. It's called the past because it's meant to be left in the past. Drop the baggage and walk upright into the future.

Consequence of Pastoral Removal FOR a Pastor's Family

Keep in mind that leaving a church, especially abruptly, is very costly and stressful not only to us but also to our family, probably more so than the stress of standing our ground against our detractors. So do not merely give in if you feel God has more for you to do in that church. As Winston Churchill expressed it, "If you're going through hell, keep going."

Realize also that the stress on our family needs to call forth the best, most understanding, most loving ministry from us. We mustn't make our wife and children pay even more due to our self absorption, anger and reflexive impatience toward them. It is hoped that we can go through these disappointments without turning our children against the Church, against Christians, against the Lord, against us.

Serving to a new church will mean the inconvenience and expense of moving, not just next door, but, specific to the pastoral role, to a new community. Long distance pastoral commutes are not often acceptable. Congregations want us to be part of their community. So, we will have to pack up and move, perhaps involving the sale of a home and purchase of another. This is stress on everyone in the family. It may uproot children from their friends and schools, maybe even mid-year. These events can leave scars, scars we may pay for from disgruntled family members. Such things are severe physical, mental and spiritual stressors.

The Consequence of Pastoral Removal FOR Our Career Prospects

If, after termination, we open ourselves to pastoring another church, unless we have already made this arrangement while being driven out, the switch to a new charge will involve considerable delay as we put our name out and begin the process of meeting with pulpit committees.

As we leave one church, especially under duress, we will naturally carry concerns for future prospects. Along with this, we might nurse fears of the ripples our shocking biblical exit might precede us. But then, would we want how easily we bow out under pressure to be determinant of our acceptability to the new congregation? All we did was read the Scripture appropriate to the circumstance. God declared that His Word is sharp; it cuts and is meant to, in order to spur repentance and redirection, for forgiveness and renewal.

Churches will assess our theology, our concept of pastoral ministry, our personal style for dealing with people, our preaching style, our Christian character and family life, etc. Again, if rattling wrong-doers by reading appropriate Scripture to what they are doing upsets the prospective church, it is probably not a good place to settle to follow God's lead for ministry anyway.

"And we know that in all things God works for the good of those who love him, who have been called according to his purpose. " (Romans 8:28)

No Recrimination

If we bail from a pastorate because of the inordinate stress that was mounted against us is too costly to us and our family, or because we assess that the nature of that church makes it unworthy of the sacrifice of our health, spiritual survival, family consequences or whatever, there is no shame in leaving.

If we choose to leave pastoral ministry permanently or for a season, it will involve pursuing other employment to provide for the needs of our family. Be encouraged. Clergy have many transferable skills to other occupations that enable them to do very well once they are established. One surprising thing will be recognition that professionals in the secular marketplace tend to earn at levels clergy would not conceive.

I think it inappropriate to feel guilt if we need to or want to pursue a secular career. Some view a call to ministry as always and necessarily a life-long commitment. I see no proof this needs to be so. Many Bible College professors, as I discovered, left pastoring for this new career. Recognize that God loves His servants whoever they are and whatever their role, as long as we do all we do to His glory. So relax in His arms and do what needs to be done, allowing God to lead step by necessary step into the future He has for us.

"When one door closes, another door opens but we often look so long and so regretfully upon the closed door that we do not see the ones which open to us." Alexander Graham Bell

"Don't stumble over something behind you."

"And whatever you do in word or deed, do all in the name of the Lord Jesus, giving thanks to God the Father through Him." (Colossians 3:17)

"Never confuse a single defeat with a final defeat."

We're fighting a battle He's already won. No matter what comes our way we will overcome.

CHAPTER 22
Have Tools, Will Serve

"**S**uccess is not final; failure is not fatal. It is the courage to continue that counts." Winston Churchill

We began this trek with thoughts of assurance for ministry. Like my father, with tools in his tool box, with the tools we now have, we should be better prepared to navigate the challenges we may face. As well, as best I could, I have provided skill guidance. Tools are only as good as our awareness of their appropriateness to challenges and to the skill with which the tools are exercised. The crucial benefit here is preparedness. Stress research verifies that severe pressure incapacitates the thinking part of our brain. Extreme pressure neutralizes our ability to invent wise means of managing the worst. What changes this is turning anxiety into excitement. The physical responses are the same, except that excitement animates rather than paralyzes. I hope that knowing that we can manage whatever comes our way will excite us in ministry.

Insurance

Years ago I commented to my wife about how we were paying premiums for years for insurance we would never use. A few years after that, the home next door blew up, taking our home with it. Suddenly insurance I belittled became essential. Insurance is never important until we need it. It is easy to coast along unprepared, like my wife and I almost did. So, think of this book as insurance, not important until it's needed. The hope is always that insurance becomes unnecessary. This book, then, provides for possibilities I hope we will not face, but many pastors have and do. Most of what they faced we may not, but if we do, devising resolutions on the spot can be very expensive. This book is our insurance policy to provide the protection we need whatever comes – help for when we need it.

In this book, we have what we need when we are least able to think things through. We have tools, diagnosis for situations for which specific tools are appropriate and instruction for their use. With these in wise synergy, we should be able to animate the best for success in almost anything thrown our way.

We began with this challenge. I'm sure it will make more sense now. So, with the pure heart of a godly pastor, walking and serving with and in the Lord's presence and power, and with a mastering pastoring tool belt clipped on our waist, go forth, with holy boldness to serve the Lord with honor. Relinquish unwise and unskilled coping mechanisms that play into the hands of detractor's complaints against us. Stay the course with tried and true templates. Stay the course through wind and storm. Keep swimming upstream; don't float in the downward current over the falls. Unnerve the nervy. Make them face what they're up to. Turn the tables on trouble. Set churches on a new course by laying aside the clinging weights that hinder churches from being the lighthouse for God they were intended to be. Celebratively build the Church of Christ that cannot be stopped, that even the Gates of Hades and its master cannot thwart. Make what Jesus visualized for His Church happen through your leadership.

Reservations

What I share is so powerful that it leaves me with some reservations. My goal is not to create fat-headed monster ministers, puffed up with power, who use tools I share to bully their congregations. That does not honor our Lord or build godliness in His flock. God honors humble, kind and loving servants. We are to serve for His glory, and the building of His Kingdom, not our own.

This concern for the misuse of what I share weighed heavily upon me until the Lord reminded me that even His pure words and truth recorded in the Bible, have been misused by the godless and distorted religious zealots, for their own purpose and gain. A distinctive characteristic of humanity that God honors is free will. All are free to choose to benefit from or defy God's goodness and transforming truth and bare consequences to them and others. So how can I ensure such will not do the same with what I present? I suppose it is accurate to declare that those disposed to misuse good are monsters at heart already. I just pray that Jesus, the Head of the Church, will guard His Church from harm and manifest His pure power through godly leadership to the building of His Kingdom.

I'm targeting a balance of tender godliness with strong managerial competence. Called and capable.

Whatever our level of skill, we need to tune our heart to pastor according to God's guidance and values:

"A new command I give you: Love one another. As I have loved you, so you must love one another. By this everyone will know that you are my disciples, if you love one another." Jesus (John 13:34-35)

"'Do not seek revenge or bear a grudge against anyone among your people, but love your neighbor as yourself. I am the Lord." (Lev. 19:18)

"We love because he first loved us. Whoever claims to love God yet hates a brother or sister is a liar. For whoever does not love their brother and sister, whom they have seen, cannot love God, whom they have not seen." (I John 4:19-20)

Christian pastoral ministry aims to introduce people to the selfless, sacrificial love of Jesus that, through personal faith, makes salvation possible, while also building and protecting a safe and loving community to nurture growth in godliness. We are God's shepherds providing for our flock's wellbeing and growth in godliness and safety. We are to love the Church the Lord is building (Matt. 16:18), in partnership with us who faithfully and lovingly proclaim God's truth (Matt. 26:20). Whatever skills we have are as nothing for the glory of God if not motivated by agape love.

"He has shown you, O mortal, what is good. And what does the LORD require of you? To act justly and love mercy, and to walk humbly with your God?" Micah 6:8

Exercise what we learn with utmost discretion.

No Enemies?

by Charles MacKay

You have no enemies, you say?

Alas! my friend, the boast is poor;

He who has mingled in the fray

Of duty, that the brave endure,

Must have made foes! If you have none,

Small is the work that you have done.

You've hit no traitor on the hip,

You've dashed no cup from perjured lip,

You've never turned the wrong to right,

You've been a coward in the fight.

Make what Jesus visualized for His Church happen, through our godly leadership!

Keep Focused On God's Goals

In May, 1952, Florence Chadwick set out to swim the twenty-six miles from California to Catalina Island. Such a swim was normal for Florence but this one held a challenge she did not anticipate. Fifteen hours into her swim thick fog set in. She looked ahead seeing nothing but a thick wall of fog, no coastline. She admitted that, unable to distinguish her goal and despite encouragement from her team that the shore was close, Florence lost heart and gave up less than a mile from shore. Many people quit a dream on the brink of its realization. It's when the challenges feel the most daunting that we're often closer to our destination than we feel ourselves to be.

For Florence, failure was not accepted as permanent. Awareness of what disoriented her empowered her. So, despite dense fog, two months later, Chadwick, with a mental image of the shoreline in her mind, pushed herself forward, completing the swim not once, but twice.

For all of us, swimming is nebulous exercise. We push water behind us with no awareness that we have actually gone anywhere unless we are able to compare our location related to a stationary object nearby. In swimming we slip and slide with forces in the movement of the water that can subtly sabotage our intent, even shoving us off course or backward. This was the world of Florence Chadwick in the Catalina Channel in 1952. Likewise for us, if we lose our perspective.

Working with people is like that – often one step forward and two steps back. We all encounter seasons of fog, not seeing where we're heading. Our goals become blurred. We encounter a challenge that can either break us or make us.

It depends on how we deal with that challenge when it arises. What can happen is that doubt can set in. Doubt in our ability, our expertise, our intentions, our credibility, or even our competence, our confidence, our courage, and being able to get and go after what it is that we're trying to achieve.

Don't lose vision, even if you cannot see. It is often darkest just before the dawn. Keep the vision of your Lord and His purposes clear in your mind's eye always. Keep focused on Jesus' declared future for His church – He declares that He will build it with strength to defy the devil himself. Victory is assured. Jesus will come to receive His righteous bride. We are the laborers to help bring this promise to pass. Do not despair. Rejoice for whatever progress you can make. If at first you don't succeed, try, try, try again.

Let's get in the Lord's current to bring to fruition His evangelistic and transforming intent.

In yet another example...

On September 28, 2018, a small group of computer programmers in Tokyo, Japan, working to invent and develop a new line of video games called Pokémon, experienced a nerve-racking computer crash erasing four years of work, apparently irrecoverably. In complete disgust all deserted the project except for a founding member of the team, Junichi Masuda. While not a programmer, as a founding member of Game Freak, Masuda had worked alongside the programmers as a composer, director, designer, producer in the development of video games. Masuda refused to believe that they had actually lost all the data for the Pokémon game. He determined to turn things around. He dived into research, seeking advice from everyone he could about how to recover data, even learning the programming language UNIX, and learning English to read its manuals. By his determination, Masuda recovered the "lost" data. Pokémon was launched, generating more than twelve billion dollars in its many versions through the years.

Jesus believes in His Church. He has predicted its victory. We have good grounds for persisting. Let us not throw in the towel in disgust. Let us determine to restore the Church to its biblical and godly roots for it, and its leaders, to grow strong and fruitful to the glory of God.

"I will build My Church and the gates of hades shall not prevail against it." (Matt. 16:18)

Let's bring the Church back to its "turn the world upside down" expectation.

If— by Rudyard Kipling

If you can keep your head when all about you

Are losing theirs and blaming it on you;

If you can trust yourself when all men doubt you,

But make allowance for their doubting too;

If you can wait and not be tired by waiting,

Or, being lied about, don't deal in lies,

Or, being hated, don't give way to hating,

And yet don't look too good, nor talk too wise;

If you can dream—and not make dreams your master;

TOUGH STUFF

If you can think—and not make thoughts your aim;

If you can meet with triumph and disaster

And treat those two impostors just the same;

If you can bear to hear the truth you've spoken

Twisted by knaves to make a trap for fools,

Or watch the things you gave your life to broken,

And stoop and build 'em up with worn out tools;

If you can make one heap of all your winnings

And risk it on one turn of pitch-and-toss,

And lose, and start again at your beginnings

And never breathe a word about your loss;

If you can force your heart and nerve and sinew

To serve your turn long after they are gone,

And so hold on when there is nothing in you

Except the Will which says to them: "Hold on";

If you can talk with crowds and keep your virtue,

Or walk with kings—nor lose the common touch;

If neither foes nor loving friends can hurt you;

If all men count with you, but none too much;

If you can fill the unforgiving minute

With sixty seconds' worth of distance run—

Yours is the Earth and everything that's in it,

And—which is more—you'll be a Man, my son!

"Now to him who is able to do immeasurably more than all we ask or imagine, according to his power that is at work within us, to him be glory in the church and in Christ Jesus throughout all generations, for ever and ever! Amen." (Eph 3. 20-21)

ONE LAST TIDBIT - **How I learned to baptize**

I find it interesting that in denominations and churches that practice baptism by immersion nothing seems to be provided to help us, as pastors, to know how to do it. So, here's what I came to by my own efforts to discover what works well.

I analyzed scientific principles for how it can work. It involves two forces of nature - gravity and buoyancy. Both are very powerful. Buoyancy in water is so strong that it virtually neutralizes gravity. While collecting water in large carboys at a local spring I often quip to fellow porters how good it is that water is so heavy, so that cruise ships can float. Isn't it amazing that hulls that sink so seemingly little into the water suspend eleven decks of ship and three thousand passengers. I want to make full use of that force in my efforts to baptize.

To do this I developed a technique that has worked very well to baptize smoothly and minimize stress on my frame. It can be difficult to lift people who can be larger than I.

When candidates are immersed their feet and legs tend to float so there is nothing to hold them in place. Besides, legs suspended in water tend to want to kick in swimming motion. To keep them from sliding in the water, probably exacerbating the lift to raise them from the water, there had to be another way.

To do it well requires control of risks that can strain our frame.

I discovered that having candidates stiffen their bodies during baptism meant that their body acts like a door on a hinge, so, with an arm behind them for reassurance, a slight push backward usually provides momentum sufficient for them to immerse. Then, when buoyancy and my arm lifts them their feet more quickly contact the floor of the baptismal tank. They don't slide. Buoyancy pops them up. I lift only the top section of their body that is emerging from the water, not their whole floating body.

As well, when moving to immerse, it's the upper part of their body that slides below the surface. If we maintain our position in line with their feet, our arm behind their back at about the level of their shoulders pulls us to the side and we have to try to lift their floating body from the side. To escape this I step to the side in the direction of their head. This positions me for a straight upward lift. The lower arm behind them to lift. A white face cloth over their nose for their comfort, and for a slight push if perhaps auto immersion is not complete.

By these means, baptismal candidates are able to relax for their immersion, with hands clasped together across the front - buried in the likeness of His death; raised in the likeness of His resurrection. All effort is provided to the baptized by the baptizer but not overwhelmingly due to careful management of all forces and factors involved.

All glory to our Lord!

APPENDICES

APPENDIX # 1
How Baptist Churches Work

I formatted this as a one page brochure (81/2 x 14 double sided quadra-fold).

Please feel free to use it. Make whatever changes necessary including changing the title to suit the present situation of your church.

How Baptist Churches Work (Congregational)

The church member's position in a Baptist church is crucial.

BAPTISTS

Worldwide there are many denominational families of Baptists. What makes them Baptist is not association with a common organization. What makes them Baptist is agreement with beliefs and policies Baptists hold in common:

Bible—sole rule for faith and conduct

For Jesus, the Scriptures were absolutely authoritative. Like the Apostle Paul, He viewed them as an accurate communication of God's message through individuals who were moved to write by the Holy Spirit. Under the Lordship of Christ, Baptists affirm the Bible is God's Word—our final authority for God's will and truth. Under the guidance of the indwelling Holy Spirit, all believers are encouraged to study and apply the Bible. (Mt. 5:18; II Tim. 3:16)

Autonomy of the local church and voluntary association

Each Baptist congregation governs itself democratically without external human control. These self-governing churches own their buildings, pay their own bills and decide the direction of their ministries, but they also voluntarily associate with churches of like faith for joint ministry and for fellowship.

Priesthood of all believers

According to the New Testament, Jesus is the only high priest of the Church. Except for Him, the Church does not have an official priesthood through which believers must approach God. Rather, the Church IS a priesthood. Through Christ, each person may approach God directly. Each believer is to fulfill the priestly function of representing and presenting Christ to others, and of bringing their needs to God in prayer. Christian ministry belongs to every believer. (Heb. 4:14-16; 7:23-28; I Pet. 2:3-5; Rev. 1:5, 6).

Two Church Ordinances

An ordinance is a worship activity Christ ordered His Church to practice. Ordinances are not sacraments, that is activities that, in themselves, channel grace or salvation to participants. Rather, ordinances are congregational activities designed by Christ to remind believers of essential gospel truths. It is the heart response of believers to these truths that prompt God's blessing. The two ordinances are:

Believer's Baptism (Matt. 28:19-20; Rom. 6)

> a. By immersion – to symbolize Jesus' death, burial and resurrections.

> b. Of believers only – as a voluntary testimony of personal faith.

The Lord's Supper — to remember Jesus' death for our sins (Luke. 22)

Individual Soul Liberty

God alone has the right to define what is proper in belief and worship. Free will is necessary to saving faith; it cannot be coerced. Every person is accountable to God to their religious beliefs and practices, and has the right to worship God as their convictions and conscience dictate (Gal. 1:26; Rom. 14:12).

Saved Church Membership

Jesus is pre-existent God who became the Son of God through birth in Bethlehem. Because He lived a sinless life He was able to pay the price for our sin by dying on the cross. Those who confess their sinfulness and, in faith, accept Jesus' death for sin as substitute for the death they deserve, are forgiven by God, granted eternal life and given the constant presence of Christ through His indwelling Holy Spirit to comfort, guide and empower, Biblically, only those thus joined to Christ and baptized in testimony of that commitment are to be received as a church member. (Acts 2:41; 8:12; 18:8)

Baptist Church Government

Baptist churches recognize the Lordship of Christ over their personal and community life. Their churches are organized biblically, under spiritually mature leaders - first pastors, then servant deacons. These lead and provide for church ministries. All aim together to discern and follow the will of the Head of the Church, Jesus (Matt.16:16-18; Col 1:18).

Separation of church and state

Religious groups should not control the State, nor should the State interfere with the ethical practice of religion within its borders. Through democratic process, all individuals and groups may and should, however, contribute to the guidance and well-being of their country.

Baptists Locally, nationally and internationally

Historically, Baptist churches have reached beyond the isolation that may develop from independent congregational government. Though self governing, they have tended to voluntarily associate with other churches of like belief, purpose and practice. At first this may merely be for fellowship or it may stem from one church establishing another. Whatever the route, churches in close proximity to each other have affiliated for encouragement, accountability and to strengthen their witness. Often these bonds of local Christian cooperation have become known as associations. The ministry roles these associations tend to develop are camp ministries, workshops, ministries with men, women and youth, and assemblies to enrich the spiritual lives of church members and adherents. Several times a year interested individuals and delegates selected by each church attend association meetings held at various association churches. These meetings may include fellowship, refreshment and spiritual blessings as well as time for reports and voting concerning ministries held in common. All are invited and welcome to attend.

In recognition of the need for cooperative effort in even larger ventures, Associations and their churches have affiliated to form denominations. By working together and combining contributions in this fashion we provide expert assistance and support services to strengthen our churches and coordinate ministries beyond the resources and capability of local congregations. Typical denominational partnership ministries are communication services, educational institutions, women's mission societies, and foreign mission endeavors. Denominational administrative offices serve churches to assist their local and worldwide ministry for Christ. Elected denominational leaders exercise their offices and moral authority to serve congregations rather than dictatorially ruling over them.

Each member and each congregation has a voice in the direction of local and denominational ministry. Each year, churches send delegates to an annual denominational assembly. These delegates listen to reports from various denominational agencies concerned with ministry both at home and on the foreign field. They vote on matters of policy, approve a budget and elect a new administrative executive (mostly volunteer) for the coming year. Inspiring worship and refreshing fellowship top off these times.

So you see, your church, association and denomination cannot progress without your active involvement. A membership of individuals active in the ministry and business of local churches is essential to their association and denomination.

The Active Church Member

What can you do?

You can be an active church member. Strengthen your church, your denomination and the cause of Christ by attending services regularly, serving joyfully and conscientiously, and attending all business meetings of your church.

1. Maintain personal devotions

A church grows as individual members grow, and there is nothing more important to Christian growth than our relationship with Christ. Each member should be diligent in their efforts to maintain a personal walk with God by daily Bible reading, meditation and prayer. Our pastor would be happy to assist you in entering into such a commitment.

2. Attend worship services

Everything left to itself deteriorates—including our lives. But your church is a source of positive spiritual input and life-giving guidance. It always welcomes opportunities to help, uplift and inspire to quality Christian living. Regular church attendance is essential to you, to your family and to your church. Come weekly to be challenged and changed toward Christlikeness. Loving greetings, congregational singing, caring prayer and anointed preaching stir the spirit within. Without them, you will be like a log removed from a fire which, in consequence, quickly loses its flame, smolders and cools. For this reason, make church attendance the priority for the sake of your own spiritual health and that of your loved ones. By faithful attendance and participation you contribute to making your church home a most exciting church to the glory of our Lord.

3. Avail yourself of Bible learning opportunities

In Hosea 4:6 the Lord warns that His people are destroyed for lack of knowledge. With all the theories and opinions current these days we know this warning is not outdated. If we are not thoroughly grounded in the truths and principles of God's Word, our lives and families may be twisted and tainted by godless thinking. Learning to live God's way is not just for children, and there is no stronger form of leadership than example. Seek out opportunities for Bible study provided by your church either on Sunday or through the week.

4. Attend midweek gatherings

Spiritual health is enhanced by involvement in weekday events planned for various needs and ages. For a midweek refresher attend a Bible study, a prayer meeting or a cell group. Enjoy in-depth interactive, question and answer, Bible study with our Pastor or other capable leader and join with other caring Christians in praying for ministries, missions, people's concerns, our country.

5. Participate in activities

Support groups, children's meetings, service ministries and social times punctuate each week. These activities are not closed cliques. We welcome you with open arms to participate in everything that may be a blessing to you and yours. As needs arise and vision grows our capable leadership is prepared to launch more ministries important to you.

6. Serve and give

The greatest source of blessing for believers is not merely receiving, but giving. In giving of ourselves we become channels of God. Church ministries depend on volunteers who make their gifts and talents available to the Lord. Find a niche or two appropriate to your abilities and feel the thrill of being used by God to bless others.

Jesus tells us to be light and salt in our world, light that shines far and wide, and salt that stimulates thirst for God and helps to preserve quality of life. Be alert to ways you may gently point others to the Savior by volunteering in the social service agencies and ministries in your community (Mt. 5:13-16)

Giving also includes finances. We talk of giving to God, but God does not take our money. The money is left here to support ministry, outreach and missions, and to purchase materials and maintain facilities and equipment. What we give returns to us to bless our lives, our families, our community and our world. By giving generously we do not lose; we all gain. Not only that, God is honored by generosity. It frees Him to bless givers.

Contact church leadership to learn its method of providing confidentiality in your giving and to enable you to receive an annual receipt for tax purposes.

7. Participate in congregational decisions and direction

We are a democracy. Major decisions cannot be made without you. It is, therefore, both your privilege and your responsibility to prayerfully seek God's will for your church, attend business meetings, contribute your opinions toward consensus and assist with the implementation of these decisions with your time, your abilities and your financial support. So, when business meetings are announced, mark them as priority appointments in your calendar. In them, we seek your input and account to you for all that transpires. By seeking God together, sharing our various perspectives and following democratic procedures, we pursue the will of God. By these means we seek to stimulate and enhance exciting ministries designed to build souls for eternity.

8. Become acquainted with our mission and outreach ministries

Your church supports mission endeavors locally and around the world and provides mission education opportunities. As you are made aware of these ministries, pray for and support our evangelistic endeavors, our outreach to youth, our encouragement of other churches in the denomination and our cooperative mission efforts around the world.

<> <> <> <> <>

Heaven on Earth

Jesus said, "By this everyone will recognize that you are my disciples, if you love one another." (Jn. 13:35 Moffat)

From I Corinthians 13, we learn that love is not merely a feeling, but a way we act towards others. To express such love, we, as believers in Jesus, join together to worship and work. The basis of our fellowship is our oneness in Christ (I Cor. 12:12-27) and our concern for fidelity to God's Word in our beliefs and in our behavior (Jn. 14:23; Mt. 5:18).

Church constitutions frame the ideals to which we as members are committed. They also set out Biblical and practical guidelines for implementing these ideals. Church constitutions are composed of a covenant, articles of faith and bylaws. The covenant made before God with one another, tunes our treatment of each other to the matchless principles of Godly love. Articles of faith express foundational Biblical beliefs we hold in common. Bylaws set a church's administrative framework to protect democratic principles and ensure orderly and responsible management of church ministries and business.

Active spiritual members give life and power to a church. Inactive, unspiritual members thwart the church's progress and sap its vitality. Determine now to be the best church member you can be so that your church may be all God wants it to be to God's glory.

In a cartoon, a little boy was drawn standing outside a candy store. The window is filled with jars and boxes of candy. On the window is a poster which reads, "Do not lick the window." We smile, but may be smiling at ourselves, for there are Christians standing outside the storehouse of God's provision, looking in wistfully and wondering how on earth they can make all these good things theirs. We don't have to stand outside licking the window. God invites us in to help ourselves to all things necessary for life and Godliness. Don't stand outside any longer. Come on in! Invite others to do likewise. Welcome new people when they come.

Membership in the Christian church is a honored privilege bought with the blood of Christ. Local church membership is also a great privilege of our free society. Exercise these blood bought privileges to the hilt! If you wish believers baptism or church membership, talk to your pastor right away.

The Perfect Church

I think that I shall never see

A church that's all it ought to be;

A church whose members never stray

Beyond the straight and narrow way;

A church that has no empty pews,

Whose pastor never has the blues;

A church whose deacons always deak

And none are proud and all are meek;

Where gossips never peddle lies;

Or make complaints or criticize;

Where all are always sweet and kind,

And all to others' faults are blind.

Such perfect churches there may be,

But none of them are known to me.

But still I'll work and pray and plan

To make my church the best I can.

Anon

Without active members Baptist churches grind to a halt.

APPENDIX # 2
Incorporational Biblical Church Structure

The biblically defined structure for Christian churches is simple – pastors and deacon/servants to help them. During the early church period that structure was adequate to support church growth that "turned the world upside down". (Acts 17:6)

Over the years church structure has become more complicated with committees and boards to address different aspects of church life. None of this is necessarily wrong, any more than Sunday Schools are wrong because they are never mentioned in the Bible. Diversifying for specialized efforts for specific ministries for different needs can be appropriate. Certainly governmentally imposed structure for charitable registration, such as trustees, is appropriate as legal agents to represent ownership of non-incorporated church real estate and serve as legal signing agents for a church.

As the litigious atmosphere developed in North America, it became a concern for churches that if a church were sued for any reason, as representative owners of church assets the trustees would be the legal representative to be sued. As such, if church assets were inadequate to pay out a suit, the savings and assets of trustees could be taken to fulfill the obligation.

This stirred churches to incorporate so that the church itself was made into a legal entity. In this manner any lawsuit against a church would involve only the assets of the church, never extending to the personal assets of members.

This legal procedure seemed wise but introduced a complication into the administrative structure of churches – a Board of Directors. How does a pastor lead a church whose structure includes a Board of Deacons, a Board of Directors – Deacons, and Directors. Who leads? How does God get a say? Where does a shepherding pastor fit in leadership of the flock?

Probably the wisest way to manage this, is to make deacons the directors, but directorship is not foremost, just sort of like trustees. They exist to be legally available to manage legal issues. When a legal issue arises, some deacons slide forward to meet the legal obligation, then dissolve back within the deacons.

In the current church there might be committees and boards with specific areas of responsibility in ministries, yet overall oversight of a church must remain clear. God is not the author of confusion. Nor should we be. For the sake of healthy churches, streamlined channels of guidance should flow from the shepherd, along with deacon-servers, under the congregation's ultimate authority and adjudication under God.

"For God is not the author of confusion, but of peace, as in all churches of the saints." (I Cor. 14:33)

APPENDIX # 3
Deacon Handbook

Rev. Dr. K. Rick Baker, Lead Pastor, Calvary Baptist Church, Oshawa, Ont., Canada,

as a seminary project, produced this in the late 1980s and has been using it for deacon recruitment and development ever since. Prospective deacons receive this in advance prior to allowing their names to stand for election in order to determine whether or not their vision aligns with that of the senior pastor. This served as an ongoing guide (position charter) to measure deacon effectiveness and compliance to the leadership model of Calvary.

This very helpful booklet is provided here with approval of Rev. Dr. K. Rick Baker in hopes it may serve to strengthen pastors, churches and the cause of Christ as they use it in their ministries.

TABLE OF CONTENTS

"For those who have served well as deacons, obtain for themselves a high standing and great confidence in the faith that is in Christ Jesus." (1 Tim. 3:13 NASB).

We live in a society that offers very little by way of security, to say nothing of care. The preservation of the family unit, which at one time could almost be taken for granted, is quickly becoming a rarity indeed, even within the household of God.

Even the church, being divinely instituted to bring honor and glory to its head, the Lord Jesus Christ, is with significant regularity becoming a reproach to the Living God through the assimilation of humanistic philosophies. To an insecure and needy household of faith, the church is closing its heart in favor of self-interest and political power struggles. This ought not to be. The Scriptures are clear with regard to the church's interpersonal responsibilities (Jas. 1:27; Gal. 6:10). Caring for the brethren is a debt the redeemed owe the loving Savior.

It is the intention of this manual to create a biblical profile and identify the scriptural function of the deacon. In what way does the deacon fulfill the interpersonal mandate within Christ's church to the glory of God?

What Is A Deacon?

The term deacon is a transliteration from the original meaning of "servant" (Beyer, 1985:152). Beyer (1985) continues by adding that the term is sometimes used todesignate a special office (cf. Phil. 1:1; 1 Tim. 3:8,12).

Acts 6: The Origin?

"But select from among you, brethren, seven men of good reputation, full of the Spirit and of wisdom ... to serve" (Acts 6:3,2 NASB).

Nichols (1964) concludes that while the seven men of Acts were not called deacons, they were called upon to serve the daily needs of the congregation, which was not too dissimilar, if at all, to that of the New Testament deacon. It must be noted, however, that the origin of delegating service precedes Acts. Moses' father-in-law, Jethro, proposed an almost parallel administrative framework of service. "Furthermore, you shall select out of all the people able men who fear God, men of truth, those who hate dishonest gain and you shall place these over them..." (Ex.18:21 NASB).It is impossible to miss the consistent character qualifications necessary throughout the two dispensations.

1 Timothy 3:8-13: The Qualifications

The deacon must be:

(a) dignified (serious-minded);

(b) not double-tongued (two-faced);

(c) not addicted to much wine (stronger expression than v. 3; [Earle, 1978: 367]);

(d) not fond of dishonest gain;

(e) holding the truth with a clear conscience;

(f) above reproach having been tested by time;

(g) the husband of a respectable, irreproachable wife (Earle, 1978);

(h) a one-woman type man (Saucy, 1974);

(i) a good manager of his household and children; and is gaining for himself an excellent standing ... in the eyes of the church and in God (Earle, 1978:369).

All Christian men should manifest these qualifications, but the deacon must.

What Is Deaconing?

One of the great misunderstandings of our church era is the role of the deacon. The vacuum created by the lack of sound teaching and direction in this area has been filled by pendulum power struggles and political infightings between deacons and pastors for church headship.

Function or Office?

Most deacons would assume deaconing is an office: an official authoritative position awarded for spiritual excellence with-in the body. However, of the over one hundred times or one of its cognates appear in the New Testament, only three times is itreferring to an office (cf. Phil. 1:1; 1 Tim. 3:8,13).It becomes intuitively obvious that deaconing is a function most of the time. As White (n.d.) points out, of the great number in the local body deaconing (serving), some are chosen for the office perhaps as a result of exceptional ability. He also concludes that one of the spiritual gifts is deaconing (cf. Rom. 12:7).

Physical Activity or Spiritual Activity?

The qualification to manage well (cf. 1 Tim. 3:12) coupled with the early examples of waiting on tables (cf. Acts 6:1-3) along with the very nature of service makes deaconing a physical activity. It is also, however, very clear that ministering to people and the restoration of the fallen is spiritual labor by the spiritual (cf. Gal. 6:1).

Deaconing, New Testament style, is both a physical and a spiritual activity.

Corporate Decision-Making or Servant-Ministering?

This writer well remembers the day he was asked to run for a deacon. This writer had been asked, (so he thought), to be a part of the political decision-making process of the local church. The picture of corporate boardrooms with long, dark oak tables danced in his head. There has been a great cost to the local church by its use of the terminology Deacon Board. By implication, the deacons perceive themselves as parallel to the world's corporate system, the principles of which they are called to reject (cf. 1 Jn. 2:15-17). The signals to a new deacon are mixed indeed. It is hard to divorce oneself from assertiveness and political ambition when secular training and church leadership structures are so similar. The term board is probably secular baggage that should be left to the world. Christian conduct is serving, self-sacrificial and loving (cf. Phil. 2:2-4). Regardless of the twentieth century connotations of deacon, the term implies service. The "board" of servants should spend their time serving the needs of others with a low emphasis on the congregationally delegated authority to make some decisions (White, n.d.).

What Are The Deacon's Responsibilities?

Having examined the Scriptural requisites, qualifications and implications of the deacon and deaconing, one must zero in to understand practical deacon functions.

Duties To His Lord

Before one starts practical service, there needs to be a decision concerning the commitment of time devoted to specifically serving the Lord. Agreement in this area may differ, however as stewards to God of all of our time, it seems consistent to devote at least a tithe of our waking hours, or eleven hours per week, to the sole service of the Lord. This time will include church services (Sunday, midweek) and other church-related activities. Allowing 6.5 hours for Sunday and midweek services, the servant of God has available 4.5 hours per week to serve.

The deacon must model a devoted, separated lifestyle constantly renewed by the Word of God (cf. Rom. 12:1-2). "A pupil is not above his teacher; but everyone, after he has been fully trained, will be like his teacher; (Lk. 6:40 NASB).

Duties To His Family

Since the deacon is qualified on the basis of a well-ordered family including a dignified, faithful wife, it is imperative that he maintain and nurture the spiritual excellence of his family. The deaconing function of the church is very much a team ministry of the married. With the constant Satanic siege on the institution of marriage within the local church, it is needful for the flock to see a godly matrimonial example in their deacons and pastors.

To an assembly inundated with the secular justification of fractured relationships, immoral lifestyles and self-actualization, a family devoted to God's blueprint for the home (Eph.5:22-6:4) is the mandatory servantship model.

Duties To His Pastor

"Obey your leaders, and submit to them; for they keep watch over your souls as those who will give an account. Let them do this with joy and not with grief, for this would be unprofitable for you"; (Heb. 13:17 NASB).

It is here that the office part of the deacon ministry seems to be over exaggerated. The deacon is not God's appointed watchdog, (or the congregation's for that matter), to assure that the overseer exercises integrity and wisdom. If the pastor cannot be trusted, he should not be watched, he should be dismissed.

The pastor is the counsellor, coach, friend, guide, helper and resource person who God has given to the church to oversee the ministry of the assembly (Bixby, n.d.). The deacons are not to be evaluators or adversaries, but members of a ministry team assembled to serve based on shared decision-making (Bixby, n.d.). It is a wise pastor who solicits the counsel of godly men (cf. Prov. 13:10; 19:20).

It is the deacon's responsibility to respect, honour and trust the ruling elder (cf. 1 Tim.5:17), not in blind faith, but through spiritual discernment. Additionally, the deacon, as well as other saints, should act as a buffer between the critics and the pastor (cf. 1 Tim. 5:19).

It is best when the pastor and deacons covenant together to sacrificially care for the needs of the flock with the pastor overseeing. Demonstrating an attitude whereby each regards the other as more important (cf. Phil. 2:3) should prevent any clash of offices in favor of the balanced cooperative necessary to accomplish the task (cf. Ps. 133:1-3).

Duties To His Church

Each individual person must be made to feel our interest in him, our concern for his total spiritual life, and our joy in his relationship to the church. This effort, more than any other, will make our church strong and vital (Nichols, 1964: 113), that there should be no division in the body, but that the members should have the same care for one another. And if one member suffers, all members suffer with it, if one member is honored, all members rejoice with it (1 Cor. 12:25-26 NASB).

The Word of God spends no time teaching how to conduct Deacon Board meetings nor how to decide the color of church carpets. The Word of God does concentrate on our obligation to care for the needs of one another that the body might grow to maturity in Christ Jesus (cf. Eph. 4:11-13). It would follow that of the agreed-upon deacon service-time, most should be spent on caring for the needs of the saints. As Dr. Eugene Berends (n.d.) points out, the leaders must model what the brethren are commanded to do. Several individuals, including Dr. H. Bixby, Dr. D. Brandon and Harold Nichols (1964), have identified the following duties of deacons toward the church: (a) ascertaining needs; (b) accountability; (c) prayer; and (d) stimulating service. Bixby (n.d.) suggests that the church be divided into family units to be distributed to the watchcare of individual deacons.

By briefly explaining the scope of each duty, one will be able to appreciate the requiredspiritual service of the deacon.

Ascertain needs

There are two kinds of needs that the deacon must be alert to: physical and spiritual. Physical needs would include health and financial. The deacon must make sure that, where possible, the church aids in meeting needs. Widows and orphans require the special attention of the deacon along with his male leadership. Spiritual needs can be attended to by the deacon or where special help is required, the pastor can be alerted. The deacon is a resource for the pastor concerning the needs of the flock.(cf. Prov. 27:23)

Accountability

The deacon is generally elected by the congregation to serve as part of the church leadership team. It is, therefore, the responsibility of the deacon to account for the administration of the church, as well as distribution of funds. The deacon can provide the necessary liaison between pastor and people to make sure they appreciate and esteem his leadership and to make sure there are no misunderstandings (cf. 1Th. 5:12-13).

Prayer

The people need to know that they are cared for. It would seem there are few better ways to demonstrate care for one another than to bring one another to the attention of God in prayer. Samuel knew the importance to God and man of intercessory prayer when he uttered, "Moreover, as for me, far be it from me that I should sin against the Lord by ceasing to pray for you; ..." (1 Sam. 12:23 NASB). As Dr. Eugene Berends, deacon at Calvary Baptist, Grand Rapids, well points out, more people leave a church for the want of care than the want of spiritual food. The two concepts really are indivisible; feeding is only effective with care.

Stimulate service

"Iron sharpens iron, so one man sharpens another"; (Prov. 27:17 NASB).

We are all redeemed to minister, to deacon (cf. 1 Cor. 12; Eph. 4:11 ff.). Sometimes, however, the hand needs to encourage the foot to do its thing or the eye has to discover the great flexibility of the hand. The servants of the church can perform a great labor for the body as they seek to first be models of service and second, encourage imitation. Paul reminded Timothy not to neglect his gift (1 Tim. 4:14).

How?

The only time people will respond to the question of their well being in a manner other than, "is when convinced it really matters to the questioner."

The only way one finds out needs is through personal knowledge; the only way one exhorts and admonishes another to activity is through personal contact.

The constant ingredient is personal relationships. It is therefore suggested that the deacon use part of his time, already designated to the Lord, as an investment in the lives of a selected group of people, (perhaps a benefit of membership?). The Deacon Caring Ministry developed by Dr. Howard Bixby suggests the following schedule of personal contact: (a) one phone call to each family unit per month; (b) two personal contacts outside of the church per year; (c) a prayer schedule that includes two family units per day, plus any other families with urgent needs. The results of this service are a tremendous blessing to the flock and a valuable informational resource for the pastor. The pastor is able to be in touch with the pulse of his flock in a way impossible without the service of the deacons (cf. Ex. 17), and the flock is content because for the most part, that their needs are tended to.

To effectively accomplish the caring ministry, the deacons and pastor must be committed to accountability. As an old math teacher of this writer used to say, "Don't expect what you don't inspect."

Conclusion

The greatest danger for the Jew was assimilation. "Thus you are to be holy to Me, for I the Lord am Holy; and I have set you apart from the peoples to be Mine." (Lev. 20:26 NASB). The greatest danger for the Christian is assimilation (cf. 2 Cor. 6:4-7:1; 1 Pet. 1:14-16). The penetration of the world's values into the church of Christ is alarming indeed. The corporate-ecclesiastic structure is an unequally yoked marriage that has invited power politics and self-interest into an institution that should be immune to such things: the church. This is not a new phenomenon; the Pharisees (cf. Jn. 11:48) as well as the disciples (cf. Lk. 22:24) concerned themselves with their status. Ministry to people with its effect on the heart makes the chase for the top a race without participants.

Pastors and deacons alike must prioritize the towel (cf. Jn. 13), let Christ be Lord of the church and agree with Paul to, "Admonish the unruly, encourage the fainthearted, help the weak, be patient with all men. See that no one repays another with evil for evil, but always seek after that which is good for one another and for all men." (1 Th. 5:14-15 NASB).

LIST OF REFERENCES

Asquith, Glenn H.

1981 Church Officers at Work. Valley Forge, Pennsylvania:

1977 Judson Press (reprint).

Barber, Cyril J. and Gary H. Strauss

1982 Leadership: The Dynamics of Success. Greenwood,

South Carolina: The Attic Press.

Berends, Eugene

The Deacon Caring Ministry of Calvary Baptist Church

(edited by Howard Bixby). Grand Rapids, Michigan:

Church Development Ministries.

Beyer, H.W.

1985 "Diakoneo."; In Gerhard Kittel and Gerhard Friedrich (eds.)

Theological Dictionary of the New Testament, abridged in one volume. Grand Rapids, Michigan: Wm. B. Eerdmans Publishing Company.

Bixby, Howard

The Deacon Caring Ministry of Calvary Baptist Church

(edited by Howard Bixby). Grand Rapids, Michigan:

Church Development Ministries.

Brandon, David R. B.

The Deacon's Handbook. Willowdale, Ontario:

Fellowship Baptist Press.

Earle, Ralph

1978; 1 Timothy.; In Frank E. Gaebelein (ed.) The Expositor's

Bible Commentary, XI. Grand Rapids, Michigan: Zondervan Publishing House.

Eims, Leroy

1981 Be A Motivational Leader. Wheaton, Illinois: Victor Books.

Gangel, Kenneth O.

1987; Leadership: Coping with Cultural Corruption.;

Bibliotheca Sacra, 144: 576: 450-459.

Getz, Gene A.

1984 Sharpening The Focus Of The Church. Wheaton, Illinois:

1975 Victor Books (reprint).

Hyles, Jack

1968 The Hyles Church Manual. Murfreesboro, Tennessee:

Sword of the Lord Publishers.

Jacobsen, Lloyd

1983 "Who Decides What Deacons Do?"; Leadership, 4: 3: 67-73}.

Nichols, Harold

1964 The Work of The Deacon and Deaconess. Valley Forge,

Pennsylvania: Judson Press.

Saucy, Robert L.

1974 "The Husband Of One Wife"; Bibliotheca Sacra,

131: 523: 229-240.

Van Wyk, Kenneth

1981 "Organizing Laity for Outreach"; In. Win Ara (ed.)

1979 The Pastor's Church Growth Handbook. Pasadena,

California: Church Growth Press (reprint).

White, John Jr.

The Deacon Caring Ministry of Calvary Baptist Church

(edited by Howard Bixby). Grand Rapids, Michigan:

APPENDIX #4
Sharing Deacons Proceedings with Non-Deacons

Demands of others that they keep private what we, as deacons, have not been able to keep.

Defrauds people by allowing them to listen in on discussions they can't contribute to. If they feel strongly about an issue they may be left with anger because they were left out or they may try to manipulate the deacon to pursue their preferences.

May introduce unseen controllers into proceedings.

Discloses opinions of individuals shared along the way to decisions:

This may cause hurt to that individual who shared with the understanding he was contributing in confidence to the decision making process, with the understanding that the decision only would be made public.

Such disclosure of private opinions may put a damper on the free exchange of opinions in the deacon meetings, hindering deacon effectiveness.

Opinions of individual deacons may be interpreted as representing all deacons.

Airing differences of opinion from deacon discussions may create the illusion of lack of unity in the Board. (The fact we disagree is no lack of unity as long as we move together toward agreement and are perceived as doing so.)

Discussing Deacons Meeting proceedings before children may sour them to church life by exposing them to unnecessary adult issues, especially if strong emotions accompany the disclosure.

Breaking Deacon Confidentiality Produces No Good, Only Damage:

to people.

to relationships.

to churches.

to the Lord's work.

The decision to take matters beyond Deacons Meetings for consideration in other quarters should be agreed to by the Deacons, otherwise Deacon discussions are confidential, even from our spouses.

APPENDIX # 5
Hedge of Protection Biblical Backing

Heavenly Father, in the name(3) and through the blood of Jesus,(4) I ask You(5) to rebuke(6) and bind Satan(7) and his influence concerning (person(s) and/or circumstance(s)).

I ask You to raise up a "hedge of protection"(8) around ___________________, which the power of evil cannot penetrate.

Restore a right heart within _______________, Lord, and guide me to actively help rather than hinder Your working.

Release Your power to heal and help _________ according to Your wisdom and for Your glory.

I thank You for hearing and answering this prayer, for it is founded on Your revealed will in Your sacred Word,(9) which states, "I will build My church and the gates of hell shall not prevail against it."(10)

or

"What therefore God hath joined together, let no man put asunder." Matt. 19:6 (11)

or

"Come to me, all you who are weary and burdened, and I will give you rest." Matt. 11:28

or...

Jesus—"The Spirit of the Lord is on me, because he has anointed me to proclaim good news to the poor. He has sent me to proclaim freedom for the prisoners and recovery of sight for the blind, to set the oppressed free" (Luke 4:18)

AMEN

Scriptural Notes for Hedge of Protection

(1) II Corinthians 10:4-5

The weapons with which we fight are not the weapons of the world. On the contrary, they have divine power to demolish strongholds. 5 We demolish arguments and every pretension that sets itself up against the knowledge of God, and we take captive every thought to make it obedient to Christ.

(2) Matthew 12:29

"Or again, how can anyone enter a strong man's house and carry off his possessions unless he first ties up the strong man? Then he can plunder his house.

(3) John 14:13-14

And I will do whatever you ask in my name, so that the Father may be glorified in the Son. 14 You may ask me for anything in my name, and I will do it.

(4) Revelation 12:11

They triumphed over him by the blood of the Lamb and by the word of their testimony; they did not love their lives so much as to shrink from death.

(5) Luke 10:17-20

The seventy-two returned with joy and said, "Lord, even the demons submit to us in your name." 18 He replied, "I saw Satan fall like lightning from heaven. 19 I have given you authority to trample on snakes and scorpions and to overcome all the power of the enemy; nothing will harm you. 20 However, do not rejoice that the spirits submit to you, but rejoice that your names are written in heaven."

Mark 16:17

And these signs will accompany those who believe: In my name they will drive out demons; they will speak in new tongues;

Matthew 18:18

Truly I tell you, whatever you bind on earth will be bound in heaven, and whatever you loose on earth will be loosed in heaven.

I John 4:4

You, dear children, are from God and have overcome them, because the one who is in you is greater than the one who is in the world. Though Christians have been given the spiritual authority in Jesus to rebuke Satan, to converse with Satan is to court his subversive influence. The wiser route, therefore, is that of Michael, the archangel, who asked God to rebuke Satan. This keeps our focus on Christ, and off self and Satan. We conquer only through Him.

Jude 1:9

But even the archangel Michael, when he was disputing with the devil about the body of Moses, did not himself dare to condemn him for slander but said, "The Lord rebuke you!"

(6) Matthew 17:18

Jesus rebuked the demon, and it came out of the boy, and he was healed at that moment.

Mark 9:25

When Jesus saw that a crowd was running to the scene, he rebuked the impure spirit. "You deaf and mute spirit," he said, "I command you, come out of him and never enter him again."

(7) Matthew 12:29

"Or again, how can anyone enter a strong man's house and carry off his possessions unless he first ties up the strong man? Then he can plunder his house.

Matthew 18:18

"Truly I tell you, whatever you bind on earth will be bound in heaven, and whatever you loose on earth will be loosed in heaven."

(8) Hosea 2:5-23

Their mother has been unfaithful and has conceived them in disgrace. She said, 'I will go after my lovers, who give me my food and my water, my wool and my linen, my olive oil and my drink.' 6 Therefore I will block her path with thornbushes; I will wall her in so that she cannot find her way. 7 She will chase after her lovers but not catch them; she will look for them but not find them. Then she will say, 'I will go back to my husband as at first, for then I was better off than now.' 8 She has not acknowledged that I was the one who gave her the grain, the new wine and oil, who lavished on her the silver and gold—which they used for Baal. 9 "Therefore I will take away my grain when it ripens, and my new wine when it is ready. I will take back my wool and my linen, intended to cover her naked body. 10 So now I will expose her lewdness before the eyes of her lovers; no one will take her out of my hands. 11 I will stop all her celebrations: her yearly festivals, her New Moons, her Sabbath days—all her appointed festivals. 12 I will ruin her vines and her fig trees, which she said were her pay from her lovers; I will make them a thicket, and wild animals will devour them. 13 I will punish her for the days she burned incense to the Baals; she decked herself with rings and jewelry, and went after her lovers, but me she forgot, declares the Lord. 14 "Therefore I am now going to allure her; I will lead her into the wilderness and speak tenderly to her. 15 There I will give her back her vineyards, and will make the Valley of Achor a door of hope. There she will respond as in the days of her youth, as in the day she came up out of Egypt. 16 "In that day," declares the Lord, "you will call me 'my husband'; you will no longer call me 'my master.' 17 I will remove the names of the Baals from her lips; no longer will their names be invoked. 18 In that day I will make a covenant for them with the beasts of the field, the birds in the sky and the creatures that move along the ground. Bow and sword and battle I will abolish from the land, so that all may lie down in safety. 19 I will betroth you to me forever; I will betroth you in righteousness and justice, in love and compassion. 20 I will betroth you in faithfulness, and you will acknowledge the Lord. 21 "In that day I will respond," declares the Lord—"I will respond to the skies, and they will respond to the earth; and the earth will respond to the grain, the new wine and the olive oil, and they will respond to Jezreel. 23 I will plant her for myself in the land; I will show my love to the one I called 'Not my loved one.' I will say to those called 'Not my people,' 'You are my people'; and they will say, 'You are my God.'"

Job 1:5, 9-10

When a period of feasting had run its course, Job would make arrangements for them to be purified. Early in the morning he would sacrifice a burnt offering for each of them, thinking, "Perhaps my children have sinned and cursed God in their hearts." This was Job's regular custom. 9 "Does Job fear God for nothing?" Satan replied. 10 "Have you not put a hedge around him and his household and everything he has? You have blessed the work of his hands, so that his flocks and herds are spread throughout the land.

Ezekiel 22:30

"I looked for someone among them who would build up the wall and stand before me in the gap on behalf of the land so I would not have to destroy it, but I found no one.

Luke 22:31, 32

"Simon, Simon, Satan has asked to sift all of you as wheat. 32 But I have prayed for you, Simon, that your faith may not fail. And when you have turned back, strengthen your brothers."

II Kings 6:15-17

When the servant of the man of God got up and went out early the next morning, an army with horses and chariots had surrounded the city. "Oh no, my lord! What shall we do?" the servant asked. Don't be afraid," the prophet answered. "Those who are with us are more than those who are with them." And Elisha prayed, "Open his eyes, Lord, so that he may see." Then the Lord opened the servant's eyes, and he looked and saw the hills full of horses and chariots of fire all around Elisha.

(9) I John 5:14-15

This is the confidence we have in approaching God: that if we ask anything according to his will, he hears us. 15 And if we know that he hears us—`whatever we ask—we know that we have what we asked of him.

(10) Matthew 16:18

And I tell you that you are Peter, and on this rock I will build my church, and the gates of Hades will not overcome it.

(11) Matthew 19:6

So they are no longer two, but one flesh. Therefore what God has joined together, let no one separate."

(12) II Corinthians 10:4

The weapons we fight with are not the weapons of the world. On the contrary, they have divine power to demolish strongholds.

(13) Proverbs 28:26

"Those who trust in themselves are fools, but those who walk in wisdom are kept safe."

(KJV) "He that trusteth in his own heart is a fool, but whoso walketh wisely, he shall be delivered."

(RSV)"He who trusts in his own mind is a fool; but he who walks in wisdom will be delivered."

Isaiah 55:8-9

"For my thoughts are not your thoughts, neither are your ways my ways," declares the Lord. 9 "As the heavens are higher than the earth, so are my ways higher than your ways and my thoughts than your thoughts.

Romans 12:2

Do not conform to the pattern of this world, but be transformed by the renewing of your mind. Then you will be able to test and approve what God's will is—his good, pleasing and perfect will.

(14) II Corinthians 10:5

We demolish arguments and every pretension that sets itself up against the knowledge of God, and we take captive every thought to make it obedient to Christ.

(15) James 5:16

Therefore confess your sins to each other and pray for each other so that you may be healed. The prayer of a righteous person is powerful and effective.

(16) II Corinthians 10:5

We demolish arguments and every pretension that sets itself up against the knowledge of God, and we take captive every thought to make it obedient to Christ.

Discipline

(17) DIVINE DISCIPLINE—Hebrews12:5-6

5 And have you completely forgotten this word of encouragement that addresses you as a father addresses his son? It says, "My son, do not make light of the Lord's discipline, and do not lose heart when he rebukes you, 6 because the Lord disciplines the one he loves, and he chastens everyone he accepts as his son."

NATURAL DISCIPLINE—Galatians 6:7-8

Do not be deceived: God cannot be mocked. A man reaps what he sows. 8 Whoever sows to please their flesh, from the flesh will reap destruction; whoever sows to please the Spirit, from the Spirit will reap eternal life.

(18) CHURCH DISCIPLINE—Hebrews 3:13

But encourage one another daily, as long as it is called "Today," so that none of you may be hardened by sin's deceitfulness.

HEBREWS 12:14-15

Make every effort to live in peace with everyone and to be holy; without holiness no one will see the Lord. 15 See to it that no one falls short of the grace of God and that no bitter root grows up to cause trouble and defile many.

Matthew 18:15-18

"If your brother or sister sins, go and point out their fault, just between the two of you. If they listen to you, you have won them over.16 But if they will not listen, take one or two others along, so that 'every matter may be established by the testimony of two or three witnesses.'17 If they still refuse to listen, tell it to the church; and if they refuse to listen even to the church, treat them as you would a pagan or a tax collector. 18 "Truly I tell you, whatever you bind on earth will be bound in heaven, and whatever you loose on earth will be loosed in heaven.

Galatians 6:1

Brothers and sisters, if someone is caught in a sin, you who live by the Spirit should restore that person gently. But watch yourselves, or you also may be tempted.

(19) DEMONIC DISCIPLINE—I Corinthians 5:5

Hand this man over to Satan for the destruction of the flesh, so that his spirit may be saved on the day of the Lord.

All church discipline lands here.

SINCERE APPRECIATION FOR ALL MY ENABLERS

During six tough years of research and writing I have needed and benefited a great deal from the expertise, support and encouragement of some wonderful people.

Six years ago, when God snapped my attention away from a book I was writing about meekness. I had no idea where He would lead me. God knew what He needed for His Church and His pastors. It was for me to search until all was revealed. It was an extended safari into deep and damaging things that dragged me down as I sought thorough understanding and God's route to resolution for each one. It seemed as though the work might never end but, as I worked, God provided a comforting vision of two hands with fingers interlocked as in prayer descending over my book and moving together to grasp it between its palms—grasping together around the substance of the book—assurance for me to let go now – "You're done Ray." Whew!

MY FAMILY

My wife, Diane, faithfully applied her teacher skills to edit my writing word by word, page by page, again and again, and stood by always encouraging. My son Jeremy's incredible computer skill kept my word processor active, despite relentless keyboard pounding. My daughter, Andrea, of Andrea Cross Photography, in her sweet, caring manner, applied her graphic skills to design the powerful cover so appropriate to my Tough Stuff theme, using a profound picture by kevron2001.

CRITIQUE

Thanks to Rev. Dr. Lester Dennis, Rev. Evan Craig, Rev. Robin Ross, John Smyth and Roan Elford who read the manuscript and provided insightful guidance.

Rev. Dr. K. Rick Baker was especially helpful in providing forthright, in-depth critique so needed as the book neared completion. It was tough to rework but the benefits to all will be multiplied by our collaboration. Thank you.

All of these I have needed to bring to you a book that moves me deeply. I pray it does the same for you, and provides you with useful guidance to transform your pastoral ministry possibilities to the glory of our Lord.

Rev. Raymond Cross Bth, BA

Don't miss out!

Visit the website below and you can sign up to receive emails whenever Raymond Cross publishes a new book. There's no charge and no obligation.

https://books2read.com/r/B-A-KZKDB-BLNAD

BOOKS2READ

Connecting independent readers to independent writers.

About the Author

Raymond Cross Bth BA describes himself as an "improvementist". Ray always looks for ways of breathing new life, creativity and healing into all of his relationships and activities – a life drive that uncovers improvements and solutions to perplexing inefficiencies and weakness. Ray applies this drive to all he experiences. His books, therefore, touch on a variety of challenges that have crossed his path, both conceptual and practical.Ray pastored Baptist churches in Ontario, Canada for thirty-five years. Since retiring from pasturing the Lord has led Ray to write a number of books about various aspects of ministry and spiritual life,

Ray has been happily married since 1971 to Diane, a nutrition expert and retired public school teacher They have two grown children and three grandchildren.

Read more at raycross.net.